P9-CFC-357

Rewarding Results

Harvard Business School
Series in Accounting and Control
Series Editor, Robert S. Kaplan

Rewarding Results
Motivating Profit Center Managers
by Kenneth A. Merchant

REWARDING RESULTS
Motivating Profit Center Managers

Kenneth A. Merchant
Harvard Business School

Harvard Business School Press
Boston, Massachusetts

Printed in the United States of America.

93 92 91 90 89 5 4 3 2 1

Library of Congress Cataloging-in-Publication Data

Merchant, Kenneth A.
Rewarding results : motivating profit center managers / Kenneth A. Merchant.
p. cm. — (Harvard Business School series in accounting and control)
Bibliography: p. 253
Includes index.
ISBN 0-87584-215-1
1. Executives—Salaries, etc. 2. Employee motivation. 3. Profit.
I. Title. II. Series.
HD4965.2.M47 1989
658.4'0714—dc20 89-32888
CIP

The paper used in this publication meets the requirements of the American National Standard for Permanence of Paper for Printed Library Materials Z39.49-1984.

To my parents, Reuben and Violet Merchant

Contents

Foreword by Richard F. Vancil ix
Acknowledgments xv

Introduction 1

1. Using Contracts to Motivate Profit Center Managers 9

2. Trade-offs in Motivational Contracts 23

3. Using Short-Term Accounting Earnings to Exert Consistent Short-Term Performance Pressure 51

4. Correcting for the Short-Term Bias in Accounting Measures of Performance 63

5. The Controllability Problem, Part I: Deciding Whether to Exclude Uncontrollable Elements from Earnings-Based Performance Measures 87

6. The Controllability Problem, Part II: Deciding Whether to Adjust for Uncontrollable Influences After the Fact 109

7. Using Motivational Contract Elements for Nonmotivational Purposes 143

8. Evaluating Contract Effectiveness, Part I: The Incidence of Myopia and Earnings Management 161

9. Evaluating Contract Effectiveness, Part II: Foregone Motivation and Excessive Compensation 197

10. Designing and Managing Good Motivational Contracts 209

Appendix: Research Method 229
References 253
Index 263

Foreword

A brief retrospective may be useful before you plunge into this book. Kenneth Merchant has already given it a subtitle, but I propose another: "Closing the Loop on Management Control Systems." Reviewing the chronology of events that began nearly fifty years ago can be illuminating. I am aware, of course, of the risks of institutional and personal self-serving, but I hope to spread more light than laurels.

Harvard Business School was founded in 1908, and by 1940, the faculty had decided to focus its energy on the development of "general managers." It was a bold stroke—and a risky one—because there were no precedents to follow. "General management" could be defined rather succinctly, but it lacked a theoretical foundation and the disciplined body of knowledge that sustains academic endeavors. The result was that many of the School's courses were either vocational (Railroads) or functional (Sales Management). Two courses that had some claim to academic respectability were Financial Accounting and Business Statistics. The capstone course, Business Policy, was required in the second year and focused on the administrative point of view.

The School discovered the need for a body of knowledge called management control during World War II, when it was mobilized to train military officers and civilian executives. Its mission was to enhance their analytical skills, helping them to optimize the management of the scarce resources available for the war effort. Business Policy was hardly the right rubric for a set of educational programs designed to win the war. Adapting, the faculty poured old wine into new bottles and called it "Management Control."

In these programs, the administrative point of view was introduced on the first day of classes. The paradigm was simple: when managers accept responsibility for the performance of pools of resources, their first tasks are to define their objectives and develop a stream of prompt, accurate information about their operations. When a problem (or opportunity) arises, they conduct a careful, situational analysis of how alternative actions will affect the performance of the unit *and* the performance of other units at higher levels. A "macro" view of the situation was most likely to yield the best solution.

Despite the power of these simple analytical tools, it was probably inevitable that the field of management control did not bloom in the postwar era. One reason was that the School was busy trying to serve the thousands of veterans who flocked to its doors. The curriculum was redesigned and integrated: Business Policy regained its premier status, and Control was merged with Financial Accounting in order to link data with analysis. All classes in the first year were required, and the faculty regarded themselves as interchangeable parts, qualified to teach any first-year course. The Division of Research continued to fund academic projects, but many of the faculty were almost anti-theoretical. The pedagogy of these true believers was grounded in the case method: "Every situation is unique; occasionally we find 'currently useful generalizations,' but they are not testable hypotheses; we use cases, not theories, 'Because wisdom Can't be Told.' "[1]

A dozen or more faculty members had been involved in designing and teaching the Management Control course during World War II, but three stood out: Ross G. Walker, Edmund P. Learned, and Charles A. Bliss. They were colleagues for more than twenty years (1937–1958), and they shaped the development of the field. But, in the oral tradition of the School, none of them published a statement of their insights and wisdom.

Finally, in the mid-sixties, three scholars each published a serious treatise on general management as seen from his particular perspective. They were contemporaries, born during World War I, but not collaborators. Collectively, however, their work was complementary. In broad terms, they were all concerned with strategy, structure, and management control.

Alfred Chandler's seminal book, *Strategy and Structure,* was widely proclaimed and showered with honors and awards.[2] Trained as an historian, he became interested in the ways that large U.S. corporations were managed; his in-depth research led not only to a lexicon of business terminology that permitted him to observe similarities and differences among the scores of large corporations that he studied, but also, even more important, to an explanation of *why* these companies had evolved over time as they introduced innovations that required changes in both their strategy and their structure.

One of Chandler's most important findings was that, as the companies grew, they adopted a form of organization called "decentralization." Administrative work is an identifiable activity of two sorts. Sometimes the administrator must be concerned with the long-run health of the company; other times, with efficient day-to-day operations. Using current nomenclature, every decentralized company has at least three generic administrative titles: a corporate manager, business managers (for each product line), and functional managers (for a plant or sales office). Chandler did not say that all firms were identical, but for those who clung to the every-situation-is-unique theory, the implicit response was, "Yes, but there are some useful similarities."

Kenneth Andrews published his treatise on general management in 1965,[3] a few months before Robert Anthony published his monograph on management control.[4] Both men were nearing the peak of their careers: Andrews was chairman of the Business Policy area, and Anthony was the chairman of the Control area. Both men cited Chandler briefly, but they had a different agenda. Chandler's work was (magnificently) descriptive, but the time had come to be overtly prescriptive. Andrews and Anthony wrote as much for their colleagues as for a broader audience, and the message was clear: the oral wisdom was to be written down. It was the end of an era.

The primary difference between the two books was scope. Andrews took the high ground, stating that corporate strategy was the "pattern of purposes and policies defining the company and its business." With that statement as his centerpiece, he developed a very useful diagram (page 41) that is widely used today. The two main tasks in corporate strategy are formulation (deciding what to do) and implementation (achieving results).

Anthony had a different, but related, agenda. Managers needed formal systems for both planning and control, but the interface between the two was not well articulated in the mid-sixties. He parsed out the territory, differentiating between strategic planning and management control.

Finally, both Andrews and Anthony devoted attention to a topic that Chandler had had no way of observing: the *process* of management. Beyond strategy and structure, there are cadres of managers making it all happen. Process, the ways that a group of people work together, can be a major strategic asset, as we will see.

My contribution to the field was my book on *Decentralization*.[5] Chandler had identified the trend toward decentralization, and fifteen years later there was a roaring fad to endow profit center managers with responsibility for the bottom line. I already knew that every profit center was unique because it shared some resources with other units in the corporation; transfer prices between profit centers for semifinished products was only the tip of the iceberg. What I needed was survey data (provided by 291 companies) and a metric for measuring the degree of autonomy for the typical profit center in each company.

A management axiom warns, "You can't hold a person responsible for activities over which he or she has no authority," but the opposite of the axiom is pervasive for profit center managers. It works by differentiating functional authority from financial responsibility. Profit center managers do not have autonomy for all the resources, but their perceived autonomy is greater than their functional authority. My conclusion was that those findings were so consistent that corporate managers must have intended the result. Thus, my subtitle: "Managerial Ambiguity by Design."

Finally, we come to Merchant's book, *Rewarding Results.*

Viewed from the perspective of Andrews's framework, both Merchant and I worked on implementation. My focus was on coordination of divided responsibility, and Merchant's (eleven years later) is on motivation and incentive systems. Given his results, the delay was worth waiting for. His book is a tour de force.

Merchant held one-on-one interviews with scores of profit center managers in twelve diverse corporations. He discovered that, when it comes to awarding incentive compensation, every situation *is* unique—or nearly so. His findings are compelling because he documents *why* corporate managers tailor incentive contracts at the start of the year but sometimes change them at the end of the year. The changes are made because incentive contracts involve too many trade-offs and are based on too many poor forecasts to allow adherence to rigid terms set at the beginning of the year.

Merchant's framework (Figure 10-1) focuses on the trade-offs, and he organizes it to display the linkages to the earlier frameworks of Andrews and myself. It is in that sense that I believe Merchant has "closed the loop" in terms of completing the paradigm for strategy, structure, and control in large decentralized U.S. corporations. If that is so, or even close, then *Rewarding Results* will surely have a bright future. Senior executives in these companies will not be surprised at Merchant's findings, but they will read his book carefully, looking for new insights. The good news for the academic community is that Merchant has presented them with a bundle of prescriptive hypotheses. There are several ill-defined trade-offs in motivational contracts at the moment, but further progress will be made. Meanwhile, I hope you will enjoy and learn from Merchant's contribution as much as I have.

Richard F. Vancil

NOTES

1. A famous essay by Professor Charles I. Gragg on the virtues of the case method, "Because Wisdom Can't be Told," *Harvard Alumni Bulletin,* October 19, 1940.

2. Alfred D. Chandler, Jr., *Strategy and Structure: Chapters in the History of the Industrial Enterprise* (Cambridge, Mass.: MIT Press, 1962). Chandler was at MIT when he wrote *Strategy and Structure,* but he moved to the Harvard Business School in 1970 and later published *The Visible Hand* (1977) and *Scale and Scope*(1989).

3. Kenneth R. Andrews, "*The Concept of Corporate Strategy,*" in *Business and Policy: Text and Cases,* edited by Christensen et al. (Homewood, Ill.: Richard D. Irwin, 1965). Reissued as a monograph by Dow Jones-Irwin, 1971.

4. Robert N. Anthony, *Planning and Control Systems: A Framework for Analysis* (Boston: Division of Research, Harvard Business School, 1965).

5. Richard F. Vancil, *Decentralization: Managerial Ambiguity by Design* (Homewood, Ill.: Dow Jones-Irwin, 1978).

Acknowledgements

Anyone who has written a serious book about people in organizations will say it was a very tough book to write. There are so many complex realities to contend with and alternate ways to present the data. To help me cope with the complexity, I asked for and received advice from many colleagues throughout the research and writing.

Special thanks are due Richard Vancil, Lourdes Ferreira, and Jean-François Manzoni. Dick Vancil was a continuing source of support and encouragement; he acted as my sounding board throughout the project and contributed in major ways to the revision of several manuscript drafts. Lourdes and Jean-François provided excellent research assistance. They accompanied me on many of the field trips, helped me review the research literature, and participated in many sessions where we tried to make sense of the disparate bits of data we had collected.

Barbara Feinberg provided invaluable editorial help. She assisted in the identification of the theme of the book and made major improvements in the clarity and cogency of the writing over the course of several manuscript drafts.

Many of my colleagues at the Harvard Business School read and made suggestions for improving the manuscript. They include Frank Aguilar, Robert Anthony, Chris Argyris, George Baker, William Bruns, Robin Cooper, John Dearden, Robert Eccles, David Hawkins, Julie Hertenstein, Robert Kaplan, Jay Lorsch, Warren McFarlan, Krishna Palepu, Robert Simons, and Karen Wruck. Others who made similar contributions include Kenneth Euske and Joseph San Miguel

(Naval Postgraduate School), C.J. McNair (University of Rhode Island), David Otley (University of Lancaster), and Michael von Breda (Southern Methodist University).

Other colleagues have contributed to this project. In particular, I would like to thank Raymond Corey, Dwight Crane, Colyer Crum, Gordon Donaldson, and Benson Shapiro, who provided important advice and encouragement at various stages of the research. And my secretary, Elisa Lusetti, prepared countless versions of the figures, and, most important, blocked access to my office door when it was best that I not be interrupted.

The Division of Research at the Harvard Business School provided generous financial support. Because of that support, I was able to visit the corporations and profit centers that were most appropriate for the research, instead of the ones that were nearest to Boston.

And last, but certainly not least, I wish to thank the 12 companies and 203 managers who participated in the research. For reasons of confidentiality, I cannot thank the managers by name. But their willingness to take time out of their busy schedules and share their experiences and ideas was obviously essential to my being able to gather the data from which this book was developed.

Introduction

I became interested in the issues corporate managers face in controlling the activities of their firms' profit center managers about six years ago while doing the research for a related book (Merchant, 1985). To a large extent, control in divisionalized firms means motivating—promising rewards for good results—and I was struck by several significant, unanswered motivational questions. I knew U.S. firms had been sharply criticized for being excessively short-term-oriented. But I did not sense that the incentives in many firms were becoming more long-term-oriented, even though the criticisms had been widely publicized for enough years for management to have responded.

I also listened to several profit center managers, who explained that they were expected to achieve budget targets even when their entities' results were affected by large, unexpected, and uncontrollable factors. They said that to protect themselves against the vagaries of these factors, they sometimes responded in deceptive ways: they negotiated for budget targets that were as achievable as possible and maintained significant stocks of "unreported profits." What is curious is that even though corporate managers know of these undesirable side effects, many of them do not lessen the pressures they place on their profit center managers for short-term performance, and they do little to eliminate the distorting effects of the uncontrollable factors from the performance measures.

To explore these and related motivational issues, I decided to conduct a field study. I wanted to understand the incentives corporate managers gave their profit center managers and the rationales they used in making their choices. I also wanted to try to make some judgments about whether, for example, the critics' conclusions were warranted and whether the problems of dealing with uncontrollables were tractable.

The study was aimed at filling a research void. The void exists because researchers who have studied motivational contracts have tended to focus on either top management or lower-level employees because the data are easier to gather. Most of their findings, however, are not generalizable to profit center levels.

This book presents the findings of what became a major field research study of 54 profit centers in 12 corporations. It describes how to design and manage the "rewards-for-results contracts" that managers of divisionalized corporations use to motivate their profit center managers to act in the firm's best interest.

The book presents data showing that all firms use multiple motivational contracts, both written and unwritten, linking profit center managers' rewards to reported results. These contracts vary considerably across corporations and across profit centers in the same corporation. Much of the variation is present because corporate managers make different choices in addressing trade-offs among desirable contract qualities, such as measurement congruence with organizational objectives, controllability, and accuracy, the ability of performance standards to provide managers with the right amount of challenge, and contract simplicity. The need to make the trade-offs among these contract qualities is caused by three primary design constraints: (1) the inability to measure directly the profit center managers' influence on shareholder value; (2) the inability to isolate in the results measures the effects individual managers can control; and (3) the desirability of using some contract elements for nonmotivational purposes.

Trade-offs Caused by the Inability to Measure Changes in Shareholder Value Directly

Because changes in entity value cannot be measured directly at profit center levels, virtually all motivational contracts for profit center managers are based on a surrogate summary performance measure—accounting earnings (or a profitability ratio such as return on net assets). This is a natural choice. Earnings is a simple summary measure that is positively correlated with changes in value; it is available on a timely basis, so it can be used to apply the consistent short-term performance pressure necessary to keep managers from becoming sloppy or wasteful; and it is reasonably objective, verifiable, and understandable.

Earnings measures, however, have an inherent short-term bias that can induce profit center managers to be excessively short-term-oriented (myopic). Corporate managers must offset this bias, and they use any of several approaches to do so. The most common is to base some rewards on leading indicators of the earnings to be reported in subsequent periods, such as market share, product development successes, or customer satisfaction. These leading indicators can be standardized across the corporation if the profit centers' missions and their managers' roles are similar. Often, however, the specific measures and their weightings should be varied to reflect the profit centers' unique critical success factors. But this variance makes the contracts more complex and the evaluations more prone to subjective biases.

Some firms attempt to offset the short-term bias by basing additional rewards on long-term profit center performance. These rewards can be incorporated in formal, written contracts or in unwritten understandings between the profit center managers and their superiors.

Written long-term contracts are used by only a few firms because they are expensive and difficult to administer. The rewards they embody are not promised to the profit center managers until years in the future. These rewards can attract the managers' attention and materially affect the balance between their short-term and long-term incentives only if they promise to be lucrative (and costly to the corporation). Written long-term contracts are also difficult to administer because reasonably challenging performance standards cannot be reliably set for long measurement periods in environments that are typically uncertain and because some managers invariably switch jobs before the multiyear measurement period has concluded.

Most firms use one or more unwritten long-term, rewards-for-results contracts. A common example involves the allocation of managerial promotions. Because the unwritten contracts are based on subjective performance evaluations, they are more flexible than written contracts. But unwritten contracts also have their drawbacks. Their terms are often implicit and not well communicated, and if profit center managers do not understand them, the contracts have no positive motivational effects. And some profit center managers do not respond well to unwritten contracts because they do not trust their superiors' promises or their subjective performance-evaluation judgments.

Finally, the short-term bias in accounting earnings measures can be partially offset by relaxing the pressure for short-term earnings. This alternative is advantageous, however, only where myopia is potentially severe and where the managers can be trusted not to become sloppy or wasteful in the short run.

Trade-offs Caused by the Inability to Isolate the Managers' Individual Contributions

The second set of trade-offs is caused by the inability to isolate only the effects of the managers' individual contributions in the results measures. The distorting effects of some uncontrollable influences can be eliminated either before or after the measurement period. They can be eliminated before by excluding certain line items of revenues, expenses, and assets from the profit center financial measures. After the period has ended, adjustments to remove all or some of the effects of any uncontrollable factors that were actually felt can be made either to the measures or to the standards used for evaluations.

It is difficult, however, to decide how to use either or both of these approaches. The before-period choices are difficult because it is desirable to include in the results measures all line items the profit center managers can influence so they will pay attention to them. But holding profit center managers accountable for line items over which they have only partial control means they bear extra risk; their rewards depend on factors they cannot control. If the firm fails to compensate them for this risk, it will bear the costs of frustration, lower motivation, and possibly managerial turnover. The key question, then, is: When is the managers' influence great enough to warrant holding them at risk for something they cannot totally control?

Deciding when to adjust for uncontrollable influences after the measurement period is even more complex. It depends on the size of the distortion, the extent to which the manager is expected to respond to the uncontrollable influence, the ability to calculate (or at least estimate fairly accurately) the size of the effect, and the profit center managers' tolerances for subjectivity in performance evaluations.

Trade-offs in Using Contracts for Nonmotivational Purposes

Most corporate managers face a third set of design constraints because they want to use particular motivational contract features for one or more nonmotivational purposes. Selecting these nonmotivational features involves trade-offs because they make the contracts more complex and because they can have adverse effects on motivation.

Some corporations base a portion of the profit center managers' rewards on corporate performance, which is virtually uncontrollable from the perspective of a profit center manager, or limit the range of performance over which rewards are linked to results. These contract features are used for many reasons: they force the managers to share some of the shareholders' risk; they protect the corporation from paying large, but undeserved, bonuses; they make managers' rewards less volatile; and/or they deliver a message to the managers that organizational cooperation is important.

Some corporations use written long-term contracts as "golden handcuffs." They delay the payment of some rewards and increase managerial retention.

And most corporations allow profit center managers to work toward earnings targets that are less challenging than is desirable for strictly motivational purposes. The achievable targets serve other purposes, such as the improvement of resource planning and corporate financial reporting.

Designing and Managing Good Motivational Contracts

Because of the importance of the profit center manager role, it is critical to the success of the corporation that the contracts used to motivate these managers be effective. Corporate managers must think about the whole combination of contracts influencing the profit center managers' behavior, not just individual contracts.

Contract design requires numerous choices, many of which involve complex trade-offs. Making the right trade-offs requires knowing the full range of feasible alternatives and their effects, positive and negative, on the profit center managers' behavior. In addition, many factors that are descriptive of the corporation (e.g., desire for short-term profit), the profit center (e.g., planning uncertainty), the profit center managers (e.g., tolerance of risk), and their evaluators (e.g., knowledge of profit center's business) are relevant to the design decisions because they can affect the severity of the trade-offs corporate managers must make in designing motivational contracts or their ability to cope with the trade-offs. Thus it is natural that contracts are different across corporations and sometimes across profit centers in the same corporation.

If the full range of design alternatives or the benefits and costs of the feasible choices in the settings in which they will be used are not explored, the contracts will be flawed. Three types of flaws are common. Some contracts actually induce profit center managers to eliminate good long-term investments and to manipulate short-term earnings reports because the importance of short-term earnings is overweighted. Overweighting is caused, in turn, by overestimation of the corporate benefits of smoothing short-term earnings reports and underestimation of the costs of stressing the short run.

A second type of flaw undercuts the positive motivational effects of the contracts. This flaw stems from the overuse of ranges of performance where results are not linked to rewards, or from the inappropriate basing of a portion of the profit center managers' rewards on corporate performance.

A third type of contract flaw is the payment of rewards that are unnecessary because they have no positive motivational impact. Some profit center managers are overcompensated because corporate managers make adjustments for uncontrollables asymmetrically: the managers are protected when they are unlucky, but benefit when they are lucky. Some profit center managers are also overcompensated because their rewards are based on an incorrect assumption about the achievability of their targets.

Because the benefits and costs of motivational contracts depend on a broad range of factors, many of which change frequently, such contracts cannot be designed once and then forgotten. Firms must continually monitor the relevant environmental changes and adapt the contractual elements to them.

I have written this book for two audiences. One is the practitioners, including the general managers, staff specialists, and consultants, who design the motivational contracts for profit center managers, and those who implement them, particularly the evaluators of performance. For this audience, I describe the practices and experiences of the 12 corporations and interpret them in terms of some new concepts and theories. Managers will recognize the choice they make, but they will find some of them described in new terms, with new slants and emphases, without the technical jargon that pervades much of the research literature.

The second audience includes academics and others who study organizations and management practices. These readers will find a framework that structures the findings of the study and many theoretical statements that link specific framework elements. They should also benefit from the rich descriptions of the contracts the 12 firms use and the profit center managers' reactions to the contracts.

Organizational theorists have been active recently in exploring some of the incentive issues I discuss. Empirical evidence to support or refute the theoretical findings is in short supply, however, because it is difficult to secure organizational access and expensive (in time and money) to gather the data. The descriptions of current practice provided here should be useful to those who are conducting research in this area.

CHAPTER 1

Using Contracts to Motivate Profit Center Managers

"The design of an effective management control system requires three main issues to be resolved. First, what are the dimensions of 'good' performance and how are they to be measured? Secondly, what are appropriate standards for performance and how are they to be established? Thirdly, how are rewards (or penalties) to be linked to results?"[1]

Controlling Profit Center Managers

The divisionalized form of organization has been called "the primary organizational philosophy in U.S. manufacturing corporations today"[2] and "American capitalism's most important single innovation of the twentieth century."[3] Essential to the rise of the large, diverse corporations that derive advantages from economies of scale and scope, this organizational form now predominates among corporations of all types of at least minimal size.[4]

Divisionalization means that the corporation is divided into multiple profit centers under the direction of general managers who are given bottom-line responsibility.[5] These managers, who run entities with a variety of labels—company, sector, group, division, area, or unit—play the key role in most decentralized corporations.

Profit center managers' roles are key because, as Donaldson concludes in a recent research report, "Companies succeed or fail in their economic functions at the divisional level."[6] In keeping with the spirit of decentralization, most profit center managers are given substantial authority to initiate, make, or approve many actions critical to the success of their business units. In particular, they must mediate the natural conflicts among the business functions; they often play a substantial, if not decisive, role in deciding on the business strategy, such as where growth should occur and how it should be achieved; and they are central figures in making the critical trade-offs between current and future performance.

When it works properly, divisionalization results in timely decisions made by informed, motivated employees. When it fails, however, severe consequences may result.

The control challenge for top management is to ensure that the profit center managers act consistently in the corporation's best interest. This challenge is difficult to meet because top managers are limited in their business-specific and day-to-day operating knowledge and in their abilities to monitor the profit center managers' actions. The profit center managers frequently know their businesses better than top management does because they can devote much more of their time to following developments in their specialized areas. Hence top-level managers usually do not have detailed knowledge of the actions they want particular profit center managers to take, and even direct monitoring of the actions taken, if it were feasible, would not ensure that the profit center managers were acting appropriately. Even in the few cases where direct monitoring is feasible and useful, it can be expensive in time and travel because the profit center managers are often widely dispersed. Most often, then, control of profit center managers is indirect; it involves *motivation.*

Motivation does not mean simply inducing profit center managers to exert greater effort. In fact, encouraging effort is a relatively minor concern at the profit center level because most of the managers have been promoted on the basis of proven abilities and attitudes toward work. But profit center managers must be motivated in several important ways, all of which serve to mobilize their hearts, minds, and energies to serve the corporation's best interests.

Sometimes the manager's attention needs to be directed.

For example, it is commonly recognized that managers have a tendency to let short-run concerns drive out long-term thought.[7] They can become preoccupied with customer problems or new-product development efforts and need to be reminded to "pay attention to inventory levels." They need information about how top management wants certain trade-offs to be made; for example, how much current profitability is to be traded off for growth, and how much time should they spend on market development as opposed to fixing flawed information systems. And sometimes they need incentives to take difficult and distasteful (personally costly) actions, such as instituting a layoff or stopping a pet development project.

Motivating through Contracts

All corporations can be said to motivate their profit center managers through written and unwritten promises of rewards for results that are usefully labeled "contracts."[8] Some of these promises are legal contracts, enforceable by the courts. Other promises are not legally enforceable but are virtually indistinguishable from legal contracts in both their form and effects. Often, they are enforced by corporate adjudication procedures or labor-market forces. If corporations renege on their promises, for example, the managers will leave, and because the firms' reputations for trustworthiness will be damaged, they will find it difficult to hire talented replacements.

Some motivational contracts, such as incentive plans, are described in writing in detail. Other, often equally important, contracts or contract elements are largely or totally unwritten. These "understandings" between managers are implemented on a case-by-case basis and used to fill the gaps left either intentionally or unintentionally in the written contracts. Sometimes these unwritten contracts are as explicit as if they were written in detail. They are communicated in ways that are so unequivocal, such as by direct, oral orders, that the profit center managers immediately understand their terms. In other cases, however, the managers must infer the terms from events (such as promotions and demotions) that occur over time.

Contract Elements

As the chapter opening quotation states, motivational contracts, which are the key to effective management control in divisionalized firms, consist of three primary elements. The first is a definition of one or more *measures* (for example, annual return on net assets—RONA) that either represent the corporate objective or, at least, are correlated with that objective.

The second element is a description of the *standards* that will be used to distinguish deficient from satisfactory performance. For example, a 20% RONA may be defined as the minimum acceptable performance for the next year, and a 35% RONA may be defined as outstanding performance.

The third element is a description of how the *rewards* (and penalties) will be linked to the performance evaluations. For example, the contract may promise no monetary rewards for performance below the minimum acceptable level (20% RONA) and a bonus of 50% of base salary for outstanding performance (35% RONA), with interpolation between those extremes. The contract may also imply that if performance persists for several years below the minimum acceptable level, the manager's job will be in danger.

Many Important Design Choices Must Be Made

Although motivational contracts consist of only three primary elements—measures, standards, and rewards (and a set of administrative provisions, such as how to treat a manager who switches positions in midyear)—the design choices are many and the selections are often far from obvious. The contract designers, whose positions vary from the compensation committee of the board of directors down to the profit center managers' immediate superiors, must make choices about each element from a vast array of possibilities. Some of the alternatives they choose are shown in Table 1-1.

TABLE 1-1
A Sampling of Motivational-Contract Design Choices

Contract Element	*Available Choices*
Performance Measurement	Profit after tax
	Profit before tax
	Operating income
	Return on equity
	Return on capital employed
	Return on assets
	Residual income
	Return on sales
	Growth
	Customer satisfaction
	Employee welfare
Performance Standard	Budget
	Flexible budget
	History
	Performance of similar entities
	Judgment of possibilities in the circumstances faced
Rewards	Salary increases
	Bonuses
	Stock options
	Increased promotion possibilities
	Recognition
	Autonomy

Motivational-contract design choices have attracted more management attention in recent years. Many corporations have learned that it is important to provide adequate incentives for their top performers and that these top performers distinguish themselves by generating the best results.[9] One important form of reward—results-dependent compensation—is becoming an increasingly large proportion of total compensation.[10] And in a recent survey of corporate directors, 66% of the respondents reported that the most important issue currently faced by compensation committees is how to develop more effective links between pay and performance.[11]

Not all motivational contracts are equally effective. Some contract designs are inherently flawed, and others do not work well in certain organizational settings.

The problems firms encounter with motivational contracts can be put into four broad categories. The first is a *failure to communicate*. Every instruction that tells profit center managers what results are important to the corporation and how they are to make important economic trade-offs can be said to be part of a motivational contract.[12] Some firms, however, do not provide these instructions, or they provide them through contracts that are so vague or complex that they fail to communicate the desired message effectively. The result is a persistence of costly ignorance.

Second, some contracts *fail to provide incentives* that make it worthwhile for the profit center managers to override some of their own selfish interests in order to do what they know is in the corporation's best interest. Although most managers want to do a good job for their corporation, it is tempting for them to do otherwise. For example, some managers make investments designed solely to increase the size of their organization (and thus their power within the corporation) or to make their own personal circumstances easier (a staff assistant); some delay taking uncomfortable or distasteful actions (such as laying off employees) until the problem reaches crisis proportions; and some simply fail to work the extra hours needed to visit important customers or to analyze decisions properly.

A third, often severe, outcome of poorly designed motivational contracts is *displaced motivation*—contracts can actually induce managers to do the wrong things. Even managers who want to do a good job will take actions that they know are not in the corporation's best interest when the corporation gives them incentives to do so.

Many critics have described examples of displaced motivation. Some have observed that the motivating contracts used in most U.S. corporations have made managers excessively risk-averse and short-term-oriented.[13] Some have observed that many contracts induce managers to "cook the books" or to resort to other manipulative actions in their zeal to meet budget targets or show steadily improving results.[14] And some have observed that motivational contracts can discourage teamwork by inducing managers to focus narrowly on their own performance measures and to ignore the effects of their actions on other corporate entities.[15]

The final potential problem with some motivational contracts is that they *cause the corporation to bear unnecessary costs.* For example, some contracts put managers' rewards needlessly at risk by basing them on measures over which the managers have no control. Because of the lack of control, the contracts have no motivational impact, but the corporation bears extra costs because the managers must be compensated for bearing the risk.

Other contracts cause corporations to bear unnecessary costs in the form of frustration (lower motivation) or turnover by providing rewards that are unfair. Unfairness occurs when managers believe their rewards are not commensurate with results, the risks they bear, or their alternate employment opportunities.

Conflicting Advice about Contract Design

Many authors have made suggestions for changing the incentives or for relieving the pressures that lead to this counterproductive behavior, but most of these are based on untested assumptions about the probable effects of various contract design choices. Only rarely do we see candor such as that in a recent article: "It must be stressed that the relationships described above . . . are totally conjectural. There is no evidence to support these 'logical' deductions."[16]

Because the assumptions are untested and because situations differ, it is not surprising that the suggestions often conflict. The conflicts arise in almost every contract design choice area. For example, one conflict involves whether corporations should offer contracts that expressly link compensation to performance. Some authors suggest that these contracts are vital because pay is a powerful motivator.[17] Some suggest that the contracts just waste money because they will not cause managers to work any harder.[18] Still others say that because the contracts are so easy to misdesign and mismanage, they may actually diminish motivation.[19]

Most existing empirical evidence does not apply directly to the issue of profit center manager motivation. Several compensation consulting firms publish surveys of practice, but their primary focus has been on incentives for top executives, and in any case their data are disclosed in broad, fragmentary terms (such as the percentage of firms having stock option plans). Academic researchers, who have become much more interested in executive compensation issues in the last decade, have also focused almost exclusively on contracts for top executives. Their statistical analyses have related corporate-level "outcome" data, such as capital expenditures, to descriptions in proxy statements of some contract elements and actual compensation awards. These types of data are not readily available for the study of the form or effectiveness of contracts used to motivate profit center managers.

What is known about the motivating effects of top management rewards-for-results contracts cannot be applied to profit center managers because the design choices and their effects are quite different for the two organization levels.[20] Objective measures of changes in entity value are available for corporations but not for profit centers. Profit can be measured for each profit center (by definition), but it is often not a reliable indicator of profit center manager performance for any of many reasons: the profit measures fail to capture the long-term implications of short-run actions; the measures do not reflect the impact on other organizational entities; and the existence of shared resources and efforts necessitates sizable and often largely arbitrary allocations of costs, assets, and sometimes revenues. Profit center performance standards are sometimes of questionable usefulness because politics and gamesmanship impinge on planning processes. And profit center managers are probably interested in a different mix of rewards from that of most interest to top executives. For example, in comparison with top executives, profit center managers are probably more interested in protecting their autonomy and in improving their promotion possibilities and less interested in stability of immediate income (after their salaries are assured).[21]

Since so little direct evidence is available, we must conclude that we know little about how rewards-for-results contracts for profit center managers are designed or how the contracts in use affect profit center managers' actions. Others have noted this point; for example, in the conclusions of recent review papers:

> There has been an enormous amount of research in the economics of contracting, but this increasingly technical research has generated few empirical implications and offers little guidance in understanding actual compensation arrangements in large organizations.[22]
>
> . . .
>
> While a variety of theories exists about the effects of various compensation policies, surprisingly little evidence exists on the extent to which compensation policies vary across firms and more importantly on the effects of pursuing alternative compensation strategies.[23]

Research Design

To address this knowledge void, I undertook a field research project whose findings and analysis are presented in this book. The purpose of the research was to understand how profit center manager motivational contracts are designed and managed in practice. The few researchers who have worked in the area have suggested that "broad-based clinical studies continue to rate first priority" because there is a dearth of good descriptions of practices on which to build conceptual frameworks and theories.[24]

Over a three-year period starting in the spring of 1985, I gathered field evidence, much of it through interviews with 203 managers in 12 corporations. (See the appendix for a more detailed description of my research methods.) I addressed three basic questions:

1. What contracts do firms use to motivate their profit center managers?
2. Why do they make the contract design choices they do?
3. What effects do the contracts have on profit center manager behavior?

I was particularly interested in gathering evidence about

whether the criticisms of U.S. management practices mentioned earlier are justified. Because these criticisms have been in writing for almost a decade, enough time has passed for managers to have received the criticism and to have reacted to it.

The 12 corporations were selected for diversity. Their annual sales ranged from $40 million to nearly $10 billion (median = $2.6 billion). Their businesses differed, and none of them competed with any of the others to any significant extent. Other variations included service versus manufacturing businesses, capital intensity versus labor intensity, high- versus low-technology products, rapid growth versus stability, varying customer bases (government versus commercial, consumer versus industrial marketing), and degree of diversification.[25]

I studied a total of 54 profit centers in the 12 corporations. These profit centers were at the first organization level where the business functions (particularly marketing and operations) came together. Despite this important similarity, the profit centers were also diverse. For example, their annual sales ranged from less than $500,000 to more than $1 billion.

Because of the sensitive nature of some of the information collected, I promised each corporation and each individual interviewed strict anonymity, so some data have had to be disguised in this book. Each corporation is referred to by a letter and a brief industry-descriptive label. (Table 1-2 shows these letters and descriptive labels and a crude indication of each firm's size.)

Design of the Book

The book is organized in three basic parts. The first part, contained in Chapter 2, describes the theme, which is that the key to designing motivational contracts for profit center managers lies in understanding the trade-offs that are necessary to circumvent some significant design constraints. The chapter starts by describing an ideal motivational contract and then goes on to show that the ideal contract is not, and can-

TABLE 1-2
The 12 Corporations

Corporation	*Descriptive Label*	*Size*
A	Diversified luxury goods	medium
B	Electronic equipment	medium
C	Distribution	large
D	Diversified industrial products	large
E	Diversified chemicals	large
F	Hospitality	large
G	Electrical connectors	small
H	High tech(nology)	small
J	Consumer products	large
K	Electronic systems	small
L	Specialty chemicals	small
M	Consumer durables	medium

Key: *Large* signifies annual sales of more than $2 billion. *Medium* signifies annual sales between $1 billion and $2 billion. *Small* signifies annual sales of less than $1 billion.

not be, implemented at profit center organizational levels. Each corporation must make trade-offs to avoid, at least partially, any of three significant design constraints: the inability to measure changes in shareholder value; the inability to measure the profit center managers' unique contributions to measured results; and the desirability of using motivational contracts for nonmotivational purposes.

The second part of the book, contained in Chapters 3 through 7, describes in detail each of these constraints and the trade-offs it necessitates. These chapters explain why there is so much variation among the motivational contracts corporations choose. The variation stems from differences across corporations and profit centers in both the feasibility of various design alternatives and the costs associated with each of the necessary trade-offs.

The third part of the book is evaluative and prescriptive. My primary intent in the research was to be descriptive, because I believe we must understand the motivational contracts being used and the factors that shape them before we can make reliable statements about whether they are the best available and, if not, how they ought to be changed. The processes of observing and explaining, however, inevitably caused me to reflect on my observations and to make some evaluations.

I noted that some firms are bearing costs that seem to be largely avoidable. They have not avoided these costs either because their contract designers are unaware of some of the design alternatives available, or because they base their choices on questionable beliefs about the effects of various contract features. Reflecting the incomplete knowledge in the field, I found numerous areas where the designers' beliefs were in conflict. The conflicts existed among designers in the same firms, as well as across firms.

Because I had direct access to the profit center managers themselves, I was able to form my own judgments about the validity of various beliefs. Thus, this book includes some recommendations for designing effective motivational contracts. These prescriptions must be considered tentative, of course, for more research on these issues is needed in other settings and with larger samples of firms and profit centers. But this book is a first step toward a more sophisticated understanding of the broad range of contract design choices that are made and how the choices are interrelated—in terms of trade-offs, substitutions, and complementarities.

Throughout the text I have quoted extensively from the interviews I conducted because I wanted to present the contract descriptions, design rationales, and reactions in the managers' own terms as much as possible. These quotations are, in effect, the data of which this book is made. They serve as direct and powerful evidence of the choices the managers have made, the reasoning behind them, and the outcomes.

NOTES

1. Otley (1987), p. 20.
2. Vancil (1978), p. 25.
3. Williamson (1970), p. 175.
4. Mauriel and Anthony (1966) found that 82% of a sample of 2,658 of the largest 3,525 firms had multiple profit centers. Reece and Cool (1978) surveyed 620 of the *Fortune* 1000 firms and found that 95.8% had multiple profit centers. Vancil (1978) reported that 296 (95%) of his 313 manufacturing firm respondents had two or more profit centers.

5. Anthony (1988) defines a profit center as "a responsibility center whose inputs are measures in terms of costs or expenses and whose outputs are measured in terms of revenues." Most profit centers are themselves subdivided into multiple responsibility centers, including revenue and cost centers, and sometimes even other profit centers.

In this book, "profit center" is defined somewhat more broadly to include those entities that Anthony defines as "investment centers"—where the managers have responsibility for some or all categories of assets and liabilities, as well as profits. This is done because in actual practice, the line between profit centers and investment centers is quite blurred. Some managers, whose performance is measured in terms of, for example, return on operating assets, are clearly investment center managers. But other managers, who are technically only profit center managers, may be held accountable for the identical sets of balance sheet accounts because their performance is measured in terms of profit and a series of management-by-objective targets, such as days' receivables and inventory turnover.

6. Donaldson (1984), p. 144.

7. This is called "Gresham's Law of Planning." See, for example, Martin (1973).

8. This view of contracts is consistent with the modern economic theory of the firm, which views organizations as "legal fictions which serve as a nexus for a set of contracting relationships among individuals" (Jensen and Meckling, 1976, p. 310). In the terminology used in this literature, managerial incentive problems are said to arise when the preferences of "principals" (shareholders or top management) do not coincide with those of "agents" (managers or lower-level employees). Principals exercise control, then, by designing contracts to motivate the agents to act in the principals' best interest. The contracting problem is made difficult because the agents' efforts cannot be monitored directly, and because the agents have private information (i.e., they are experts who know more about the relevant aspects of decision making than do the principals), their efforts cannot be accurately inferred from measures of output. (All these features are accurate descriptions of the situation at profit center organization levels.) See also Fama (1980), Cheung (1983), Hart and Holmstrom (1987), and Levinthal (1988).

9. In a recent survey, the Hay Group (1988, p. 2) concluded, "Within recent years, contingent compensation [based on performance and improvements in productivity] has emerged as a key issue for American management."

10. For example, Reibstein (1987) and "Merit Increases Will Shrink Next Year as Emphasis Shifts to Incentive Pay," *The Wall Street Journal* (1987).

11. Sibson & Company (1987).

12. Using Arrow's (1974) terminology, contracts can be viewed as including both operating rules and enforcement rules. Operating rules tell managers what to do, and enforcement rules specify the rewards and penalties. The operating rules will not be followed unless some rewards or penalties are at least implied.

13. For example, Curran (1988), Winter (1987); "More Than Ever, It's Management for the Short-Term," *Business Week* (1986), and Hayes and Abernathy (1980).

14. For example, Wang (1988), Jereski (1987); "Cooking the Books," *Dun's Business Month* (January 1983); and Hudson (1983).

15. This is the so-called "externality" problem described in many economic writings and management accounting textbooks. See, for example, Atkinson and Kaplan (1989), Chapter 13.

16. Kerr (1982), p. 64.

17. For example, Jensen and Murphy (1988), Foulkes (1985), and Wilson (1973).

18. For example, "Management Bonuses: Do You Need Them?" *Chief Executive*, (1979).

19. For example, Kohn (1988), Pearce (1987), and Hamner (1975).

20. Uyterhoeven (1972, p. 84) also concludes that "the middle manager's job is quite different from that of the top-level general manager."

21. Eaton and Rosen (1983) provide evidence to support this latter preference.

22. Baker, Jensen, and Murphy (1988), pp. 593–594.

23. Ehrenberg and Milkovich (1987), p. 1.

24. Vancil (1978), p. 142. The other major work in this area was a field study: Solomons (1965).

25. The amount of diversity 12 corporations can represent is, of course, limited. The 12 corporations obviously do not represent all industries, and they do not face all the situations that can influence contract design choices. For example, none of the corporations studied is highly vertically integrated. Thus, transfer pricing is a minor annoyance to the managers involved; it is not a major organization-design constraint.

CHAPTER 2

Trade-offs in Motivational Contracts

Designing motivational contracts for profit center managers is difficult because the managers play varied and often ill-defined roles and operate in uncertain and changing environments. Research findings have pointed the way toward ideal contracts in simpler, more certain situations.[1] Even though such contracts are impossible to implement in their entirety at profit center organization levels, they are useful as standards by which to evaluate the contracts firms actually use because they highlight the trade-offs designers must make.

Identification of these trade-offs is the focus of this chapter. The chapter describes the ideal contract, compares it with the contracts used in the 12 corporations that participated in the study, and explains how constraints in the corporations' and profit centers' situations necessitate the design trade-offs.

The Ideal Motivational Contract

The ideal motivational contract for employees in reasonably simple, self-contained, stable work situations has six primary characteristics: (1) performance measures that are congruent with the overall corporate goal of maximizing shareholder value; (2) controllable results measures; (3) accurate results measures; (4) preset and challenging performance standards; (5) rewards that are meaningful, but at minimum cost; and (6) simplicity.

Performance Measures Should Be Congruent with the Corporate Goal of Maximizing Shareholder Value

The results for which employees are held accountable should be congruent with corporate goals.[2] Congruence is necessary to encourage employees to act in the corporation's best interest.

It is generally agreed that the primary goal of profit-making corporations is to maximize shareholder value (subject to some constraints, such as compliance with laws and adequate concern for employees, customers, and other stakeholders).[3] The value of any economic asset is calculated by discounting the expected future cash flows for time and risk. Thus employees should be rewarded for their contributions for increasing the cash flows the corporation expects to receive, accelerating the receipt of the cash, or increasing the likelihood that the cash will actually be received as expected (decreasing the risk).[4]

Any results measures used to assign rewards should be evaluated for their congruence with changes in shareholder value. Using measures that are not congruent with these changes creates perverse incentives that virtually ensure employees will misdirect their efforts.

Results Measures Should Be Controllable

The prescription that results measures should reflect only what the managers can control is included in most management writings. Here are some representative expressions of it taken from researchers in accounting, organizational behavior, and economics, respectively:

> It is generally agreed that it is better to evaluate managers on their *controllable* performance, and to filter out the uncontrollable factors.[5]
>
> A man should be held accountable for only that which he alone can control.[6]

> To the extent we are able to separate the results of managerial actions from the effects of exogenous factors—factors management cannot control—we are clearly much better off.[7]

The rationale for this prescription is that the more performance indicators are influenced by uncontrollable events, the less informative they are about the desirability of the actions the manager has taken.[8]

To the extent possible, uncontrollable business risks, such as changes in material costs and economic conditions and the shocks of random events, are best left with the shareholders. The shareholders, as owners, have implicitly agreed to bear these risks. Furthermore, they are better able to bear them because their rewards, unlike those of employees, come from a diversified portfolio.

Corporations that hold employees accountable for uncontrollable influences must bear some costs of doing so. Random distortions in performance evaluations cause employees' rewards to become more dependent on the vagaries of luck. Employees, being risk-averse, must be compensated for bearing that risk.[9] Thus firms that hold managers accountable for the effects of factors they cannot control will bear additional compensation costs. If they do not provide adequate additional compensation, they will bear alternate costs, in loss of motivation and, probably eventually, turnover.

Second, they must bear the costs of counterproductive, risk-averse behavior, unless they are able to prevent this behavior through stringent controls. Employees whose performance evaluations (and rewards) are affected by factors they cannot control may compensate by acting to lower their exposure to the uncontrollable factors. For instance, they may fail to develop or implement ideas for investments that are in the corporation's best interest but that involve some risk. They may also create budgetary slack or engage in some form of income-smoothing behavior to protect themselves against uncontrollable environmental shocks.

Third, corporations must bear the cost of lost time. Employees whose performance is evaluated partly on uncontrollable factors may waste effort arguing about the effects of those factors.

Results Measures Should Be Accurate (Verifiable and Objective)

Results measures should accurately reflect the quantity being measured. The term "accuracy" embodies two qualities: verifiability and objectivity.[10] Measurement verifiability means that the measurement dispersion is small; the measures can be "substantially duplicated by independent measurers using the same measurement methods."[11] But low dispersion is not sufficient to provide accurate measures; the measurement must also be objective—free from personal bias.[12] Objectivity is increased where the measurement is done or verified by persons who are independent of the rewards linked to the measures.

Where either verifiability or objectivity is lacking, the measures do not reflect the aspect of performance being measured. The noise or bias in the measures obscures the signals provided about the managers' performance, and the likelihood that performance will be evaluated incorrectly increases sharply.[13] Poor evaluations, in turn, lead to poor corporate decisions, such as about who should receive incentive compensation and who should be promoted, and cause profit center managers to become frustrated and less motivated.[14]

Inaccurate performance measures cause the corporation's overall motivational contract costs to increase for reasons quite similar to those stemming from the inclusion of uncontrollable distortions in the measures. The vagaries in the evaluations caused by the measurement inaccuracies force the profit center managers to bear additional risk, and they have to be compensated for doing so.

Performance Standards Should Be Preset and Challenging

Standards used to evaluate performance should be set before the measurement period, and they should also be challenging. This prescription comes from a sizable body of behavioral research. For example, the authors of a review of more than 100 studies in the psychology literature concluded that "specific, hard goals [induce] better performance than medium, easy, do-your-best, or no goals."[15]

The rationale for having preset standards is based on the realization that most people are goal-oriented. They respond to the challenge of trying to meet a performance standard even when the corporation does not give them monetary rewards for that achievement. They judge personal success by how well they achieve a predetermined goal, and they work to improve their chances of being successful. Thus, preset standards are motivating.

The rationale for having challenging standards is to motivate employees to do their best. Too-easy targets lead to underperformance because people can reach them with less than maximum effort, or they can slack off after they reach the target. Targets that are too difficult are not motivating because they are seen as unattainable.[16] Psychological studies have shown that optimum motivation occurs when targets are set on the basis of past performance to be achievable between 25% and 40% of the time.[17]

Results-Dependent Rewards Should Be Meaningful, But At Minimum Cost

All employees' actions can be interpreted as furthering the individuals' self-interests.[18] Thus, results-dependent rewards (or penalties) should be sufficiently meaningful to offset other incentives employees have to act contrary to the corporation's best interest.[19]

In general, meaningfulness is related to the size of the reward (or penalty) promised (or threatened) and to its timeliness, because rewards long separated in time from performance lose much of their incentive effect.[20] The rewards that are meaningful to a particular employee, however, depend on personal circumstances and tastes. For example, some employees are greatly interested in immediate cash bonuses, whereas others are more interested in increasing their autonomy, in improving their promotion possibilities, or in merely doing a good job for their corporation.[21] The corporation can provide meaningful rewards at the lowest possible cost if it tailors the rewards to employees' preferences.

The Contract Should Be Simple

Ideally, firms should use only one, simple motivational contract that describes the results the corporation wants and the rewards for employees who produce them. Simplicity is desirable because it eases administration of the contract and, more importantly, facilitates communication of the contract terms. Without effective communication, employees cannot be properly motivated.

For employees in well-defined, stable roles, ideal motivation occurs only where a single, simple contract with all of the six qualities described above is used. When any one of these qualities is missing, the firm suffers. Table 2-1 summarizes the resulting negative consequences.

Motivational contracts with all of the ideal qualities can be designed for some workers. Piece-rate contracts used for some factory workers, for example, are virtually ideal because the measures are congruent with the employees' contributions to shareholder value, controllable, and accurate; the performance standards are preset and challenging; and the rewards are meaningful and set to be competitive but not excessive.

For profit center managers, however, the ideal is impossible to achieve. Corporate managers use multiple contracts to motivate their profit center managers, and some of the contracts appear far from ideal.

Multiple Motivational Contracts

All 12 firms in this study use multiple motivational contracts that promise profit center managers rewards for results. The contracts are quite varied, but those with potentially the most significant motivational effects fall into four

TABLE 2-1
Qualities of the Ideal Motivational Contract, and Effect If Quality Is Missing

Contract Element	*Quality*	*Effect if Quality is Missing (Everything Else Equal)*
Performance Measurement	Congruent with corporate goals (maximize shareholder value)	—Displaces motivation
	Reflects only what the manager can control	—Must compensate managers for bearing extra risk —Induces risk-averse behavior —May cause managers to argue about the fairness of their evaluations —Can create frustration that leads to lower motivation
	Accurate (verifiable and objective)	—Forces possibly unfair evaluations that will lead to poor decisions and reduce motivation —Must compensate managers for bearing risk of unfair evaluations
Performance Standard	Preset, challenging	—Lowers motivational impact
Rewards	Meaningful, at minimum cost	—Lowers motivational impact or creates excessive costs
Overall	Simple	—Lowers motivational impact —Causes higher administrative costs

categories: (1) threats of penalties for missing short-term profit budget targets; (2) promises of incentive compensation for annual performance; (3) written promises of rewards for long-term performance; and (4) unwritten promises of rewards for long-term performance.

PENALTIES FOR MISSING SHORT-TERM PROFIT BUDGET TARGETS

The vast majority of profit center managers in the 12 corporations face the same budget contract: they are asked to make their budget targets and told that if they fail to do so, at least more years than not, they will face potentially severe consequences. Most of the firms place the greatest emphasis on meeting *annual* budget targets, but some also place significant emphasis on meeting *quarterly* targets and those for even shorter periods.

Managers who fail to achieve budget targets usually lose out on many rewards, and they may be assessed some organizational penalties. Bonuses and salary increases are obvious rewards that will be reduced if budget targets are missed. Often even more important, the managers also lose credibility, which in turn harms their promotion possibilities and their ability to sell their ideas and compete effectively for corporate resources. They are also likely to lose some autonomy, as top management is more likely to intervene in the profit centers' affairs where budget targets are being missed. A profit center manager in corporation H (high tech) saw a clear link between budget achievement and managerial autonomy:

> If our profit before tax is according to budget and profitability is greater than 20% [a corporate-determined minimum acceptable performance level], the people at corporate allow me to do pretty much what I want. I may get some comments and questions, but not in an approval/disapproval mode. Last year, in fact, when we were having a good year, [my boss] and I agreed to disagree on the amount of money I was spending on marketing. (He thought I was spending too much.) If I wasn't meeting budget, however, I would get a lot of pressure to get profits up. [Corporate] is very much a fair-weather friend. I want to be able to run the show here. Meeting plan is the way that is accomplished.

Although this "make-the-budget-or-else" contract provides a potentially significant threat, the targets are set almost as minimum performance standards that effective, hardworking managers can expect to meet, even if they run into some bad luck.

All of the evidence I gathered on this subject suggests that a large majority of the profit center budget targets are set so they can and will be achieved. The corporate and profit center-level managers estimated high probabilities of budget achievement; they reported that historically their budget targets were met far more often than they were missed; and they reported that budget overachievements are likely to be larger than the underachievements.

When I asked the managers and controllers to estimate the probability they held when their budget was approved that the target would be met, most expressed confidence that they would meet it.[22] These data are shown in Table 2-2.[23] Of the 44 profit center managers responding to the subjective probability question, 39 (89%) reported a probability estimate of at least 75%. Even more striking, 24 (55%) reported a probability of 90% or greater, with 7 (16%) reporting they were 100% certain they would meet the target, whereas only 3

TABLE 2-2
Subjective Probability at Time of Budget Approval of Achieving Budget Target

Entity		*Probability Estimates*			
		Profit Center Level		*Level of Immediate Superior*	
Corporation	*Profit Center*	*General Manager*	*Controller*	*General Manager*	*Controller*
A	1	90%	85%	b	b
(Diversified	2	0	40	b	b
luxury goods)	3	80	95	90%	100%
	4	75	—	78	—
	5	80	—	b	—
B	1	88	a	50	a
(Electronic	2	90	70	a	50
equipment)	3	23	a	30	a
C	1	100	100	a	a
(Distribution)	2	90	b	a	a
	3	90	90	a	a
	4	90	a	75	70
	5	75	—	75	b
	6	60	—	75	b
D	1	100	b	78	a
(Diversified	2	90	b	55	a
industrial	3	b	80	a	a
products)	4	99	b	a	a

TABLE 2-2 (*Continued*)

Entity		*Probability Estimates*			
		Profit Center Level		*Level of Immediate Superior*	
Corporation	*Profit Center*	*General Manager*	*Controller*	*General Manager*	*Controller*
E	1	30%	38%	10%	a
(Diversified	2	75	50	50	a
chemicals)	3	b	a	a	a
	4	85	—	a	50
	5	73	50	a	—
	6	b	a	a	a
F	1	b	—	95	—
(Hospitality)	2	90	—	90	—
	3	95	—	95	—
	4	b	—	80	—
	5	100	—	100	—
	6	b	—	a	—
G	1	90	a	100	100
(Electrical	2	80	a	100	70
connectors)	3	97	b	100	100
	4	63	a	100	90
H	1	b	b	b	—
(High tech)	2	100	—	b	a
	3	b	—	b	a
	4	90	a	a	—
	5	99	b	a	—
J	1	93	b	a	b
(Consumer	2	95	b	b	b
products)	3	100	99	b	b
	4	95	a	99	70
	5	80	80	a	80
K	1	83	90	a	80
(Electronic	2	75	—	a	80
systems)	3	b	—	b	75
L	1	90	78	b	a
(Specialty	2	85	>50	b	a
chemicals)	3	100	80	b	a
	4	100	—	100	b
	5	80	—	a	a
M	1	80	80	80	b
(Consumer durables)	2	80	b	a	a

— = position does not exist.
a = was not interviewed.
b = did not answer question.

(7%) felt they had less than a 50% chance of doing so. The median response was 90%; the mean was 85%.

The interviews convinced me that these high probabilities of success are not specific to the year of interview. A number of managers spoke proudly of their record of budget achievements. For example, the manager of profit center 3 in corporation G reported that in 33 years as a manager, he had never missed a budget.

The managers' records of actual achievement support their high achievability estimates. I was able to collect data on the budget performance of 39 of the 54 profit centers for the year just completed. The data, displayed in Table 2-3, show that of the 39, 29 (74%) met or exceeded their budget

TABLE 2-3
Evidence About Actual Achievement of Budget Targets

Entity		*Meet Budget Target?*	
Corporation	*Profit Center*	*Prior Year*	*Current Year (latest estimate)*
A	1	Y	Y
(Diversified	2	Y	Y
luxury goods)	3	Y	Y
	4		Y
	5		Y
B	1		
(Electronic	2	N	
equipment)	3	N	
C	1	Y	
(Distribution)	2		
	3		
	4	Y	
	5		
	6		
D	1	Y	Y
(Diversified	2	Y	Y
industrial	3	Y	
products)	4	Y	Y
E	1	N	Y
(Diversified	2	Y	Y
chemicals)	3	N	
	4	Y	Y
	5		
	6		

TABLE 2-3 (*Continued*)

Entity		*Meet Budget Target?*	
Corporation	*Profit Center*	*Prior Year*	*Current Year (latest estimate)*
F (Hospitality)	1	Y	Y
	2	N	Y
	3	Y	
	4	Y	
	5	Y	Y
	6	Y	
G (Electrical connectors)	1	Y	
	2	N	
	3	Y	
	4	N	
H (High tech)	1	N	
	2	Y	
	3	Y	
	4		
	5	Y	
J (Consumer products)	1		
	2	Y	
	3		
	4	Y	N
	5	Y	
K (Electronic systems)	1	Y	N
	2		N
	3	Y	Y
L (Specialty chemicals)	1		Y
	2		Y
	3	Y	Y
	4	N	
	5	Y	
M (Consumer durables)	1	N	
	2	Y	Y

Y = yes, actual profit > budget.
N = no, actual profit < budget.
blank = no information.

targets.[24] At the time of the interviews, on average conducted in the middle of the fiscal year, I also obtained the latest estimates of success in the current fiscal year from 22 profit center managers, and 19 (86%) reported they would achieve their budget targets.

Finally, the controller of one firm provided five-year histories of the budget performance of three of the profit centers in which interviews were conducted. He reported that these profit centers achieved their budgeted profit targets in 12 of the 15 profit center-years. Furthermore, because the overachievements were considerably larger than the misses, the average actual profit performance for those years exceeded the budget targets by 39.5%. Thus, it appears that many profit center managers are rewarded for attaining a budgeted profit target they are virtually certain to attain.

Although the terms of this "make-the-budget-or-else" contract are not written down, the profit center managers understand them very well and are influenced by them. The following comments are representative of managers' perceptions:

> What is the effect on people who miss plans? It isn't pleasant. They will be seen as substandard performers. Everybody knows who the bad guys are . . . they miss forecasts regularly. We get rid of most of them (group controller in corporation D).
>
> Corporate management says that good managers don't miss forecasts (profit center controller in corporation E).
>
> This is not a company that gives a pat on the back for choosing a lofty goal and missing it by 2% (profit center manager in corporation J).

Where the profit center managers are struggling to meet budget targets, this contract usually has such powerful effects on their behavior that it dominates all the other motivational contracts.[25]

Incentive Compensation Awards for Annual Performance

A second type of motivational contract used in the 12 firms for profit center managers promises cash rewards for annual performance measured in financial (and sometimes nonfinancial) terms. These short-term incentive contracts tend to be complex, and they are quite varied across firms. Many of the contract terms are communicated clearly in writing, but some firms' contracts have unwritten features that allow evaluators room to exercise judgment and discretion.

Table 2-4 outlines some of the major features of the firms'

TABLE 2-4
Overview of Major Features of 12 Corporations' Short-Term Incentive Compensation Contracts

	Corporation											
	A *Diversified Luxury Goods*	*B* *Electronic Equipment*	*C* *Distribution*	*D* *Diversified Industrial Products*	*E* *Diversified Chemicals*	*F* *Hospitality*	*G* *Electrical Connectors*	*H* *High Tech*	*J* *Consumer Products*	*K* *Electronic Systems*	*L* *Specialty Chemicals*	*M* *Consumer Durables*
1. Profit center managers included in contract?	yes	yes	yes	yes	yes	yes	yes	yes	yes	yes	yes	yes
2. Is contract uniform across the corporation?	a few exceptions	yes	yes	yes	a few exceptions	no	yes	yes	a few exceptions	yes	a few exceptions	yes
3. Size of awards (% of salary):												
target	20%	30%	50% is common	30%	35%	15–25%	20–25%	80–100%	10–20%	20–25%	60%	25%
maximum	60%	54%	50%	unlimited	unlimited	40%	unlimited	140%	30%	40–50%	60%	45–67.5%
4. "Pain-sharing" limits on awards?	yes, <3% corp. earnings	no	no	yes, corp. ROC determines size of bonus pool	yes, corp. PAT determines size of pool	no	no	no	yes, corp. oper. profit growth determines size of bonus pool	yes, no payout if corp. EPS & ROI <80% of plan	no	no
5. Results measures (weighting in parentheses if explicit)	PAT (35%); cash flow (35%); 2 personal objectives (30%)	worldwide ROA (40%); worldwide sales (30%); corp. sales (30%)	PBT (50–100%); 1–5 key objectives (0–50%)	list of 6–12 measures; ROC most important	PAT (50–100%); corp. PAT (0–50%)	oper. profit (50–60%); personal ratings (30–50%); group profit (5–15%)	PBT, bookings; shipments, quality, efficiency, delinquencies	ROS (35%); ROA (15%); profit growth (50%)	list of 5–25 objectives	PBT (50%); 1 or 2 personal objectives (20%); corp. EPS and ROI (30%)	ROA (80%); corp. ROI (20%)	oper. inc. (50–75%); group or corp. earnings (25–50%)
6. Target performance level	subjective (CEO)	budget	budget; prior year actual	budget	budget	budget	budget	timeless standard	budget	budget	timeless standard, but influenced by budget and CEO subjectivity	budget

7. Adjustments made for uncontrollables?	rarely	rarely	yes	yes	yes	rarely	no	no	yes	rarely	yes	yes
8. Award cutoff levels												
lower	80% target	sales: 90% budget; ROA: 80% budget	prior year actual	none	67% budget	85% budget	100% budget	none	none	80% budget	20% ROA	80% budget
upper	110% target	sales: 115% budget; ROA: varies by profit-ability level	105–110% budget	none	133% budget	105–110% budget	none	ROS = 50%; ROA = 100%; profit growth = 100%	none	150% budget	35% (or lower if budget lower)	130% budget
Award at lower cutoff (% of salary)	0	15%	0	0	0	0	0	0	5%	12–15%	0	0
9. Shape of results/ award function	linear	linear	linear	linear	linear except flat between 90–105% of budget	step function	linear	linear	step function	linear	linear	linear
10. Awards												
form	cash	cash	cash	cash	⅔ cash; ⅓ restricted stock	cash	cash	cash	cash	cash	cash	cash
timing	annual	annual	annual	annual	annual	annual	quarterly, but based on annual performance	annual	annual	annual	quarterly, but based on annual perform-ance	annual

Key:
PAT = profit after tax
PBT = profit before tax
ROA = return on assets
ROC = return on capital
ROS = return on sales
ROI = return on investment

short-term incentive contracts. Several similarities are obvious. One is the heavy weighting placed on financial measures of performance. Although most firms use multiple measures of performance, the incentive rewards they promise are based primarily on performance measured in accounting terms, most commonly profit or return on assets (line 5 of Table 2-4). In addition, the performance standards are typically the annual budget targets (line 6); rewards are earned only for performance that meets or exceeds the targets. Both profit center managers and their superiors are well aware of the central importance of the earnings measures and the budget standards, as the following typical quotes illustrate:

> Operating income is all that's important. We also have goals for return on capital, program accomplishments, accounts receivable, and inventories, but if we don't make our operating income targets, nothing else matters (a profit center manager in corporation E).
>
> If I didn't make my budget [profit target], I wouldn't expect to make a bonus, no matter what else happened. If I do make my budget, I expect a bonus (a profit center manager in corporation J).
>
> If [the profit center managers] make their operating profit targets but miss the others, it doesn't cost them much. If they miss their market share objective, it doesn't cost them much this year, but it may cost them down the road, of course. [This corporation has] a slavish obsession with short-term profit (a group vice president in corporation J).

The firms' short-term incentive contracts have a few other similarities. The rewards generally increase linearly with results (line 9), and they are usually given in cash at the end of each year (line 10).

The firms' short-term incentive compensation contracts are different, however, in a number of important ways. The target awards—the rewards profit center managers earn by achieving their performance targets—vary markedly, from 15% to 100% of base salary (line 3), with a median in the range of 25–30%.[26] Seven firms use a single contract for all their profit center managers, whereas the other five tailor some aspects of their contracts, particularly the bases on which the rewards are assigned, to specific profit center characteristics (line 2). Nine firms base part of the rewards on corporate or group performance; the other three base them only on profit center performance (lines 4 and 5). Six firms make some adjustments for uncontrollable influences that distort the results measures; the other six either do not make such adjustments or make them only under extreme circumstances (line 7). Nine firms define results levels below which no bonuses will be awarded, and a different nine define a level above which no extra bonuses will be awarded (line 8). The reasons for these contract differences are explained in the chapters that follow.

Written Promises of Rewards for Long-Term Performance

A third type of motivational contract promises in writing rewards based on the long-term (multiyear) performance of the profit center or higher-level entities, particularly the corporation. Ten of the 12 firms offer one or more such contracts for their profit center managers.

The terms of these contracts vary significantly. Table 2-5 provides an overview of the firms' treatment of two important contract features: the bases for assigning rewards and the rewards' form. This table shows that only three firms link rewards directly to multiyear profit center financial performance; six link them directly to corporate financial performance; and six base them on organization level.

Table 2-5 also shows that only two firms provide cash awards for long-term performance. Much more common are grants of restricted stock, phantom stock, or stock options, whose values are difficult to estimate. The contracts tend to be quite lucrative when the firm's stock is performing well, but often have little or no value when the stock price is down. Again, the reasons for the variation in the firms' long-term contracts are explained in the chapters that follow.

Unwritten Promises of Rewards for Long-Term Performance

The final type of motivational contract involves unwritten, but potentially important, promises of rewards for managers

TABLE 2-5

Overview of the Bases for Assignment of Rewards and the Form of the Rewards of 12 Corporations' Long-Term Contracts

	Corporation											
	A *Diversified Luxury Goods*	*B* *Electronic Equipment*	*C* *Distribution*	*D* *Diversified Industrial Products*	*E* *Diversified Chemicals*	*F* *Hospitality*	*G* *Electrical Connectors*	*H* *High Tech*	*J* *Consumer Products*	*K* *Electronic Systems*	*L* *Specialty Chemicals*	*M* *Consumer Durables*
Bases for rewards:												
Profit center financial performance	X							X			X	
Corporate financial performance	X	X							X	X	X	X
Organizational level	X			X	X		X		X	X		
Form of rewards:												
Cash		X										X
Stock (restricted, phantom, options)	X	X		X	X		X	X	X	X	X	X

who perform well over an extended period of time. These contracts vary widely in their terms—the rewards promised and the bases on which they will be given. And they can be communicated in various ways, ranging from explicit oral orders to tacit understandings about the ways things are or have to be. For example, some profit centers managers told me that if they do what's right, the corporation will "take care" of them. But if they act foolishly, they will be punished with demotion or loss of reputation, subjectively assigned bonuses, or their job.

Such a contract given to a profit center manager in corporation C (distribution) is described by an executive vice president:

> I just had lunch with one of our young managers, and one of these [long-term/short-term] issues came up. He is having a tough year and is worried about it. We discussed some specifics, and I just told him to do what's right. I think he got the message. It's important that we have a long-term relationship of trust. I can't write down what I want him to do, and there is always the danger that some judgments will be influenced [so as to make this year's profit target at the expense of the long-term].

One common unwritten contract, which is important for virtually all profit center managers except those nearing retirement, involves promises of career advancement for those demonstrating superior managerial ability over time. It is rare that profit center managers are told directly what they must do to earn a promotion. They infer the results and personal characteristics that lead to advancement by observing over time whom top management chooses to promote. The managers know that the terms of the contract vary across the organization: what applies in one group of profit centers (for instance, a consumer products group) may not apply in another (for instance, a defense group). Furthermore, the managers know that the terms may change with changes in top management or corporate or group strategies.

In many cases, the results leading to promotions are apparently not dissimilar to those leading to other rewards, such as bonuses, salary increases, and greater autonomy: the managers who are promoted are generally those who meet their financial targets consistently. For example, a profit center manager explained his understanding of his firm's promotion contract as follows: "Profit is important, and turning it in in a predictable fashion is important. If you do both, you get rewarded and promoted."

One important difference between this promotion contract and most of the written contracts, though, is that the long-term rewards are not based solely on an individual profit center manager's performance. They involve some degree of competition among managers both within and outside the firm.

How the Actual Contracts Deviate from the Ideal

Individually and often collectively, the motivational contracts the firms use lack many of the characteristics of the ideal contract described earlier. *Congruence* appears to be lacking because the controllable results weighted most heavily for purposes of assigning rewards are short-term accounting measures of performance, particularly profit and return on assets, and research has shown that these accounting-earnings-based measures are not reliable indicators of changes in shareholder value. Rappaport explains the shortcomings of accounting numbers as indicators of changes in shareholder values and presents evidence documenting those shortcomings. His most significant conclusion is that "earnings growth does not necessarily lead to the creation of economic value for shareholders."[27] Still, firms tend to provide the greatest rewards to profit center managers who are best at producing (or at least reporting) short-term accounting earnings.

Controllability seems to be lacking because the rewards promised to virtually all the firms' profit center managers are based on measures that are affected by a wide range of influences the managers cannot control. These influences include economic conditions, competitors' actions, and other managers' successes and failures. Even in the six firms that make some adjustments for uncontrollable influences, many such influences go unadjusted.

Measurement accuracy seems to be lacking because many of the measures on which rewards are based lack some degree of verifiability or objectivity. Even accounting earnings measures, among the most verifiable of the results measures used, are not totally verifiable because flexibility in accounting rules sometimes leads to widely varying earnings numbers, all of which are technically "good accounting." Objectivity is a concern because many contracts, even those that are explained in some detail in writing, allow superiors substantial subjectivity in evaluating profit center managers' performances. In particular, superiors' decisions about whether and how to adjust for uncontrollable influences often have a heavy subjective component.

The performance standards are not always *preset and challenging*. Some standards are really not set until after the measurement period has ended. This occurs where firms allow evaluators considerable latitude to decide after the period whether the standards were fair.

In addition, for most profit center managers the most important preset performance standard—the annual profit budget target—is certainly less challenging than the targets with a 25% to 40% chance of achievement that prior research has shown to provide the ideal amount of challenge. The firms set their budget targets with the expectation that the profit center managers will achieve them. In essence, they define success as reaching budgeted profit targets, and they contract for success, not for results that maximize shareholder value.

The results-dependent rewards are not always *meaningful*. Their size is not a problem because profit center managers seem to be motivated by the possibility of earning bonuses whether their bonus expectation is 20% or 70% of salary. But a potential deviation from the ideal of providing meaningful rewards occurs because most firms limit the profit range within which extra short-term rewards, particularly bonuses, are provided for additional favorable results. Outside this range, the rewards are obviously not meaningful because there is no link between rewards and results.

In addition, the firms' rewards for long-term performance are often not meaningful to managers. The reasons are that the long-term rewards are: (1) not given promptly; (2) based heavily on aspects of performance managers cannot control; (3) uncertain because they depend on the future price of the corporation's stock; or (4) insignificant in comparison with the rewards for short-term performance.

Contract *simplicity* is also often lacking. Some of the contracts, particularly the written short-term and long-term ones, are quite complex. Many of the profit center managers claim that their firms' contracts are so complex they do not understand how the rewards are calculated.

Overall, then, we must conclude that both individually and collectively the motivational contracts the firms at profit center organization levels use deviate significantly from the ideal. The roles profit center managers play and the environments in which they manage, however, make the deviations from the ideal at least partly inevitable; design trade-offs are necessary.

Constraints and Trade-offs

Contract design trade-offs stem from three important constraints: (1) the inability to measure changes in shareholder value directly; (2) the inability to isolate the profit center managers' unique contributions to results; and (3) the desirability of using some motivational contract elements for other than motivational purposes. These constraints and the trade-offs they necessitate are presented in Figure 2-1, and each is described below.

Design Constraint #1: Inability to Measure Changes in Shareholder Value Directly

The first set of trade-offs follows from the inability to measure changes in shareholder value directly. Although several

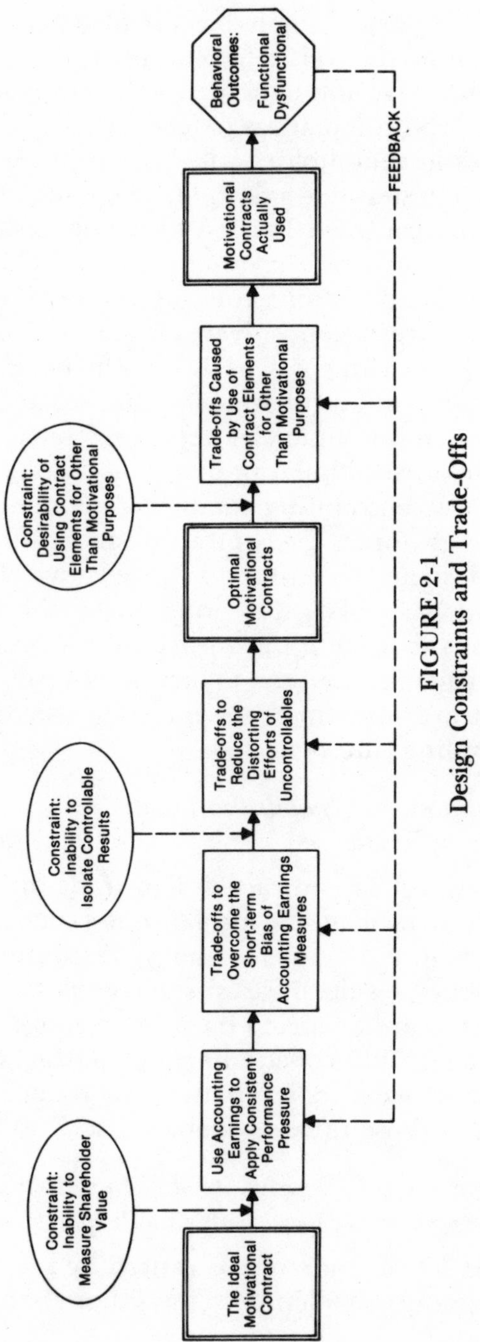

FIGURE 2-1
Design Constraints and Trade-Offs

consulting firms are trying to sell the idea of direct measurement of shareholder value for incentive purposes, virtually no companies have implemented their suggestions. Almost invariably, corporate managers feel they are unable to measure changes in shareholder value at profit center organization levels accurately enough to make the measures usable in a motivational contract. Instead they emphasize short-term accounting earnings as a useful proxy.

There are good reasons for this choice: the accounting-earnings measures are positively correlated (and thus somewhat congruent) with changes in shareholder value; they are relatively objective and verifiable; and because they are already prepared for financial reporting purposes, they require almost no additional preparation costs.

Use of these accounting measures for motivational purposes, however, forces the contract designers to make a series of choices designed to minimize the negative effects of these numbers. In particular, they must offset the known short-term bias in the accounting measures and direct the profit center managers' attention to key long-term performance factors that are sometimes absent or obscured in the summary accounting numbers.

Design Constraint #2: Inability to Isolate Managers' Unique Contributions to Results

The second set of contract design trade-offs is caused by the inability to isolate the profit center managers' unique contributions to the results achieved. Accounting measures, and many other results measures that could be used for contract purposes, are distorted by a broad range of uncontrollable influences. This constraint leads contract designers into decisions about whether to eliminate or reduce the effects of some or all of these uncontrollables, and if so, how.

Design Constraint #3: Desirability of Using Motivational Contract Elements for Nonmotivational Purposes

The third set of trade-offs is caused by the desirability of using some contract elements for other than motivational purposes. Sometimes designers knowingly choose to use motivational contracts containing elements that are not ideal for motivational purposes because those elements better serve other organizational purposes, such as corporate risk reduction, managerial retention, or improvement of corporate financial reporting, resource planning, and control.

Making Wise Trade-offs

The contracts the firms use deviate from the motivational ideal because each of these constraints forces designers to make trade-offs. Each trade-off involves a cost—the sacrifice of one or more of the ideal contract qualities—and the designers' task is to make the trade-offs so as to minimize these costs.

Wise trade-offs can be made only with a good understanding of the full range of feasible design alternatives, the outcomes (positive and negative) produced by each design choice, and the relative importance of these outcomes in a given profit center or corporation where the contract is to be used. Because the alternatives, outcomes, and desires vary across situations, it is inevitable that designers select quite different contracts.

Some trade-offs cause some contract features and even whole contracts to be designed for a particular narrow purpose. Thus, only the *combination* of contracts, not the individual contracts, can be compared with the ideal.

NOTES

1. My understanding of this ideal stems from discussions with managers during this and other field research projects, and from my reviews of textbooks and summaries of research findings. In addition to the writings cited in the chapter, Holmstrom and Tirole (1989), Holmstrom (1987), and Horngren and Foster (1986) were particularly helpful. A few of these ideas appeared in two of my earlier works (Merchant, 1985; Merchant and Bruns, 1986).

2. Charles Horngren (1986) has credited Robert Anthony (1964, p. 362) with introducing the term "goal congruence" to the accounting literature. The term now appears in virtually all textbooks in management accounting, control, compensation, and general management. See, for example, Horngren and Foster (1986) and Henderson (1985).

3. See, for example, Treynor (1981) and Mason (1988).

Donaldson (1984, p. 22) observes that in fact top-level managers tend to direct their efforts toward increasing *corporate wealth,* not shareholder wealth. They want to maintain access to a generous supply of funds, which includes cash, credit, and corporate purchasing power, to ensure survival and a high degree of corporate self-sufficiency. Managers focusing on corporate wealth tend to be conservative in borrowing and in paying dividends. This desire for self-sufficiency causes them to settle for less than maximum corporate growth when the growth places strains on the firm's pool of available capital.

The distinction between maximization of shareholder and corporate wealth is not of major importance when goals for profit center managers are being considered because the primary difference between the two concepts is in the way investments are financed. Profit center managers are almost invariably not involved in these capital structure decisions. Their task is to invest whatever funds are made available to them from whatever sources in ways that will generate the most wealth, regardless of whether the wealth will be disbursed as dividends or retained.

4. This point has been made in both the academic and practitioner literature. In an academic review article, Holmstrom and Tirole (1989), for example, state that a "manager's true performance . . . is equal to the increment in the expected present discounted value of profits." In a *Harvard Business Review* article, Mason (1988, p. 72) concludes that, "Executives' financial rewards must be linked more clearly and more emphatically to shareholders' if increasing shareholder value continues to be the first priority of U.S. corporations." And in a *Business Week* article analyzing the causes of the recent spate of LBOs, Dobrzynski (1988, p. 31) writes, "Mostly [managers] are mispaid—with pay and bonuses tied to accounting profits instead of value creation, calculated by such measures as return to shareholders."

5. Magee (1986), p. 265 (emphasis in original).

6. Dalton (1971), p. 27.

7. Michael Jensen, quoted in "A Roundtable Discussion of Management Compensation" (1985), p. 29.

8. One clear exception to this general principle occurs in a few settings where it is possible to compare managers' performance with that of other managers facing the same environmental circumstances. Where this so-called relative performance evaluation can be made, considering uncontrollables does actually provide additional information about how the managers have performed, even though profit center managers cannot control the other managers' results. See Baiman and Demski (1980), Holmstrom (1982), and Antle and Smith (1986).

There may be another exception, depending on how one chooses to define "controllable." Zimmerman (1979) and Baiman and Noel (1985) find that it is desirable to hold managers accountable for some categories of costs, such as corporate overhead and capacity costs, for which they have no direct control because doing so conveys information to them about how their decisions affect areas outside their control. One could argue, however, that the managers do in fact control these costs, even if they are not incurred directly in the managers' immediate organizations.

Both of these situations are discussed further in Chapter 6.

9. This statement follows directly from the definition of risk-aversion, and it is used as a basic tenet in much theoretical research in economics. See, for example, Nalbantian (1987), p. 12.

10. McKeown (1971), p. 28.

11. Accounting Principles Board (1970), p. 37.

12. Staubus (1977), p. 49.

13. For example, Ivancevich et al. (1977, p. 465) argue that "individual performance assessment must be made with as much objective data as possible."

14. Kopelman and Reinharth (1982, p. 40) conclude that reward systems "that tie performance more closely to rewards are likely to generate higher levels of performance, particularly after a year or two."

15. Locke et al. (1981), p. 131. Similarly, Donaldson (1984, p. 139) concludes, "Goals must be boldly stated and clearly defined to influence organizational behavior."

16. See, for example, Locke et al. (1988).

17. This is the conclusion of Dunbar (1971) who synthesizes the findings of Stedry (1960) and Stedry and Kay (1966). Other, more recent, studies show similar findings (see Rockness [1977] and Chow [1983]). These probabilities of expected achievement are how textbook prescriptions for targets that are "tough but attainable" (Newman et al., 1987) or "currently attainable" are made operational.

18. See, for example, Culbert and McDonough (1980).

19. This is an important argument in Locke's (1968) often-cited theory of motivation and incentives.

20. For example, Costello and Zalkind (1963) conclude that the timing of the reinforcement (reward) determines the speed with which learning takes place and how lasting its effects will be.

21. A key element of Etzioni's (1988) theory of "socio-economics" is the acknowledgment that many social and moral interests, such as a sense of duty, a sense of identity, and a feeling of self-worth, provide powerful motivators for most human beings. Also see Mahoney (1964).

22. To solicit subjective estimates of budget achievability, I asked the following question: At the time your profit budget for this year was approved, what did you feel the probability was that it would at least be achieved?

To improve the accuracy of the responses, I asked the question in several forms, using suggestions made by Chesley (1975) for eliciting subjective probabilities. For example, if the interviewee responded that he or she felt the probability of achieving the budget was 90%, I sometimes asked if that meant "the budget was relatively easy to make." This often made the managers think more deeply about their responses. On no occasion, however, did it cause a respondent to alter his or her probabilistic estimates. I also gathered data for each profit center from multiple sources where possible. The multiple respondents' answers to this subjective-estimate question were generally consistent.

23. This data set is incomplete for two reasons. First, some interviews were not possible because the role did not exist (particularly profit center controller), because the role was not filled, because the person in the role was too new or otherwise not knowledgeable about the relevant questions (not part of the management team), or because scheduling could not be arranged. Second, some individuals did not answer the budget-achievability question either because they were not asked it (they were interviewed early in the research process, before budget achievability had been identified as a focal issue) or because they were unable or unwilling to put a probabilistic estimate on the likelihood of budget achievement.

24. This data set is incomplete for the same reasons as for Table 2-2. In addition, data on the current estimate of budget achievement were not collected when the interview occurred early in the fiscal year.

25. This finding of the central importance of the budget contract is consistent

with that of Hofstede (1967), who conducted a major field study of manufacturing managers in five corporations in the Netherlands.

26. This is quite similar to Vancil's (1978, p. 317) finding of a median bonus of 24.8% of salary for profit center managers.

Sibson (1981, p. 245) presents the results of a survey showing more detailed, but still comparable, data. This survey shows that the bonus percentage varies with the salary level. For general managers earning $50,000, for example, the average annual bonus is 27% of salary, whereas for managers earning $100,000, the average bonus is 35%.

27. Rappaport (1986), p. 27. Many other authors, including Rich and Larson (1987), Edwards (1986), National Association of Accountants (1986), Brindisi (1985), Merchant (1985), and Curtis (1985), have described similar limitations of accounting earnings measures as proxies for economic income.

CHAPTER 3

Using Short-Term Accounting Earnings to Exert Consistent Short-Term Performance Pressure

> "Without pressure for short-term results, you'll just have people squander money."

Accounting earnings (and earnings-derived measures such as return on assets) reported for periods of one year and less are by far the most important performance measure in contracts used to motivate profit center managers. Critics say this choice is flawed because it causes managers to be excessively short-term-oriented. Even in the face of this criticism, however, corporate managers have maintained their emphasis on accounting performance measures.

They have reasons for their choice. They feel that consistent short-term performance pressure is essential to motivate most profit center managers properly; that this pressure is usually best applied with a single, concise, bottom-line, summary performance measure that allows the managers operating autonomy, with control exercised on a management-by-exception basis; and that the best bottom-line performance measurement alternative available is accounting earnings.

Accounting measures have some significant advantages over possible bottom-line alternatives: cash flow, inflation-adjusted earnings, and changes in shareholder value. In particular, accounting measures are at least somewhat congruent with changes in shareholder value; the numbers are more objective and verifiable than are the bottom-line alternatives; they are inexpensive to prepare because they are already produced for financial reporting purposes; and, because they are in such common use, the profit center managers generally understand them quite well. Thus it is not surprising that accounting earnings numbers are the most important measures in the vast majority of the contracts used to motivate profit center managers.

The Advantages of Applying Short-Term Performance Pressure

All 12 firms studied purposely use accounting earnings measures to maintain some short-term performance pressure on their profit center managers. The terms of the budget contract, in particular, require the profit center managers to achieve annual, and sometimes quarterly, monthly, and even weekly, earnings targets.

In most cases the short-term performance pressure is intended to be considerable. To document this idea, I sent a questionnaire to the most senior financial executive with whom I had contact [generally the chief financial officer (CFO)]. One of the items (the full questionnaire is shown as Figure A-2 in the appendix) asked these executives whether they agreed with the following statement: "Most general managers in my corporation are under considerable profit pressure." Executives from 11 of the 12 firms responded, and ten of the 11 agreed with this statement; three agreed strongly.

Most profit center managers accept the pressure they feel for short-term earnings because they recognize its advantages. They know that most people respond better to specific, predetermined, short-range targets than to being told merely to "do their best." Here is a representative expression of that belief, by a manager in corporation H (high tech):

> [Managers] need very specific [short-term] objectives. If you tell them you want them to develop something for [two years in the future], they can't deal with that. You have to break it down into little bites, such as "develop a working prototype by the fourth quarter." A [target two years out] wouldn't generate much motivation.

His belief is widely shared and has been supported by findings in a broad variety of psychological studies.[1]

The short-term performance pressure provides two basic advantages. First, it increases the likelihood that managers will be stimulated to search for new and better ways to make their operations more efficient, because "Necessity is the mother of invention." Second, applying the pressure in a consistent short-term fashion helps ensure that managers do not allow their operations to become sloppy or wasteful.

Performance Pressure to Stimulate Creativity

Many profit center managers described examples of improvements they made because they felt short-term earnings pressure. For example, a profit center in corporation B (electronic equipment) had a fortuitous experience:

> Last year we delayed some discretionary expenses for the last half of the year. This turned out to be good because we learned how lean we could be. It forced us to experiment. We had been doing maintenance every five weeks, but we learned that we could go to a schedule of every eight weeks. Also, our utility conservation program is now routinized, and that can save us $1 million each year. The impetus to cut expenses made us test what we can do.

Similarly, in a profit center in corporation H (high tech), which was squeezed for additional profit during a recent budget review, the profit center controller said:

> The managers here were angry at first, but after redoing the budget, they feel better. We took a harder look at our people and what we were doing. The process was good, and it turned out all right. It forced us to do some analysis we hadn't had to do before, and we let some deadwood go.

Finally, one profit center in corporation L (specialty chemicals) faced performance pressure because the cost of one raw material that accounted for 50% of the material costs for a major product line doubled in a three-month period. The profit center manager was unable to raise prices fast enough to offset the cost increase, so the profit center lost volume, and profits declined sharply. It was corporate policy not to protect the profit center from the effects of this uncontrollable price increase (for reasons that are described in Chapter 6), so profit center personnel received no bonus payout in the second quarter of the year. Omitting the bonus, in turn, created severe morale problems. Production quality deteriorated, and a union was threatened for the first time in the corporation's long history.

One of the profit center manager's responses was to start a quality improvement program that energized the work force, increased product demand, and lowered production costs. The manager felt that this program would not have been started without the performance pressure. His conclusion from the experience: "Great ideas are born of necessity."

Consistent Performance Pressure to Prevent Sloppiness

Whereas periodic performance pressure stimulates creativity, consistent pressure is useful in a different way—it helps prevent sloppiness.[2] Managers who feel pressure are less likely to let down and allow waste and slack to creep into their operations. Here are some representative expressions of this belief:

A profit center manager in corporation M (consumer durables): "Intermediate checks are necessary to ensure that we'll meet the annual goals."

A group vice president in corporation H (high tech): "You have to take it one step at a time. If we allow losses in the short run, we may just get losses . . ."

A corporate manager in corporation D (diversified industrial products): "We don't want to get into a position where we have to play catch up."

And a profit center manager in corporation F (hospitality), in whose operation cleaning costs were a significant proportion of total costs:

> We usually fall behind early in the year because we get a little lackadaisical. For example, this year we bought and used too much cleaning supplies. The people were not trained to use

the right amounts. They poured in 2 ounces per gallon instead of ½ ounce, and I did not stay on top of them.

Performance evaluations based on short measurement periods can be used to apply this desirable consistent performance pressure.

Although short-term performance pressure is desirable in virtually all profit center situations, it is particularly valuable when profitability is high and when growth is slow. High profitability gives managers an opportunity to report acceptable profits even when employees are sloppy and wasteful. And high growth provides a form of expense control because managers are often unable to increase discretionary spending at the rate revenues are increasing.

The Importance of a Bottom-Line Performance Measure

In theory, consistent short-term performance pressure could be maintained by focusing on multiple measures or on some of the individual line items that make up the summary performance measure. In divisionalized corporations, however, contract designers have strong reasons to base their motivational contracts for profit center managers primarily on a single, bottom-line, summary accounting-based performance measure.

Such measures have been used for many years and are reasonably well understood, so they are less expensive to communicate and administer than are varying series of measures. In addition, contracts based on a properly designed bottom-line measure orient the managers' attention in an unobtrusive way consistent with the spirit of decentralization. Corporations are decentralized partly to take advantage of the profit center managers' superior knowledge of their businesses. Global, summary performance measures do not force the managers to achieve each of a series of targets (such as quality, collection of receivables, and line items of revenues and expenses) that may not fit together in an ideal way. The managers are allowed to use their unique information and capabilities to make trade-offs among all the aspects of performance if they think they can improve overall performance by doing so.

Defining the bottom line in financial terms is natural because corporate success is usually described in financial terms. The designers' choice, then, is which financial bottom-line measure to use.

Choices of Bottom-Line Measures

In addition to accounting earnings (and its derivatives), designers of motivational contracts can consider three basic financial bottom-line measurement alternatives: cash flow, inflation-adjusted accounting earnings, and change in shareholder value. Cash-flow measures are highly volatile, easily manipulated in the short run, and potentially misleading, particularly for entities in growth phases of their life cycles. Thus, their use in incentives plans has been rare, although a few examples of successful applications have been described.[3]

Many academics and consultants have suggested replacing historical cost accounting measures with various forms of inflation-adjusted measures. For example, Dearden recently suggested that accounting depreciation numbers should be based on replacement cost values because, particularly for older assets, historical-cost depreciation numbers are not meaningful.[4] And some authors suggest that inflation-adjusted returns on stockholders' equity (that is, the return on equity minus the cost of equity capital) is the ideal measure for incentive compensation.[5] A number of U.S. firms experimented with inflation accounting in the late 1970s when inflation was in double digits, but interest has since waned. Corporate managements have resisted these suggestions because of measurement cost, lack of measurement accuracy, and the difficulty and cost of teaching managers to understand measures with which they are unfamiliar.[6]

Some authors have recently suggested basing motivational contracts directly on changes in the operating entity's value.[7]

There are no market-based measures of the value of profit center entities, so measuring value requires estimating the entities' future cash flows and discounting them for risk and the time value of money. To measure changes in value, the estimates have to be made twice, at the beginning and the end of the measurement period. The problem is that the more uncertain the future, the less reliable these numbers. Some corporations have used these shareholder value calculations for strategic planning and for valuing acquisitions, but they have been slow to endorse their use for setting incentive compensation.

Because use of these alternative bottom-line measures is rare, I did not expect to find them being used extensively in any of the 12 corporations studied, and I had no major surprises. The only exceptions I found were two relatively minor uses of cash flow measures of performance in corporation A (diversified luxury goods). One exception was a one-time (one-year) corporatewide emphasis on cash flow to reduce the level of debt, which had risen sharply in connection with two large acquisitions. The other was a permanent use of operating cash flow measures of performance in one relatively small group of profit centers where the profit center managers were believed not to influence investments or the line items of revenue and expense requiring significant accounting accruals (accounts receivable, inventories).

Two other corporations, E (diversified chemicals) and M (consumer durables) had considered implementing cash flow measures of performance. Corporation E was planning to implement them in one group of profit centers operating in mature markets to induce the profit center managers to hasten disinvestment. A profit center controller explained:

> This year we're going to have a cash flow goal [in the profit centers operating in mature markets]. Up to now we only had a net income goal. If we have a cash goal, we'll watch capital and marketing terms more closely, and we'll lower our [discretionary] expenses.

The manager of executive compensation in corporation M felt that his corporation's plan should be based at least partly on cash flow, but he had been unable to convince senior managers. He noted:

> Shouldn't we be driving some businesses for cash? Should operating income be the objective all the time? Maybe we should have two or three indicators. I raise the issues, but [senior corporate managers keep saying they] want to keep [measurements and the compensation plan] simple.

Except for the two examples in corporation A and the pending situation in corporation E described above, the key bottom-line performance measures in all profit centers studied were based exclusively on historical cost accounting numbers. The dominance of this choice stems from the advantages of the traditional accounting measures and the central role they play in corporations' external reporting. Corporate managers consider accounting numbers meaningful indicators of performance. They know that to a large extent outsiders measure their performance by the accounting returns they generate.[8] And in general they are comfortable recognizing higher or lower profits and returns as reasonably reliable indicators of improved or declining performance.

Accounting numbers also have the advantages of being understandable, reasonably accurate, and inexpensive to produce. Because accounting has been used for so long, virtually all managers understand its rules, at least in a rudimentary sense. The accounting rules are reasonably accurate (objective and verifiable), since the Financial Accounting Standards Board's (FASB's) statements largely determine, for example, when a sale is a sale, and auditors are skilled at verifying the application of the measurement rules. This accuracy is important to minimize disagreements about the measures on which important incentive contracts are based. And the accounting numbers are relatively inexpensive to produce because most of them are already required for reporting to external parties, including investors, creditors, and government regulators.

Even where managers are uncomfortable with the signals the accounting numbers provide, they are reluctant to experiment with other bottom-line measures. They feel that measurement is important to the organization and that experiments with significant uncertainty about the potential benefits are too risky to attempt. For example, the president of corporation L (specialty chemicals) was convinced that in many cases the ROA measures on which his corporation focused were at times not good indicators of the value or changes in value of his business units. He had listened to a number of consultants who proposed implementing shareholder-value measures of performance (based on estimates of future cash flow) at the business-unit level, but he decided he wanted to see some evidence about other corporations' experiences with these measures before implementing them. His reasons: (1) "I don't want incentive compensation tied to others' estimates of residual value" [at the end of the planning horizon]; and (2) "It's too important. When you screw around with your measures and incentives, you're playing with the heart of the corporation."

Thus, there are good reasons to support the emphasis most corporations place on short-term accounting earnings. Earnings measures are not perfect, however. Table 3-1, which compares bottom-line performance measurement alternatives, shows that the most severe problem with the accounting earnings measures is incongruence with corporate goals. Short-term earnings measures have an inherent short-term bias because they fail to recognize on a timely basis the positive effects of good long-term decisions.

Fortunately, the short-term bias problem with earnings can be offset, unlike most of the weaknesses of the other measurement alternatives. This problem and the approaches managers can take to offset it are discussed in Chapter 4.

Earnings or Profitability Measures?

If corporate managers wish to hold their profit center managers accountable for balance sheet line items (assets and liabilities), they must also choose whether to base their contracts on a profitability ratio (such as return on assets) or on a residual income measure calculated by subtracting a capital

TABLE 3-1

The Advantages of Accounting Earnings over Other Bottom-Line Performance Measurement Alternatives

Desired Measurement Qualities	*Accounting Earnings*	*Inflation-Adjusted Accounting Earnings*	*Changes in Entity Value*	*Cash Flow*
1. Congruence with goal of maximizing shareholder value	Fair—short-term bias problem	Possibly better than earnings in situations of significant inflation	Excellent	Worse than earnings
2. Accuracy:				
Verifiability	Excellent	Fair	Poor	Excellent
Objectivity	Excellent	Fair	Poor	Excellent
3. Simplicity	Well understood; inexpensive to produce	Not well understood; expensive if appraisals of assets needed	Not well understood	Well understood; inexpensive

charge from earnings. Many arguments have been voiced against ratio measures and in favor of residual income measures of performance.[9] Still, the vast majority of corporations emphasize ratio measures [see surveys by Walsh (1987) and Reece and Cool (1978)].

The 12 firms considered here are representative of the larger samples. In all eight firms where profit center managers are accountable for assets (and sometimes liabilities), the firms calculate a profitability ratio. One firm, H (high tech), calculates residual income for profit centers, but also calculates a return-on-assets (ROA) measure (with the capital charge excluded) for inclusion in its short-term incentive compensation contracts.

Corporate managers' choice to emphasize ratio measures is based on the belief that the advantages of residual income-type measures, if any, would be more than offset by the confusion they would cause and the implementation costs. Here are some representative observations:

> We don't use residual income because we don't want to get into arcane accounting. Everybody understands what we've got [return on operating assets], and it seems to work (controller of corporation B—electronic equipment).
>
> The theoretical sophistication of measurement is just overhead (a group vice president in corporation D—diversified industrial products).
>
> Residual income is too much of an intellectual challenge for operating types to cope with (controller of corporation E—diversified chemicals).

NOTES

1. Locke et al. (1981) provide a review of the psychology literature. Also see Hrebiniak and Joyce (1986).

2. This relationship is a key element in Leibenstein's (1989) theory of firm hierarchy.

3. For example, Berkey Photo, Inc. started providing incentives for its 17 profit center managers in terms of both quarterly profits and cash flow in 1979. The immediate result was that the operating units generated two and a half times as much cash flow as they had in 1978, and management felt the increase came from

"excess" working capital, not short-term management ("Bonus Program Is Boosting Cash Flow," *Industry Week*, January 7, 1980).

4. Dearden (1987), p. 86.
5. For example, Brindisi (1985).
6. See Hertenstein (1987).
7. Rappaport (1986) describes the advantages of using shareholder-value measures to evaluate strategies and mergers and acquisitions. He also suggests that basing incentive compensation plans on value measures would motivate executives to make decisions consistent with the long-term interests of their corporations, but he describes only a hypothetical example of how it would work. Stewart (1985), Ubelhart (1985), and Brindisi (1985) are also on record suggesting that shareholder-value measures could be useful in improving the link between managerial incentives and the real benefits accruing to shareholders.
8. Hopwood (1974) describes this tendency of managers to want to evaluate their subordinates with the same performance measures they are evaluated on as the "contagion effect."
9. For example, Henrici (1983), Dearden (1969), and Solomons (1965).

CHAPTER 4

Correcting for the Short-Term Bias in Accounting Measures of Performance

> "Every company needs a balance between short-term and long-term performance. If you focus all your needs on the long term, the CEO won't be around to enjoy the results. If you focus all your needs on the short term, the company will go out of business."
> *Chairman of Corporation A*

Although most contract designers conclude that accounting earnings is the single best measure on which to build motivational contracts, they know that accounting measures have weaknesses. The weaknesses cause some profit center managers who are rewarded for generating earnings not to work toward the corporation's true objectives.

The most pervasive and significant weakness is an inherent short-term bias.[1] This bias is particularly significant because trade-offs between short-term and long-term performance are among the most important decisions profit center managers are asked to make, and corporate managers often provide cues for making these trade-offs through motivational contracts. Contracts based on short-term accounting earnings measures are reasonably effective in communicating the importance of short-term performance, as was discussed in Chapter 3, but they are not effective in providing long-term incentives.[2] This problem occurs because the managers can increase short-term earnings by taking actions that are not in the long-term best interest of their profit center or the corporation. Thus, holding profit center managers accountable for short-term earnings causes them to be excessively short-term-oriented in the absence of balancing incentives. This excessive short-term orientation is often referred to as management myopia.

Motivational contract designers correct for the myopia-inducing short-term bias in accounting earnings measures by adding any of a number of contracts or contract features designed to encourage the profit center managers to think longer term. The designers' choices from among the alternatives available account for much of the contract variation we observe across firms.

Each choice involves a trade-off, however. In the quest to have managers pay more attention to long-term considerations, corporate managers sacrifice one or more of the other desirable contract qualities—particularly measurement accuracy, preestablishment of standards, meaningfulness of rewards (or their costs), and/or contract simplicity.

Short-Term Bias and Its Effects

Accounting earnings measures tempt profit center managers to act myopically in either of two areas: investments and operating decisions.

INVESTMENT MYOPIA

Holding managers accountable for short-term earnings induces them to reduce or postpone investments that promise payoffs only far in the future, even when those investments clearly have a positive net present value. This dysfunctional behavior can be labeled "investment myopia."

Investment myopia occurs because accounting rules require firms to begin recognizing the costs of investments when they are made, but do not allow them to record gains to be earned in subsequent accounting periods until such gains are realized. The accounting rule makers generally emphasize measurement accuracy over timeliness. They argue that gains should not be recognized at the time of investment because the critical income-producing activities have not yet taken place and the anticipated earnings are uncertain and cannot be measured in an objective, verifiable way.

The short-term bias is exacerbated because accounting rules are purposely conservative. To protect against overstatement of earnings, the rules require firms to expense investments in research and market development projects and other projects with uncertain returns and little liquidation value immediately, and they require capital investments to be expensed over periods that are typically shorter than the investments' return horizons.

The motivational effect of these basic measurement rules is perverse. Whenever the remaining accounting measurement horizon is shorter than the investment payback period, managers can increase short-term earnings by reducing their investments.

Operating Decision Myopia

The second form of myopia is operating decision myopia. Even managers who are not making long-term investment decisions can act myopically by destroying good will the profit center has built up with customers and employees. For example, they can ship hastily assembled, lower-quality product in a last-minute attempt to boost current period sales and earnings. This action may cause returns to increase and customer satisfaction to deteriorate, but the cost increases and losses of future revenues will not be recognized in the current accounting period. Alternatively, the managers can treat employees insensitively, through forced overtime, brusque communication, or forced vacations, thereby causing morale problems and turnover that will harm the profit center in the long run.

Solving the Short-Term Bias Problem

Corporate managers, well aware of the short-term bias in short-term accounting earnings measures, take any of a number of actions to try to eliminate, or at least reduce, myopia. When they are aware of the potential for specific myopic actions, such as layoffs of key development personnel, they often try to prevent those actions. Some, for example, require profit center managers to seek approval before they act, and others establish policies prohibiting certain myopic actions and then follow up to ensure that the policies are followed.

In many situations, however, these prevention controls cannot or should not be used, for any of several reasons. For example, corporate managers may not know the profit centers' businesses well enough to know how the long-term/short-term trade-offs should be made. The control actions may be too costly, particularly in managers' time, to use frequently when the profit center is geographically separate from corporate headquarters. Or, the profit center managers may resent the interference with their operating autonomy.[3]

The more general solution to the myopia problem is to change the motivational contracts. The problem can be addressed with any one of four approaches: (1) track one or more leading performance indicators in addition to the accounting earnings measures; (2) offer written contracts promising rewards for long-term profit center performance; (3) offer unwritten contracts promising rewards for long-term profit center or individual performance; or (4) reduce the pressure the profit center managers feel for short-term results.

Leading Performance Indicators

One common approach is to promise rewards for results measured in terms of leading indicators of profits (and cash flows) to be earned in subsequent accounting periods. The measures used as leading indicators include market share, growth, bookings, collections of receivables, achievement of specific milestones in a development project, and audit and safety ratings. Such measures are leading indicators of performance because they reflect the economic effects on shareholder value of specific management accomplishments and failures more quickly than do the accounting measures.

Basing motivational contracts on leading indicators induces profit center managers to consider factors whose effects will appear beyond the short-term accounting horizon. The leading indicators direct the managers' attention to longer-term concerns, and when linked to rewards, they tilt the balance of incentives toward longer-term actions.

The leading indicators need to be weighted heavily to attract the managers' attention. For example, one profit center manager in corporation K (electronic systems), many of whose products were still being developed, was promised 20% of his annual bonus for reaching developmental milestones and meeting timetables for introducing new products. He noted: "If I was evaluated strictly on profit, I would not be running the level of R&D I have been running. If they want profit, I can give them profit. I'll cut R&D in half."

Table 4-1 summarizes the leading indicators used in one or more of the profit centers studied in each of the 12 corporations.[4] The table shows that all of the corporations track at least one leading-indicator measure at profit center-organization levels in addition to the bottom-line financial measures. The most widely used leading indicators are inventory control (used in nine of the 12 corporations), expense control (eight), accomplishment of specific tasks (seven firms), customer or distributor satisfaction (seven), product quality (six), and sales growth (six).

Sometimes the indicators are standardized across the corporation; sometimes they are tailored to specific profit centers as part of a management-by-objectives (MBO) system. The code letters in Table 4-1 (x and y) show the organizational level at which the measurement-choice decisions are made. An x means top management has decided to track one or more measures for *all* profit centers in the corporation. The standardization has occurred in three corporations—B (electronic equipment), G (electrical connectors), and H (high tech)—all firms in which the profit centers are relatively homogeneous. A y means that the supplemental performance measures vary across profit centers; in other words, they are tailored to the profit centers' missions, settings, or circumstances. In most cases, these measurement choices are made by the profit center managers' immediate superiors (who are lower in the corporate hierarchy than chief operating officer [COO] in all corporations except A, G, and M),

TABLE 4-1
Use of Leading Indicators in 12 Corporations

	Corporation											
	A *Diversified Luxury Goods*	*B* *Electronic Equipment*	*C* *Distribution*	*D* *Diversified Industrial Products*	*E* *Diversified Chemicals*	*F* *Hospitality*	*G* *Electrical Connectors*	*H* *High Tech*	*J* *Consumer Products*	*K* *Electronic Systems*	*L* *Specialty Chemicals*	*M* *Consumer Durables*
Leading Indicator												
Accomplishment of specific task (e.g., R&D project mile stone)	y			y	y				y	y	y	y
Market share	y			y	y				y		y	
Sales growth		x		y			x	x	y		y	
Bookings				y			x			y	y	
Product quality				y	y	y	x		y	y		
On-time delivery							x					
Customer/distributor satisfaction				y	y	y			y	y	y	y
People management (development, morale)			y	y	y	y						y
Capital spending (accomplishments vs. plan)				y								
Audit rating						y						
Facility ambience/cleanliness						y						
"Conduct of the business" (e.g., affirmative action)			y						y		y	
Safety					y	y						
Productivity							x	x	y			
People count (e.g., reduction)	y										y	
Receivables management (days' receivables)	y		y		y			x			y	y
Inventory management (inventory turnover)	y		y	y	y	y		x	y	y		y
Expense control (e.g., SG&A as % of sales)	y		y	y		y		x	y	y	y	

Key:
x = tracked in *all* profit centers.
y = tracked in *some* profit centers.

often in consultation with the profit center managers themselves.

When contract designers add leading indicators to motivational contracts, they are attempting to make the contracts more congruent with the corporate goal of increasing shareholder value, which is a long-term concept. Congruence is not easily attained, however, because the indicators vary considerably in their reliability as indicators of forthcoming profits, both in general and in specific profit centers. For example, reaching milestones in a product-development project does not ensure that the product will be commercially successful, but tracking these accomplishments provides a probabilistic indicator of profits to be earned several years, and sometimes even decades, in the future. The leading indicators also vary in the time by which they lead the earnings reports. Bookings, for example, is a reliable indicator of forthcoming sales, and probably profits, but its measurement may precede the accounting earnings numbers by only months.

Some indicators, such as expense control, seem not to lead the earnings measures at all because successes and failures are reflected immediately in the accounting earnings measures. Many firms feel, however, that expense control and some of the other indicators are not weighted sufficiently in the summary earnings measures, which are mere linear aggregations of dollars. They feel that poor expense control in the current period will show up as much more significant problems in subsequent periods and that the performance area is important enough to direct managers' attention to it.

This was the reasoning of a profit center manager in corporation E (diversified chemicals):

> [One of our] "hot buttons" is MAT [marketing, administrative, technical] spending. If MAT [as a percentage of sales] is up, that's very bad. It's perceived as not well controlled. [The subsidiary president's] orientation is that we must always be careful with MAT spending. If it increases in good times, it's there in bad times.

In most of the profit centers in corporation E, MAT's direct effect on profit is relatively small because it typically runs only 7% of sales, so if rewards were based solely on profit performance the managers would be affected only marginally if they did not control MAT tightly. But some executives in corporation E give extra weight to MAT as a percentage of sales to help ensure that the profit center managers do not lose sight of their MAT expenses.

The contract designers' task is to combine accounting earnings with a set of leading indicators in a measurement package that is congruent with the profit center managers' effects on shareholder value. They must choose which indicators to use and how to weight them, individually and in total, to offset the short-term pressures profit center managers feel. Often they choose indicators, such as new-product development or quality, that reflect the profit centers' strategies—the approaches corporate managers have asked the profit centers to take in generating shareholder value. Other indicators, such as expense or inventory control, can be important for profit centers that are following quite different strategies.

Selecting sets of leading indicators and varying their weightings to form a single composite measure that induces each manager to act precisely in the corporation's best long-term interest is challenging.[5] Still, these indicators are useful because they provide incentives for the profit center managers to think beyond the short-term accounting period.

Although including these indicators in the motivational contracts improves congruence, in adding them designers are explicitly trading off some of the ideal contract qualities. The mere choices of some of the leading indicators and their weightings can create perceptions of subjectivity and unfairness across the organization. In rapidly changing environments, particularly, the weightings are left to the discretion of the profit center managers' immediate superiors who usually exercise this discretion after the measurement period is over. Thus, the managers do not know before the measurement period how they are to make decisions that involve trade-offs between conflicting goals. And there is often some loss of measurement objectivity and verifiability with use of some of the leading indicators, such as customer satisfaction, facility ambience, and conduct of the business.

Perhaps most significant, however, are the costs of contract congruence and simplicity if the leading indicators are not used properly. If the wrong indicators are chosen, congruence with goals will deteriorate. And if too many indicators are used, the profit center managers can become distracted by contracts that are no longer simple because they contain multiple, sometimes conflicting, targets.

A consultant who participated in the design of corporation K's (electronic systems) short-term incentive plan expressed his concern about distraction:

> The more [individual measures] you choose, the less the focus on each. Take, for example, a manager with a bonus target of $35,000. If he has five financial targets and five individual targets, they are worth only $3,500 each. The manager can ignore one of them with little cost. If you put all of the money in just a few baskets, you get real focus. But it is somewhat narrow to focus on just one, so we suggest companies focus on two or three [individual measures].

Similarly, a group vice president in corporation M (consumer durables) asked the profit center managers reporting to him to set targets for only one or two measures in addition to operating return on assets even though the corporate guidelines called for four to six measures. His reasoning: "It gives focus. The fewer you use, the better the managers' abilities to achieve the objectives." And a profit center manager in corporation A: "I can set as many personal objectives as I want, but the guideline is two. If I set five or six of these objectives, they won't all get done."

Written Contracts Promising Rewards for Long-Term Profit Center Performance

A second option for offsetting the short-term bias in accounting earnings measures is to add one or more contracts promising rewards for results measured over an extended period. An extended horizon captures more of the gains received from investments and thus reduces the incidence and severity of investment myopia.

As was mentioned briefly in Chapter 2, two corporations

(A—diversified luxury goods and H—high tech) have chosen this option. They offer their profit center managers an additional contract that promises rewards for profit center performance over a multiyear period. It is too early to determine the actual incentive effects of these contracts because neither program has been in place long enough to have provided the profit center managers with a stream of rewards. Because these contracts are unique among those of the firms in my sample, however, I will describe them briefly.

The Contract at Corporation A

Three years before my study, corporation A implemented a restricted stock plan for its most senior managers. Seventeen managers are covered by the contract, including the chief operating officer and the managers who report to him directly, among whom are the managers of the largest profit centers. The chairman said about the contract: "I consider this my long-term plan. Every company ought to have long-term and short-term plans. The long-term plan protects against a short-term emphasis. But I restrict this plan to the top people who are the decision makers on the long-term decisions." The plan awards restricted stock on the basis of the corporation's return on shareholders' equity (ROE) over a three-year period. Awards are given for ROE performance exceeding 12% up to a maximum award for an ROE of 20%.

The plan provides a direct incentive for the profit center managers because the awards can be affected by plus or minus 10% depending on three-year after-tax earnings at the profit center level and by plus or minus 10% depending on each individual's accomplishment of two personal goals, up to a limit of 100% of the target award. The personal goals, negotiated between the profit center managers and the chief operating officer, can include targets for financial measures, such as earnings, sales, expenses, or cash flow; or targets for nonfinancial measures, such as market share, inventory turnover, people count, and accounts receivable exposure.

The payouts under this contract can be lucrative. With good corporate and, if necessary, profit center and individual performance, and an increasing stock price, the total annual payout can exceed five times the maximum short-term bonus a profit center manager can be paid.

The actual incentive effects of this contract are difficult to determine, because the plan is so new. Corporate managers felt that even though the plan had been in existence for three years, some managers did not fully understand it. The corporate managers were confident that the participants were aware of one important plan feature: the bases for the awards. But they felt that the incentive effects would be greater once the managers realized how lucrative the awards could be.

The Contract at Corporation H

One year before my study, corporation H started a stock option plan that includes profit center managers. In the plan, 0.5% of the corporation's outstanding shares of common stock are made available for distribution to profit center managers and other key personnel in the operating entities. (Another 0.2% are reserved for top management.)

The shares are allocated to the group level of the organization (one level above profit center) on the basis of the groups' prorated shares of the following specific combination of results:

$$P_1\left[\frac{P_1 - P_2}{0.2(S_2)}\right] + P_2\left[\frac{P_2 - P_3}{0.2(S_3)}\right] + P_3\left[\frac{P_3 - P_4}{0.2(S_4)}\right]$$

where: P_1 = profit before tax for most recent fiscal year
P_2 = profit before tax for year before P_1 year
P_3 = profit before tax for year before P_2 year
P_4 = profit before tax for year before P_3 year
S_2 = net sales for fiscal year prior to most recent
S_3 = net sales for fiscal year before S_2 year
S_4 = net sales for fiscal year before S_3 year

The formula captures three years of profit improvements and normalizes them for group size.

The shares are then allocated to eligible personnel in each group at the discretion of the group vice president. Presumably, but not necessarily, the vice presidents of the various groups will use a similar form of proportioning. The options will be granted at market price. Typical grants are expected to be in the range of 5,000–10,000 shares, but individuals will not necessarily receive a grant each year. The options vest at 20% at the end of each of the first, second, and third years following the award year, and 40% at the end of the fourth year. The options will expire four years after they are vested.

Again, it is too early to say whether the new long-term contract will have a significant incentive effect, but the plan came about because of pressure from profit center managers for a long-term incentive plan. The chairman had long resisted such a plan. His reasoning:

> Stock option plans don't work. There is so much volatility in stock prices despite steady earnings per share. Timing is everything with options. It creates a selling pressure on the stock. It gets to be too much. Why not give the whole company away every year? Do present stockholders have no rights?

Trade-offs Required in Using Written Long-Term Contracts

Like all the approaches to reducing the short-term bias in accounting measures of performance, implementing long-term contracts such as those used in corporations A and H necessitates trade-offs. The potential reduction in myopia causes increased reward expense, increased evaluation subjectivity or managerial risk bearing, and additional administrative problems.

The increased reward expense stems from the multiyear time lags in giving rewards. Actions that profit center managers take today are not rewarded until three years from now. The problem is, in the words of one profit center manager: "[The long-term payoff] is so far in the future, and so uncertain, that I just don't think much about it."

To provide a long-term incentive that balances the many monetary and nonmonetary rewards profit center managers are given for short-term results, the long-term performance rewards have to be quite large. Because of the long payoff horizon of the long-term incentives, even equal annual payoff potential for the long- and short-term rewards still favors the short term.

The evaluation subjectivity or managerial risk-bearing problem occurs because of the difficulty of setting long-term performance standards at the right level of challenge. The planning uncertainty for most profit centers increases markedly as the horizon recedes. Neither corporation A nor corporation H has chosen the obvious alternative of calibrating its long-term incentives with the targets set as part of its strategic planning because management does not want its profit center managers to think conservatively when doing their long-term plans. The success of the corporation A plan depends on its profit center managers being comfortable with considerable subjectivity, as the performance targets are set by the COO. The success of the corporation H plan depends on its profit centers managers being comfortable with uncontrollable risk. Its long-term rewards, being competitive, are based to some extent on a factor the profit center managers cannot control—the performance of other profit centers that do not face the same industry conditions.

Potentially severe administrative problems create a third impediment to the implementation of long-term incentive contracts. Managers are more likely to retire or transfer between jobs over a multiyear period than over a one-year period. The resulting complexity makes such contracts difficult to communicate and costly to administer.

The costs of these trade-offs are usually significant. Only two of the 12 corporations studied have implemented written long-term motivational contracts because their managers have concluded that the costs of these trade-offs outweigh the benefits.

Unwritten Contracts Promising Rewards for Long-Term Performance

A third method of correcting for the short-term bias in accounting measures of performance is to use unwritten contracts that promise rewards for good long-term performance, or at least lack of penalties for taking risks and failing. For example, in corporation A (diversified luxury goods), the chairman made it clear to his profit center managers that he wanted and expected them to take risks, and he altered the reward structure accordingly. A profit center manager explained:

> We're not restricted by anything the corporation does. We spent millions of dollars trying to build [a new type of product] in the United States. No bank would have gone along with the costs that were adding up, but [the corporation] kept funding it. We failed; we designed something we couldn't manufacture. But I didn't lose my job. Corporate wants us to take risks.

The corporations that use unwritten long-term contracts reinforce them by making examples of managers who make good (and bad) long-term/short-term trade-offs. An obvious reward is to promote managers who are good at developing their businesses over a long period. The profit center managers are quick to observe the bases used to assign this important reward. For example, a profit center manager in corporation J (consumer products) said: "There are rewards for taking the long-term perspective. My boss got promoted because he was seen as being the best long-term builder of the business. He was not the best short-term manager."

Other managers are penalized for acting myopically. A group vice president in corporation L (consumer durables) expanded on this point:

> Delaying a needed expenditure and causing commercial damage is stupid. If a [profit center] manager did that, I would talk to him. We may miss a product introduction window, and this business needs new products.
>
> Such an occurrence has never happened to me, but I remember that it did happen in [another division of a corporation in which he used to work]. A manager shrank his R&D department when he had a number-one market position. There was a horrendous price paid two and three years out, and the division had to go into a major turnaround situation. The manager was fired.

Unwritten long-term contracts can be effective in improving overall contract congruence, but communicating their terms is often difficult. The performance standards are often neither preset nor well understood, and the rewards are uncertain. When there is lack of understanding, the contracts have little motivational impact on profit center managers.

The unwritten contracts, and the performance evaluations associated with them, also suffer because they are heavily subjective. Consequently, improvements in congruence and the costs of profit center managers' perceptions of evaluation unfairness depend largely on the evaluators' skills.

REDUCED PRESSURE FOR SHORT-TERM PERFORMANCE

A final approach to balancing short-term and long-term incentives is to reduce the pressure the profit center managers feel for short-term performance by setting more easily achievable budgeted profit targets. As was described in Chapter 2, budget targets are on average highly achievable: the managers' median estimate of the probability of achieving annual budget targets was 90%, and achievement was perceived to be certain in seven profit centers.

Reducing pressure for short-term results has desirable effects in some profit center situations because it allows the managers to make long-term discretionary investments and reduces their need to take short-term actions with probable long-term costs. For example, the COO of corporation G (electrical connectors) said he wanted one of the six profit center managers reporting to him, in particular, to have a long-term orientation. This manager ran a profit center with considerable long-term potential, but it was losing money because significant production problems were causing low yields and high delinquency rates. The corporation offers significant rewards for short-term performance and has no meaningful long-term contract. To ensure that the profit center manager focused on the long term, the COO ordered him to make the production improvements and told him not to worry about the short-term losses. He also lowered the profit center's annual budget target to ensure that personnel in the profit center would achieve their target and earn some incentive compensation.

The major cost of deemphasizing short-term performance is a potential loss of concentration on short-term results and the attendant risk of some sloppiness. Thus I was not surprised to find that the profit center managers who had the most budgetary flexibility were usually long-time employees of their firms who had proven their effectiveness over an extended period. Top management trusted them to make good judgments about consuming the budget slack and relied on them not to allow short-term sloppiness.

The manager of one high-performing group of profit centers in corporation A (diversified luxury goods) is such a trusted manager. "Sandbagging" (knowingly submitting budget proposals containing slack) has been routine in this group, and the group has exceeded its targets every year. The corporate chief executive officer (CEO) accepts the group's sandbagging because he trusts the group vice president to ensure that his managers make the proper short-term/long-term trade-offs. He noted in a seemingly unconcerned manner: "[This group president] beats [his target] no matter how clever I am."

Within the group, the manager of profit center 3, who is recognized as perhaps the best manager in the group, has the most budget slack, which gives him highly achievable budget targets. He admitted to being able to deliver 50% more profit than was forecast in his budget without any cuts in discretionary expenditures or any windfalls.

Slack is allowed in this profit center by design. The group controller noted that profit centers "with less attractive track records are asked for better numbers."

Reducing the pressure on profit center managers for short-term performance does not necessarily result in a longer-term focus. It does, however, help provide a better short-term/long-term balance by preventing the managers' short-term concerns from driving out their long-term concerns.

Long-Term Contracts with Little Motivational Effect

Not all so-called long-term contracts reduce the short-term bias problem. Nine of the 12 firms have long-term contracts that provide rewards based on corporate financial performance or the managers' organization levels, as described in Chapter 2. Because the rewards are not tied to results the profit center managers can control to any significant extent, however, by and large their only motivational effect is a weak form of attention-directing.[6]

For example, corporation J (consumer products) has implemented a phantom stock plan providing awards that vest over a seven-year period. The vice president-administration described the firm's intent in implementing this plan: "We meant to mute the managers' total concentration on the current year. We wanted to give individuals a stake in future years." For this purpose, corporation J's plan is a success. This contract, and those like it in the nine firms using such contracts, give profit center managers a stake in the corporation's long-term performance and thus encourage a sense of belonging to an entity larger than just one profit center. They also help deliver the message to the profit center managers that long-term performance is important. And they can increase social control within the firm, since profit center managers can in some circumstance monitor each others' actions.[7]

These uncontrollable long-term incentive contracts have little or no direct motivational effect on profit center managers, however, because the rewards are not linked directly to any specific actions the managers might take. Most profit center managers are goal-oriented individuals who want to manage their own entity and be rewarded for their accomplishments. None of them with whom I talked felt that the motivational effect of these uncontrollable long-term plans was significant.

A representative reaction came from a profit center manager in corporation M (consumer durables), whose company has implemented a contract providing long-term incentives based on three-year corporate ROE. He lamented: "I wish we had a long-term incentive based on unit performance. That way I would feel motivated to make investments that would pay out in two or three years." Similarly, the compensation consultant who participated in the design of the incentive compensation plans for corporation K (electronic systems) said of that firm's stock option plan: "These options have evolved to be a right, not an incentive. The grants are based strictly on the managers' level in the corporation . . . I think we can classify these plans as incentive plans only if individual performance is related to the grant."

Reducing Myopia

In considering how to eliminate or reduce the short-term bias caused by emphasizing accounting earnings performance measures, contract designers must make two judgments. How severe is the potential myopia? Which approach(es) should be used to deal with it?

Assessing the Potential Severity of the Problem

Myopia is a potential problem in any profit center where the manager is evaluated on accounting earnings, but the severity of the problem varies markedly across profit centers (and corporations). Operating-decision myopia occurs in almost every profit center. Investment myopia, however, occurs only in profit centers that must invest for the future, and the potential risk varies directly with the size of the investments and the speed of the payback.

Corporate managers understand these differences. In corporation G (electrical connectors), for example, the COO was asked how much time each of the four profit center managers studied should devote to thinking long term (with a horizon of more than one year). He replied: "For two of them, zero. They are not in a position to do what needs to be done two years down the road. They need to compete for each order to maintain market share. They can't expect much more than 10% growth."

Similarly, executives in corporation C (distribution) felt they had no noticeable investment myopia problem in their distribution profit centers because the period covered by the financial measures exceeded the profit center managers' thinking horizons. The distribution profit centers are not capital-intensive, so their managers make few long-term investments. Furthermore, corporate managers described distribution as a "reactive" type of business in which the tactics change but the strategies are constant. Thus the distribution profit center managers are not acting myopically even if they spend all their time focusing on improving annual and even quarterly profits. Corporate managers in corporation C had considered implementing a long-term incentive plan, but decided not to. The CFO explained: "Our feeling is that the distribution business is a short-term business. If we do well in the short term, we'll do well in the long term."

Investment myopia is more severe in growing corporations and profit centers than in those that are stable or declining.[8] And it is most severe in entities with long product-development, manufacturing, or selling cycles because the accounting-treatment lag between the costs of investments and the gains from those investments is greater. Designers of motivational contracts must address the myopia problem most carefully in these profit centers.

WHICH ALTERNATIVE(S) TO USE?

Designers have four basic options for eliminating or reducing short-term bias. In deciding which method(s) to use, they must consider the trade-offs described above.

If the potential costs of myopia are small because a long-term focus is not important to the profit center strategy, short-term pressure should not be reduced. The short-term focus is too important.

Some leading indicators can be measured in almost all profit centers, although contract designers must recognize that the benefits of some indicators can vary across profit center settings. Some indicators are redundant: in some profit centers, for example, market share is largely redundant with sales. And some leading indicators do not lead the accounting numbers by enough time to make them worthwhile. Bookings, for example, is not particularly useful when sales follow closely, although the measure can help reduce operating-decision myopia by reducing managers' temptation to accelerate shipments at the end of a measurement period just so that sales can be recorded.

The costs of using the various leading indicators also vary. Some indicators cannot be measured accurately, as is true for market share when there are numerous substitutes for a profit center's products. Some indicators are less useful where, because good historical performance data are lacking, it is not possible to set reasonable, challenging targets objectively. And there is sometimes a danger that the profit center managers will lose their focus on the most important success factors if they are given targets for each of a series of other, less important indicators.

Despite these drawbacks, it appears beneficial to use one or more leading performance indicators in virtually every profit center to offset the short-term bias in the accounting performance measures. The leading indicators are effective precursors of changes in value that are not perfectly correlated with earnings measures, and they are relatively easy and inexpensive to use. It is probably best to use a small set of indicators for each profit center so that the message does not become too diffuse.

If the firm's profit centers are reasonably homogeneous, a common set of indicators can be used. Generally, however, the indicators should be tailored to the specific critical success factors for each profit center to avoid a problem of measurement unfairness caused by applying identical measures to substantially different types of profit centers. Many firms struggle with this measurement tailoring because their managers are accustomed to thinking of short-term measurement primarily in earnings terms. Furthermore, if corporate managers choose measures that are differentiated across profit centers, they must convince profit center managers of the equality of their incentive possibilities. Corporation L (specialty chemicals) was among the firms struggling with this measurement-differentiation issue, as a group vice president explained:

> Our current system does not work well for the business conditions [the corporation] is facing today. Having one basis of measurement for all our [profit centers] suggests they are all the same, but they are not the same. [For example,] it does not recognize that some managers are minimizing losses and others are maximizing profit. In our system of the future, we must define excellence, and in each case that definition may be different.

Similarly, a vice president in corporation B (electronic equipment) noted that top-level managers in the firm were just starting to address this issue: "Our [incentive plan] is too centrally determined. We have corporate people deciding how the progress of each entity is to be measured. Our senior executives are on a learning curve in terms of strategic differentiation. They are just now recognizing that different entities do different things for you."

Written long-term contracts can also be used in any profit center by extending the measurement horizon, but their costs are substantial. The costs stem from: (1) the provision of rewards that must be sizable to offset the immediacy of the short-term rewards; (2) the motivational deterioration caused by increasing the subjectivity allowed in performance evaluations (measurement and setting of performance standards); (3) the risk of faulty contract design, which is high because the designs are not easily reversible—little feedback is received about the effectiveness of the contracts for years;[9] and (4) the administration of contracts that often contain complex provisions necessitated by the virtual certainty that some managers will not remain in their positions for the full measurement period. These administrative difficulties increase with the rate of turnover in a particular firm or profit center industry.

Because of the size of these costs, written long-term contracts should be implemented only where the potential benefits to the corporation are large. The largest benefits occur where the danger of investment myopia is highest. It is not surprising, therefore, that in the two corporations that have implemented written long-term contracts (A and H), the profit center managers have substantial authority to initiate and curtail long-term investment programs.

Unwritten long-term contracts can also be used in virtually every profit center. But the success of the implicit contracts is tenuous. It depends on expectations that both the profit center managers and the superiors with whom they have the unwritten contract (or understanding) will remain in their jobs for the foreseeable future. Because evaluations are necessarily heavily influenced by subjectivity, success depends on the profit center managers' trusting their evaluators. And it depends on effective, if sometimes implicit, communication of the terms of the contracts.

Individually and in combination, these four approaches—use of leading performance indicators, written or unwritten long-term contracts, and relaxation of short-term pressure—can reduce or eliminate the myopia caused by applying short-term earnings pressure. These approaches move the balance of incentives in the direction of long-term performance. If corporate managers so desire, they can even be used to tell profit center managers that the long run is all that matters. Thus myopia is not inevitable.

Decisions about whether to use these approaches require some difficult trade-offs, however. Corporate managers must tailor their approaches to the demands of the situation. They should not implement any of the approaches if they feel that the myopia-reducing benefits are less than the monetary costs and the costs of additional evaluation subjectivity.

NOTES

1. Short-term bias is one specific type of what Hirst (1981) calls "incompleteness." He defines an incomplete performance measure as one that "reflects only some of the activities and/or outcomes associated with task performance" (p. 771).

2. Larcker (1987) finds that the adoption of a short-term compensation plan by commercial banks is associated with decreases in discretionary expenditures.

3. The costs of these "action controls" are discussed in Merchant (1985), pp. 127–129.

4. The mere existence of a measure of an aspect of profit center performance does not necessarily mean it affects performance evaluations as, for example, most of the accounts in disaggregated financial statements are not used individually as performance indicators. In assessing the set of performance measures actually forming part of motivational contracts, I looked for evidence either that the measure was explicitly included in incentive compensation agreements or that it was reported to be a part of basis for the profit center managers' performance evaluations.

5. Ridgway (1982) describes the problems associated with single, multiple, and composite (multiple measures with explicit weightings) performance measures.

6. Larcker (1983) finds that firms with long-term compensation plans spend more in long-term projects, and Brickley et al. (1985) find a positive relationship between shareholder wealth and the implementation of a long-term compensation plan. The causality behind these findings is not clear, however. The long-term plans might be inducing the increased expenditures and wealth, but it is also possible that firms that spend more in long-term projects are more prone to offer long-term incentive plans. Furthermore, neither study provides evidence that the increased investment is coming from profit center levels of the firms; the incentives may just be effective only for corporate managers.

7. Social control, which involves employees monitoring each others' performance, is often described as a primary benefit of profit-sharing-type plans, of which these uncontrollable long-term incentive plans are one type. See, for example, Schroeder (1988). But social control is effective only where the employees have knowledge of both the actions that are desirable and the actions that are taken. This knowledge is often lacking for profit center managers' actions.

8. This observation is similar to one of the major conclusions by Kotter (1982), who classifies the differences in general managers' job demands on two dimensions: the relative importance of long-run and short-run responsibilities, and the extent to which lateral relationships are demanding.

9. Etzioni (1988) makes this point.

CHAPTER 5

The Controllability Problem, Part I: Deciding Whether to Exclude Uncontrollable Elements from Earnings-Based Performance Measures

A major constraint in designing motivational contracts for profit center managers is an inability to isolate the managers' individual contributions to the measured results. An aspect of performance is totally controllable by a profit center manager if the measures are affected only by his or her actions. Accounting earnings (and many of the leading indicators of profit center performance), however, are not totally controllable because they are affected by the actions of other managers in the corporation and any of a number of randomly occurring business risk factors, such as changing economic conditions, competitors' actions, and business calamities.[1] These uncontrollable factors present a problem because they add noise to the measures that can disguise the managers' contributions (or lack of them) and lead to unfair evaluations.

Contract designers can reduce (and sometimes even eliminate) some of the distorting effects by using either or both of two complementary approaches. Before the measurement period begins, they can define the highly important earnings measures to include only the line items over which the profit center managers (or their employees) have direct authority. After the measurement period has ended, they can calculate (or estimate) and adjust for the effects of any remaining uncontrollable risk factors, using techniques such as variance analysis.

Not all firms use these approaches freely, however, because the contract designers do not want their firm to bear the costs of the trade-offs associated with them. The costs stem from decreased measurement congruence if the managers are protected from the effects of factors to which they should be responding; decreased measurement accuracy if the adjustments involve subjective judgments or crude estimates of the effects of uncontrollable factors; a failure to preset performance standards if the adjustments are made after the performance period has ended; and compromised simplicity if complex procedures are put in place to deal with the many types of possible uncontrollable factors.

The approaches to dealing with the effects of uncontrollables and the trade-offs their use requires are discussed here and in Chapter 6. This chapter focuses on the before-period approach to reducing the problem of uncontrollables—design of accounting earnings measures. Chapter 6 focuses on the after-period approaches of adjusting for the effects of uncontrollables.

Design of Accounting Earnings Measures

The effects of some uncontrollable influences can be eliminated or reduced by the choices of accounting line items to include in the bottom-line performance measures on which motivational contracts are based. Line-item accountability is not an issue for corporate managers, as all the corporate line items are included in the measures for which they are held accountable. The most commonly cited income-statement measure of corporate performance—after-tax earnings (or earnings per share)—includes all the income-statement accounts; and the corresponding asset-profitability measure—after-tax return on equity—includes all the income-statement and balance-sheet accounts.

At profit center levels of the organization, however, the

motivational contracts need not include the full set of accounts; the definition of the bottom-line financial measures involves a number of choices. Figure 5-1, taken from Solomons' classic study on the measurement of divisional (profit center) performance, provides a simple illustration of this point.[2] The income statement presented in this figure includes four measures of profit: variable profit, controllable

FIGURE 5-1
A Form of Divisional Income Statement

	$	$
Sales to outside customers	xxx	
Transfers to other divisions at market value	xxx	
Variable charges to other divisions for transfers not priced at market value	xxx	
		xxx
Less:		
Variable costs of goods sold and transferred	xxx	
Variable divisional expenses	xxx	
		xxx
Variable profit		xxx
Add (deduct):		
Fixed charges made to (by) other divisions for transfers not priced at market value	xxx	
	xxx	
Less:		
Controllable divisional overhead	xxx	
Depreciation on controllable fixed assets	xxx	
Property taxes and insurance on controllable fixed assets	xxx	xxx
Controllable operating profit		xxx
Add (deduct):		
Nonoperating gains and losses		xxx
		xxx
Less:		
Interest on controllable investment		xxx
Controllable residual income before taxes		xxx
Less:		
Noncontrollable divisional overhead	xxx	
Incremental central expenses chargeable to division	xxx	
Interest on noncontrollable investment	xxx	xxx
Net residual income before taxes		xxx
Less:		
Taxes on income		xxx
Net residual income after taxes		xxx

Source: Solomons (1965), p. 72.

operating profit, controllable residual income before taxes, and net residual income after taxes. Any manager held accountable for any one of these measures is, by definition, a profit center manager. Some of these measures, however, include line items that are not controllable because the profit center managers have little or no direct authority over them.

Determining Which Measures Are Linked to Motivational Contracts

Looking at real-world situations and determining the measure(s) for which profit center managers are actually held accountable through one or more motivational contracts is often not easy. Including a measure in a written incentive compensation contract is certainly clear evidence of accountability. But many profit center managers are also implicitly held accountable for all results measured at the profit center level because the measurements affect, for example, their reputations and prospects for promotion. This might lead one to conclude that if a profit center measurement exists, the profit center manager is at least implicitly held accountable for it. But that conclusion is not totally correct either, as some corporations distinguish between measures of the entity's performance and measures of the manager's performance. In assessing accountability, I was careful to try to learn how the profit center managers' performance was being evaluated for all purposes (such as bonuses, promotions, continued employment) and how the performance measures affected those evaluations.

Table 5-1 summarizes my conclusion about the line items included in the earnings measure for which the profit center managers are held accountable. It shows the title the firms give their primary profit center earnings measure and some of the major categories of income-statement accounts included in it.[3] Profit center managers in all the firms are held accountable for sales, direct material and labor, and discretionary expenses either incurred or contracted for by someone in the profit center. After that, the unanimity breaks down as, for example, managers in only seven of the 12

TABLE 5-1
Accounts Included in Profit Center Profit Measure

	Corporation											
	A *Diversified Luxury Goods*	*B* *Electronic Equipment*	*C* *Distribution*	*D* *Diversified Industrial Products*	*E* *Diversified Chemicals*	*F* *Hospitality*	*G* *Electrical Connectors*	*H* *High Tech*	*J* *Consumer Products*	*K* *Electronic Systems*	*L* *Specialty Chemicals*	*M* *Consumer Durables*
Net sales	x	x	x	x	x	x	x	x	x	x	x	x
Direct material and labor	x	x	x	x	x	x	x	x	x	x	x	x
Variable overhead	x	x	x	x	x	x	x	x	x	x	x	x
Depreciation of fixed assets	x	x	x	x	x		x	x	x	x	x	x
Local and contracted for nonlocal discretionary expenses	x	x	x	x	x	x	x	x	x	x	x	x
Allocated other-nonlocal discretionary expenses	x			x	x			x	x		x	x
Gains and losses on disposition of assets	x			x	x		x	x		x	x	
Interest	x			x	x			x				
Federal income taxes	x				x							
Label for Profit Measure	Earnings after Tax	Operating Income	Inc. before Int. and Taxes	Operating Profit	Net Income after Tax	Controllable Profit	Pretax Profit	Profit before Taxes	Profit from Operations	Operat. Profit	Division Contribution	Operating Profit

x = line item is included in measure of profit.

corporations are held accountable for gains and losses on disposition of fixed assets, those in only four are held accountable for interest, and those in only two are held accountable for taxes.

Table 5-2 summarizes the asset and liability accounts included in either profit center level investment profitability ratio measures (such as return on assets) or in management-by-objectives targets (such as days' receivables), as was discussed in Chapter 4. Again the firms' practices show great variation. Four firms do not measure investment profitability at the profit center level. Most of the firms restrict the investment measurement to three asset categories: receivables, inventories, and fixed assets, and some calculate a "net assets" number by deducting accounts payable (and sometimes other short-term liabilities). Two firms construct virtually an entire profit center balance sheet and hold the managers accountable for entity equity.

Relating Line-Item Accountability, Authority, and Controllability

I concluded from the data shown in Tables 5-1 and 5-2 and my knowledge of the profit center managers' roles that the controllability principle does not explain the firms' choices of income-statement and balance-sheet line items to include in motivational contracts for profit center managers. In addition to the business risks that affect many of these line items, discussed in Chapter 6, many of the managers are held accountable for line items over which they have no direct decision-making authority.[4]

The simple explanation of these data is that corporate managers are signaling the profit center managers about the line items of revenues, expenses, assets, and liabilities that top management wants them to try to *influence*.[5] The profit center managers are held accountable for some line items over which their authority is limited, although they have some influence over them.

Much of the variance in line-item accountability, as shown in Tables 5-1 and 5-2, is caused by differences in the profit

TABLE 5-2
Asset and Liability Accounts Included in Bottom-Line Profitability Measures

	Corporation											
	A *Diversified Luxury Goods*	*B* *Electronic Equipment*	*C* *Distribution*	*D* *Diversified Industrial Products*	*E* *Diversified Chemicals*	*F* *Hospitality*	*G* *Electrical Connectors*	*H* *High Tech*	*J* *Consumer Products*	*K* *Electronic Systems*	*L* *Specialty Chemicals*	*M* *Consumer Durables*
Assets:												
Cash					x			x				
Accounts receivable		x	x	x	x			x	x		x	x
Inventories		x	x	x	x			x	x		x	x
Fixed assets		x	x	x	x			x	x		x	x
Intangible assets					x			x			x	
Liabilities:												
Accounts payable			x	x	x			x			x	x
Other liabilities												

x = line item affects bottom-line calculation

center managers' roles. These differences and the accountability/role relationships can be illustrated by describing two extreme examples. Joe, the manager in the first example, has a relatively narrow managerial role, and he is held accountable for a restricted profit number called "controllable profit." Harvey, the manager in the second example, runs his business with almost total autonomy, and he is held accountable for a broadly defined bottom-line measure: before-tax return on assets, with assets defined as profit center equity.

An Example: Performance Measured in Terms of Controllable Profit

Joe is the manager of a restaurant in corporation F (hospitality) that functions as a profit center. His restaurant employs 41 people and has annual revenues of slightly more than $1 million. With the help of three assistant managers, Joe is responsible for day-to-day operations and short-term planning. He recruits and supervises the employees and makes sure that the corporation's policies are followed, service standards are upheld, costs are controlled, and assets are protected. He is authorized to spend up to $500 without securing approval.

Joe prepares the budget for the restaurant, and is accountable for a measure of the restaurant's profits called controllable profit. The categories of costs included in controllable profit are as follows: food (30% of sales), hourly labor and labor-related (20%), management labor and labor-related (10%), and other controllable costs, which include supplies, utilities, and maintenance (10%). The controllable profit margin runs around 30% of sales.

Joe is not held accountable for many significant direct and indirect costs of running the restaurant because he is judged to have little or no influence over them. These include rent, insurance, depreciation, real estate taxes, training, advertising and promotion, division and region administration, real estate development, interest, and income taxes. Furthermore, if a large maintenance expense is deemed necessary, such as painting the building, he may get a "budget adjustment" to cover that specific item. And Joe's risk is somewhat limited in a way that is like the deductible on an insurance policy: if an on-site accident causes significant damage or a lawsuit, he is charged only $500 because "it takes a lot to make up for something like that." Joe is not held accountable for any asset or liability balances.

Despite these limitations on his accountability, Joe clearly feels that he is a general manager. He has authority to take actions that influence both sales and costs, and he can earn a bonus of up to 36% of salary based on controllable profits earned and the quality of service provided in the restaurant. (Quality of service is measured through formal on-site operational audits and ratings by "secret shoppers.") Furthermore, Joe bears many of the risks of being a manager, since controllable profit is affected by many business risk factors. For example, if a competitor opens a restaurant across the street, if a labor shortage exists in the area, or if food prices increase sharply, corporation F gives Joe no relief for bonus purposes.

An Example: Performance Measured in Terms of Profit Before Tax and Return on Assets

Harvey is the manager of a profit center in corporation H (high tech) that develops, manufactures, and markets diagnostic test instruments for one specific industry segment. Harvey is an entrepreneur at heart; he founded the business in 1974 as a consulting company that gradually started building one-of-a-kind pieces of equipment. By 1979, orders started coming in for larger quantities, but the company was undercapitalized. To take advantage of the growth potential, Harvey sold the business to corporation H and became an employee/manager.

Harvey's profit center has performed excellently; sales have increased over sevenfold in five years to an annual level of about $15 million. The profit center, which has 140 employees, is very profitable, with gross margins approaching 70%.

As manager of the profit center, Harvey has almost as

much authority over his business's operations as he did as an owner/manager. Harvey described corporation H as like a mutual fund: "They do the investment banking, and they own all of the stock." The corporate staff provides only a few services, such as cash management and preparation of federal tax returns. The profit centers write their own checks, and their cash is moved each night into a central account.

In one sense Harvey feels he has even greater autonomy now than before the acquisition because he is freed from financing concerns. He noted that in contrast to the pressures he felt when he was an owner/manager, "I [now] believe there are no limits on manpower, capital, or product development." Harvey's profit center has very little interdependence with other corporation H operating entities because the corporation's management philosophy is to allow successful businesses to continue being successful; they do not force synergy.

Corporation H places very few constraints on Harvey (and the other profit center managers). The most significant constraint for some managers is a minimum performance level of 25% growth and 20% return on assets. If actual or projected performance falls below these levels, the profit center managers must explain their problems and proposed solutions to the corporate Profit and Growth Committee and, in essence, "get help." But because of his business's superior performance, Harvey is not affected by this constraint.

The only policies and procedures manual in corporation H is an accounting manual that dictates measurement rules and reporting formats and timetables. There are no approval limits on hiring people or spending capital as long as performance commitments are met because, as Harvey observed, "[corporation H] does not spend much time on capital. It has lots of cash. It is worried more about growth potential." Prudent managers do, however, secure their superiors' approval for multimillion-dollar commitments for purchases of land or buildings.

Harvey is allowed to prepare his own plans and budgets, and he admits that he is "very conservative" in projecting revenues and profits. Top management has accused him of sandbagging, but it does not force him to raise his targets. Instead it takes a "negative reserve" at the corporate level to offset the conservatism in Harvey's plan (and those of other profit center managers) to make the consolidated corporate plan more realistic.

Corporation H offers Harvey and the other profit center managers a potentially lucrative bonus based on their profit center's return on sales, return on assets, and growth in profit before tax. In calculating profit, Harvey's profit center is allocated corporate general and administrative (G&A) expenses based on a formula of 2.5% of the profit center's total cost (cost of goods sold plus all operating expenses). It is allocated group G&A expenses based on a proportion of the total costs in the group. It is assessed a capital charge at a rate of 4–5% of net assets employed (which equals entity equity). The capital charge rate is varied monthly with the corporation's borrowing rate. The profit centers are charged 1% over the corporate composite borrowing rate for the net balances in the working capital accounts, or credited with interest income if they have generated excess cash during the year. And all group assets are allocated to the profit center level by the group executive in a way that "all net assets are accounted for."

The Two Examples Compared

These two examples illustrate the strong relationship between influence and accountability across the sample of profit centers studied. Harvey's actions can affect the amounts appearing in many more accounts than Joe's, so it is understandable that his performance measurements are much more inclusive than Joe's.

This explanation is not complete, however, because Harvey, in particular, is not held accountable for some expense and investment line items that he can undoubtedly influence; for example, his actions can cause the corporation to qualify or not qualify for some federal income tax credits. Conversely, he is charged with several categories of expenses over which he seems to have no influence, such as corporate G&A expenses. These line items "at the influence margin" present the most challenging measurement system design choices.

Decisions About Line Items at the Margin

Concluding that profit center managers at the extremes, such as Joe and Harvey, should be evaluated in terms of different bottom-line measures is easy. Not all choices about line-item inclusion are so easy, however, because profit centers managers often have some, but not complete, influence over certain line items. The following sections describe some choices made in these less obvious decision areas.

FEDERAL INCOME TAXES

Many profit center managers, such as Joe, have no influence on federal income taxes. The effective corporate tax rate is determined by decisions made above them in the management hierarchy and by the skill of the corporation's tax preparers.

In two corporations (A—diversified luxury goods and E—diversified chemicals), however, corporate executives have chosen to hold their profit center managers accountable for taxes because they feel that some of the managers' decisions should reflect tax expenses and savings. An assistant controller in corporation E explained how he allocated the tax benefits:

> We compute our taxes by legal entity and then break them down by product line. We look at the major tax credits, such as investment tax credits and R&D tax credits, and break them down according to whoever generated the transaction. When we go through this exercise, we are asking ourselves, What's the closest to reality? What's the most equitable?

Corporation A goes through a similar tax-allocation exercise. The controller explained that his corporation's change to after-tax reporting has had significant, measurable benefits:

> Up until 1984 our measurements were on a pretax earnings basis. It was a joke because the divisions ignored tax accounting. They have a lot to say about our taxes. They can work to get investment tax credits. They can increase export sales and get DISC and FISC allowances. They can make charitable contributions with excess and obsolete inventory and deduct the fair market value instead of carrying cost.
>
> Until we changed to after-tax measurements, we were a statutory tax rate payer, right at 48% or 46%. Now we're in the 40.5% range. We got $1.8 million in ITC in 1986. We wouldn't have gotten $1 million if we weren't on an after-tax basis.

These two corporations calculate after-tax numbers to induce their profit center managers to consider the potentially important economic implications of taxes.

Corporate managers in corporation H (high tech) have made the opposite decision. They have decided not to hold their profit center managers, such as Harvey, who can, like the profit center managers in corporations A and E, affect corporate tax rates, accountable for taxes. Top management at corporation H is well aware that its policy of evaluating profit center managers on a pretax basis may result in inferior decisions. The chief financial officer of H noted: "Our evaluations are based on pretax numbers. Occasionally we will get a decision that is not best on an after-tax basis. We try to catch it and talk the managers into the right decision."

Corporation H's managers' decision to base their profit center manager evaluations on pretax numbers, even with the knowledge that taxes sometimes are important, reflect cost-benefit concerns. They have concluded that the amount of influence Harvey and the other profit center managers have on taxes is not material. The corporation is not highly capital intensive, so investment tax credits are small; very little of the business is overseas; and the profit centers do not have tax loss carryforwards. Thus, variations in effective tax rates are caused mostly by changes in the tax laws and skill in corporate tax-return preparation and very little by the profit center managers' actions. Furthermore, the corporation is still relatively small (less than $300 million in annual sales), so top financial managers (the people with tax expertise) have some visibility into the profit center operations; they can intervene and "correct" some decisions made suboptimally on an after-tax basis. Finally, the corporate offices operate with a small financial staff. Moving to an after-tax measurement basis would require adding some people and administrative cost, and management is not convinced that the benefits would be greater than the additional cost.

Assignments of Corporate General and Administrative Expenses

Deciding whether to assign corporate general and administrative (G&A) expenses to profit centers involves more complex trade-offs than assignments of taxes—the methods of assigning G&A costs are not always easy to discover and the assignments sometimes work against motivation. G&A costs are assigned to profit centers in seven of the 12 firms. Expenses are sometimes assigned through direct charges for services, but often they are allocated on bases such as total assets, employees, or revenues.[6]

The seven corporations that hold their profit center managers accountable for assigned corporate G&A expenses do so for either of two basic reasons. The first is that they realize these expenses can be influenced somewhat and charging them is likely to increase profit center/corporate staff communication and, it is hoped, generate constructive conflict that will help keep the corporate costs in line.[7] They realize that corporate staff managers have incentives to increase some categories of G&A costs to augment their bases of power and to make their lives easier; furthermore it is important that someone bear the cost of these increases and exert pressure on the corporate groups to keep the costs in line. Profit center managers can perform this role. In corporation A (diversified luxury goods), for example, the controller noted, "The purpose of having a 'fully loaded bottom line' is that it allows the division managers to apply pressure on corporate to keep their costs in line."

A second reason for assigning corporate G&A expenses is

that if the assignments are made on some reasonable basis, meaning that they are somewhat associated with the actual factors causing the costs to be incurred, the profit center managers' evaluations are based on a closer approximation of the full costs of their actions than they would be if G&A expenses were not allocated. As an assistant controller of E (diversified chemicals) observed: "When we allocated full costs, the managers began to see things they had never seen before." A profit center controller in corporation D (diversified industrial products) agreed: "The interest on debt and administrative charges are taxation without representation. But there is no fair way to do it. If [corporate] doesn't pass it on, the [profit centers] will forget some of these costs when it comes to pricing products. We're a monopsony; we live in a world that is cost-driven."

Because reasonable allocation bases are necessary to provide the right information signals and incentives, some corporations have gone to considerable effort to study what drives their corporate costs. Corporation E (diversified chemicals), for example, in implementing a policy of pushing as many costs as possible down to the operating units, increased the direct charges of corporate expenses to profit centers and reduced the pool of expenses that had to be allocated by over one-half, to approximately 1% of sales.[8] Some large categories of costs felt to be clearly outside the scope of existing businesses, such as the costs of basic corporate R&D, new-venture activities, or litigation related to discontinued businesses, were not charged to profit centers at all.

In other corporations, corporate G&A expenses are allocated on bases that everyone recognizes as crude—often entity sales, assets, or number of employees—but the corporate managers seem not to worry much about the crudeness. For example, the controller of corporation A (diversified luxury goods) observed: "Our allocations are based on sales and net assets. That's not the perfect way, but there is no perfect way, so we haven't changed what we do."

These crude, non-usage-based allocations are not made because of positive effects they might have on motivation.

They are made either to provide information that is useful for evaluating business entities, not managers, or to provide signals to profit center managers that their financial performance is not as rosy as it might appear from the operating performance line on the profit center accounting reports. For example, an assistant controller in corporation E (diversified chemicals) acknowledged that the profit center managers "are being held accountable for things they can't control, but they control the important items, and [the allocations] help us answer the question about whether we are generating a reasonable profit on each of our product lines." And the controller of corporation G (electrical connectors) noted, "We try to charge as many costs to [the profit centers] as we can. We want them to see the full costs so they don't feel too profitable."

In five of the 12 corporations, corporate G&A expenses are not assigned to profit centers at all. In most of these firms, the corporate managers believe that the profit center managers really can have only an insignificant influence on the corporate expenses or that the allocations are essentially arbitrary.

Corporate managers in corporation K (electronic systems) think that assigning the G&A costs to profit centers would be worthwhile, but they have not done so "for political reasons." The philosophy of the top-level managers in this young (12-year-old) corporation that has grown by acquisition has been to give the profit center managers almost complete autonomy. The top managers "haven't taken the corporation allocation issues on yet" because of fear that the profit center managers would resist the allocations as signals of increasing corporate control of their entities.

The profit center managers' reactions provide evidence of both advantages and disadvantages in assigning corporate costs. Some profit center managers prefer to be assigned the full range of costs because they feel the assignments give them more power over the corporate functions and, therefore, greater control over their own destiny. A profit center manager in corporation E (diversified chemicals) noted: "The corporate charges give us an element of control over the [corporate] functions. If we can't reach an agreement on the budget, I can't order the manager to do something, but I can appeal to a higher authority. Of course I tend not to want to do that."

Such comments are consistent with Vancil's conclusion that "profit center managers perceive that their autonomy is greater if they have to pay for the cost of corporate resources than if they do not have to pay for them."[9] This is not the pure autonomy that exists where an entity is isolated from the rest of the corporation; it is autonomy in the sense of the managers being able to control the results by which they are being evaluated in situations of significant organizational interdependence. Control of their own destiny is a quality most profit center managers value highly.

On the other hand, negative feelings set in where the profit center managers perceive that their power to control the corporate expenses is minimal and where their performance is adversely affected by the assignments. For example, a manager in corporation H (high tech) noted:

> There are certain things you can't control that other people can, such as corporate G&A. Assigning these costs can lead to bad feelings. The numbers aren't large, but it bugs me that they have gone up. We're below 20% profit this year, and I'm fighting for everything I can get. When corporate changes the rules, even a tenth of a percent can hurt because it can be a significant part of the margin we're trying to close.

Most profit center managers, however, are not concerned about their G&A charges and allocations because the amounts are small and the actual assignments do not vary much from budget. Harvey, the manager in corporation H who consistently earned maximum bonuses, said he spent no time worrying about the allocations. And profit center managers in corporation L (specialty chemicals), whose allocations of corporate expenses had just been raised from 1% to 1.25% of sales (for bonus purposes, not standard entity financial reporting), seemed unconcerned. One noted, "It's not worth having battles. Division managers should be running their businesses."

Overall, then, choices about whether to hold profit center managers accountable for corporate G&A expenses present some difficult trade-offs. The benefits of assignment are positively related to:

- the extent to which it is possible to tie the G&A expenses to the factors that cause the costs to be incurred;
- the extent to which it is desirable to have the profit center managers exercise influence on the particular item of cost, which, in turn, is related to the extent to which the profit center can control the factors used as the basis for assignment (the factors causing the costs to be incurred); and
- the extent to which the information is useful for decision making at the profit center organization level.

Some of the costs of assignment are due to the adverse motivational effects caused either by the profit center managers' frustrations at being held accountable for factors over which they have little control or by the managers' fear that corporate managers are usurping their authority. And, of course, administrative costs must be incurred to establish and maintain the cost assignment apparatuses. Since these benefits and costs vary widely across corporations, it is not surprising that the firms' G&A assignment practices also vary.

WORLDWIDE PRODUCT PERFORMANCE

Tables 5-1 and 5-2 show only some of the major choices corporate managers make about the line items for which they hold their profit center managers accountable. The categories in these tables can be disaggregated to show that many more choices must be made. For example, management in corporation B (electronic equipment) recently made a decision—to hold its domestic profit center managers accountable for the worldwide performance of their products—that is unlike that made in any of the other corporations. Because of its uniqueness, the affected accounts are not broken out separately in either table.

In corporation B, the managers of the domestic profit centers are responsible for a family of products. They have direct control over the domestic sales of their products, but overseas sales, which account for almost 40% of total corporate sales, are handled through a separate international organization. In the recent change, the managers of the domestic profit centers were made accountable for the total worldwide performance of their products. The sense of accountability for the worldwide numbers is strong. The managers are asked to submit worldwide plan numbers, and the worldwide accomplishments directly affect their incentive compensation.

The change to a worldwide measurement basis was made for four stated purposes: (1) improve understanding of the businesses on a global basis to better identify competitive advantages and use them effectively; (2) produce a superordinate financial statement for both domestic and international general managers to use in determining strategy and measuring progress in achieving objectives; (3) minimize the issues around internal transfer prices and focus management attention on customer needs; and (4) allow comparison with competitor statements. The effect is that while the international operations are outside the range of the domestic managers' formal authority, holding the managers accountable for the worldwide numbers encourages them to think internationally and to develop informal forms of influence.

The profit center managers in corporation B generally favored the change, even though it increased their responsibility for factors they cannot totally control. One profit center (division) controller noted: "Worldwide income statements give us an incentive to recognize that we are an international business. If we don't pay attention to what's happening internationally, we may lose market share." Similarly, a group controller's reaction:

> I support the change. It will cause us to interact more with our international divisions and joint venture partners. It is consistent with our philosophy that managers are held ac-

countable for things they can influence, even if they can influence them only a little. The price of this change is that it will cost us some incentive compensation for a year or two.

Conclusion

In reviewing the many examples of choices corporate managers make about line items for which to hold their profit center managers accountable, I concluded that the most important explanatory factor is the managers' degree of influence: there is a strong relationship between what managers can influence and what is included in the measures on which their motivational contracts are based. The key issue that corporate designers struggle with is, in the words of an assistant controller in corporation M (consumer durables), "how to come up with measurements that operating managers can 'own.' "

If the profit center managers' influence on a given category of revenue or expense is truly zero or if corporate managers do not want them to pay attention to certain line items where their influence is small or their involvement would be costly or annoying, these items should not be included in the performance measures. Corporation E (diversified chemicals), for example, which has a philosophy of charging profit centers for as many corporate costs as possible, does not charge them for corporate research, voluntary waste-cleanup costs, or the costs of litigation unrelated to actions taken by personnel in the profit center.

Profit center managers with some influence over particular line items often do not have total authority over those items. I concluded that a good influence/authority match occurs in the profit centers of only four (C, F, G, and K) of the 12 corporations. The match occurs because the personnel affecting the profit centers' revenues and costs report to the profit center managers. The profit centers in these corporations operate independently of other profit centers, and they are not allocated the costs of staff entities.

The influence/authority match is less complete in the other

eight corporations because of organizational interdependencies: the profit centers have to rely on other corporate entities as customers or as suppliers of products or services, and their performance measures are affected by the performance of personnel in these other entities. Thus these profit center managers are held accountable for factors over which they have less than complete authority and, consequently, less than total control. Corporate managers could conceivably choose to eliminate the potentially distorting effects of the organizational interdependencies, but their measurement system design choice shows they do not want to do so: they want the profit center managers to consider these factors over which they are judged to have some influence in making their decisions, even when their influence is less than complete.

Influence by itself, however, does not provide a simple, definitive rule to follow in defining bottom-line results measures because many of the choices require comparison of expected benefits and costs. The benefit from including additional line items in the bottom-line results measures is improved decision-making congruence. This benefit is positively related to both the size of the line item and the extent of the profit center managers' influence on it.

But the costs of adding additional line items must often be borne in several forms. For some line items, additional administrative expenses are needed to establish and maintain the measures that provide accountability. And sometimes motivational and emotional costs are caused by profit center managers' frustration at being held accountable for items over which they have little influence. These latter costs can be manifested in decreased morale and possible turnover or in the need to compensate the profit center managers for bearing the risk.

NOTES

1. These factors add noise to the accounting performance measures [Lambert and Larcker (1985)].

2. Solomons (1965), p. 72.

3. Decisions about definitions of profit are typically made at the corporate level, so only one definition is shown for each corporation. This is a simplification, however. Where profit centers are in substantially different lines of business, this decision is sometimes decentralized to operating-unit levels. Differences may also exist where a profit center has been recently acquired, since the corporation has not yet changed the profit center's accounting system to match that of the rest of the corporation. Either or both of these situations has caused differences in the measures of profit in corporations A, D, E, F, J, K, and L.

4. This finding is similar to that of Vancil (1978), who shows that most managers are held responsible for factors over which they have less than complete authority. He presents evidence gathered from a large-scale survey of the practices of 291 manufacturing corporations and shows the lack of correspondence between what he calls the firms' authority and responsibility structures. Eccles (1985, pp. 214–216) also notes the increase in interorganizational communication and beneficial conflict created by allocation of the costs of shared resources.

5. This "influenceability" principle was recently identified and described by John Dearden (1987, p. 86). He states: "I propose as a guideline for drawing up the profit budget that the company include only items that managers can influence."

Antle and Demski (1988) conclude, similarly, that managers should be evaluated in terms of all information relevant to answering the question of whether the managers supplied the desired behavior. In the terminology of principal-agent theory, an item has information content if a manager's "supply of inputs is able to affect the probability distribution of the output statistic" (p. 701). In Dearden's terms, the items with information content, then, are those the manager can influence.

6. Vancil (1978, pp. 100–105) discusses the various methods of assigning costs to operating entities.

7. This beneficial effect has been noted by other researchers, including Eccles (1985, pp. 214–216) and Vancil (1978, pp. 129–130).

8. Johnson and Loewe (1987, p. 21) describe a similar study undertaken by the Weyerhaeuser Company in the early 1980s. This study involved "carefully analyzing the activities that drive the consumption of corporate resources" in order to charge the costs to the operating entities causing the resources to be consumed. They report, for example, that the uncharged costs of the Financial Services Department, a corporate staff unit responsible for all central accounting, were reduced from $11 million to $250,000.

9. Vancil (1978), p. 304.

CHAPTER 6

The Controllability Problem, Part II: Deciding Whether to Adjust for Uncontrollable Influences After the Fact

"We have more personality clashes than tornadoes."

A second major category of choices corporate managers make about uncontrollable influences relates to the types of adjustments that are mandated or allowed once the measurement period has ended. These adjustments can be made for any of a number of business risks that are not controlled for in the profit center budget (or other preset evaluation standards) because they cannot be forecast accurately.

This chapter shows that the firms' adjustment practices vary widely in the types of uncontrollables for which adjustments are made and in the ways in which the adjustments are made. It also describes the trade-offs managers must make in deciding when to make adjustments and shows that one of the most important factors affecting those trade-offs is the perceived cost of allowing subjectivity in performance evaluations.

The chapter begins by describing two examples that illustrate much of the variation in practice across firms. The examples show that managers in corporation C (distribution) are inclined to adjust for the effects of many influences that the profit center managers cannot control, whereas those in corporation H (high tech) almost never make such adjustments.

An Example: Adjusting for the Effects of Uncontrollables in Corporation C

Fred is the manager of a profit center in corporation C that distributes liquor throughout eastern Missouri from its headquarters in St. Louis. The actual results for 1983 and 1984 and the goals for 1985 for this profit center were as follows:

		Operating Profit (000)	*Inventory Turns*	*Days' Sales Outstanding*
1983	Actual	$512	15.0	30.6
1984	Actual	547	12.2	32.0
1985	Minimum	570	12.2	32.0
	Plan	577	13.7	30.9
	Maximum	720	14.7	27.4

For purposes of awarding bonuses to Fred, the profit factor was weighted 60%, and the other two factors were weighted 20% each. If the minimum operating profit was not reached, Fred was to receive no bonus. If the maximum level of performance was reached on all three factors, he would earn a bonus of 50% of salary.

During the 1985 annual planning process, Fred and his superiors were aware of:

- a federal excise tax (FET) increase scheduled for October 1, 1985;
- contemplation of a consolidation of operations of the St. Louis profit center with those of a profit center headquartered in Kansas City; and
- the expiration of the Teamsters contract at the rectifying plant where a major private brand is produced.

The impact of each of these items caused group management to consider adjustments that had bonus implications.

The *FET increase* was planned for and an increase in sales was forecast because of expectations that customers would try to "beat the tax increase." Results around the nation were mixed, but in eastern Missouri sales were up significantly, and operating profits for the St. Louis profit center were $798,000 for the year. Group management realized that the figures were extraordinarily good, but it thought they were the result, to some degree, of the efforts of Fred and his management team. Consequently, the figures were accepted for the bonus award as measured; no adjustments were made.

Some time after the 1985 bonus parameters had been established, group management decided to *consolidate* the St. Louis and Kansas City operations to make the physical distribution system more efficient. The work, which took place in November and December 1985, caused some unusual expenses to be charged to the St. Louis profit center. These expenses were deducted from the 1985 operating results, but the practical effect was nil, since the profit center's actual operating-profit performance already exceeded the bonus program maximum. If this had not been the case, an adjustment to the St. Louis profit center's actual results would have been made; the expenses would have been removed.

With the pending *expiration of the labor contract* at the production facility, group management decided to require each distributor location to increase private brand inventory by the equivalent of one month's sales to protect against a possible work stoppage. At the close of the fiscal year, group management judged it necessary to adjust the actual inventory turn number by an estimate of the impact of this centralized decision. A group staff vice president estimated that without the adjustment the inventory turn number would have been 12.0; with the adjustment it became 13.0. This adjustment increased Fred's bonus by just over $1,000 (2% of salary).

A No-Adjustment Philosophy in Corporation H

Managers in other corporations do not make adjustments for uncontrollables either because they feel they are unable to separate the uncontrollable effects accurately or because they want the profit center managers to bear the full business risk. Primarily for the latter reason, executives in corporation H almost never adjust for uncontrollables for bonus purposes.

All the profit center managers interviewed in corporation H gave examples of factors over which they had little or no control, such as economic conditions, interest rates, and the successes or failures of major customers, that were not adjusted for. For example, in one profit center that sells automation and video graphics products to television networks and stations, sales were virtually flat in a recent year, and the budget was missed by a substantial margin. The major problem was that the merger and takeover activities in the communications industry had caused many potential customers to delay capital expenditures. Although it was agreed that the slowdown was not the fault of the profit center manager, executives made no adjustments for purposes of assigning bonuses. Similarly, in another profit center, a customer that had been forecast to buy fully 15% of the unit's total output got into financial difficulty and, in fact, later went out of business. No allowance was made here for bonus purposes either.

Corporate executives explained that they treated their profit center managers as entrepreneurs (which most of them were before selling their company to corporation H) who must bear the risk of running their own business. They allow the profit center managers considerable autonomy, ask them to build their businesses, and pay for results, with no excuses allowed. Some representative quotes from the president:

> What I want is Renaissance people running the [profit centers], people who can use all legal and ethical means to grow the business. What I don't want is someone who wants to be told what to do—that's a clerk. . . . The right kind of guy for us is creative; he builds something. . . .
>
> We don't pay for effort; we pay for results.

From a group vice president:

> The main thrust of our management style is that we consider opportunities for new business as more important for the [profit center managers] than managing what they've got. We

> don't compete by taking another 10 cents of product costs out; we compete by developing new ideas.
>
> Results have an awful lot to do with telling whether a manager is good or bad. I had one who had terrific results. I didn't agree with his management style at all, but I would not have fired him.

These two examples are of the extremes. Corporation C has essentially told its profit center managers that they should do their best and the corporation will protect them from some of the factors they cannot control. In corporation H, on the other hand, the actual reported results are all-important. The managers are told not to look to the corporation for relief.

The Firms' Adjustment Choices

The two examples above illustrate the basic controllability choice, but the practices of most corporations fall between the extremes. Most corporations adjust for some, but not all, types of uncontrollables, and the adjustments they make are partial, not total.

The practices can be distinguished in terms of five primary choice areas: (1) the purposes for which adjustments are made (such as job retention, bonus awards); (2) the person(s) making the adjustments; (3) the types of uncontrollables for which adjustments are made (such as economic conditions, acts of nature); (4) the methods of making adjustments (objective calculation, subjective judgment); and (5) the direction of adjustments (are they always made in favor of the profit center managers?).

The firms' practices vary considerably in most of these areas, as shown in Table 6-1. The following sections describe the practices in some detail and the trade-offs contract designers face in each area.

Purposes of Adjustments

When discussing after-the-measurement-period adjustments for uncontrollables, it is important to distinguish the

TABLE 6-1
Similarities and Differences Among the Firms' Treatments of Uncontrollables

	Corporation											
	A *Diversified Luxury Goods*	*B* *Electronic Equipment*	*C* *Distribution*	*D* *Diversified Industrial Products*	*E* *Diversified Chemicals*	*F* *Hospitality*	*G* *Electrical Connectors*	*H* *High Tech*	*J* *Consumer Products*	*K* *Electronic Systems*	*L* *Specialty Chemicals*	*M* *Consumer Durables*
Purposes of adjustments made: Are the effects of at least some uncontrollables taken into account when evaluating PC managers for purposes of:												
job retention?	yes	yes	yes	yes	yes	yes	yes	yes	yes	yes	yes	yes
short-term bonus awards?	yes, but rare	yes, but rare	yes	yes	yes	yes, but rare	no	generally no	yes	yes, but rare	yes	yes
long-term bonus awards?	no	no	N/A	no	no	N/A	no	no	no	no	no	no
Decision maker(s) for bonus adjustments	immediate superior; CEO has to approve	immediate superior; corporate executives have to approve	immediate superior	immediate superior	bonus pool–compensation committee; individual–immediate superior	immediate superior; group executive has to approve	COO	CEO	immediate superior	top management; compensation committee has to approve	immediate superior, CEO	immediate superior

Types of adjustments: Are adjustments made (at least sometimes) for the effects of uncontrollables:												
decisions made (or approved) by personnel at higher organization levels?	yes	yes	yes	yes	yes	yes	no	yes	yes	yes	yes	yes
economic factors?	no	no	yes	yes	yes	yes	no	no	no	no	no	no
competitive factors?	no	no	rare	no	yes	rare	no	no	no	no	no	no
true "acts of nature"?	yes	no	yes	yes	yes	yes	no	no	no	yes	no	no
Method of making adjustments	subjective	subjective	variance analysis, subjective	flexible plan, subjective	subjective	subjective	subjective	subjective	subjective	subjective	subjective	subjective
Direction of adjustments always in favor of managers?	almost always	yes	yes	subjective-yes; flex. plan-no	no	yes	yes	yes	yes	yes	yes	yes

purposes for which those adjustments are made. Corporations use the results measures for assigning a broad range of rewards and penalties, and the firms do not treat uncontrollables identically for all purposes.

One major difference is in the treatment of uncontrollables for purposes of assigning various forms of awards. As is shown in Table 6-1, the firms' practices for purposes of judging managers' abilities to retain their jobs and to earn long-term bonus awards are essentially identical. All the firms seem to follow the controllability principle for job retention purposes—they will not remove profit center managers from their positions because of negative influences on the performance measures that are known to be uncontrollable. None of them follows the controllability principle for purposes of assigning explicit long-term bonus awards—they assume that over a several-year period the favorable and unfavorable uncontrollable influences tend to even out. The firms differ considerably in their treatment of uncontrollables for short-term bonus purposes, however.

Here are four representative descriptions of how managers alter their treatment of uncontrollables depending on the purpose:

The CEO of corporation A (diversified luxury goods): "I put importance on achieving the targets, but I believe things change up and down. If a target is missed, I'm not going to kill the guy. He needs to tell me why and how he's going to do for the rest of the year. If there are extenuating circumstances, I'll forgive him. But his bonus will suffer."

The COO of corporation G (electrical connectors): "If a manager missed a budget for uncontrollable reasons, I'd allow him to keep his job, but he probably wouldn't earn a bonus. There would be no fund to pay the bonus from. He might get a raise if I judged he did a good job under the circumstances."

A profit center manager in corporation B (electronic equipment):

> The system is compassionate in that [if you miss your budget] you don't lose your job. But you get no bonus.

> [My boss] would not hold me accountable for things I can't control. If I have a bad year, my bonus would be cut, but he wouldn't hold me accountable. To me being held accountable means losing my job. Bonus is just an added incentive for performance . . .

A profit center manager in corporation J (consumer products): "Several years ago I missed my budget badly because of a number of brand failures. I got no bonus, but they had enough confidence in me that I kept my job."

Most of the following discussion is about the ways firms deal with uncontrollables for bonus purposes, because the practices are easiest to observe and the variation is the greatest. I observed that one firm (corporation G—electrical connectors) will not make adjustments for uncontrollables for bonus purposes under any circumstances; the bonus pool calculation is absolute. Corporation H's policy, described in the example above, is almost that definite. Four other firms (A, B, F, and K) have an explicit policy of not making adjustments, but they leave open a slight possibility of making exceptions under very unusual circumstances. The other six firms make adjustments for uncontrollables under some, but not all, circumstances.[1]

Decision Maker(s)

Adjustments for the effects of uncontrollable influences are generally made by the profit center manager's immediate superior. These people can best judge whether the effect was truly uncontrollable, and if so, what the size of the adjustment should be.

I noted two types of exceptions to this general rule. In six corporations, approvals for adjustments have to be made at higher organizational levels. In corporation K (electronic systems), requests for bonus adjustments were initiated by the profit center managers (or their immediate superiors), and approvals were necessary at all higher organization levels and the compensation committee of the board of directors. The purposes of this elaborate administrative procedure were to keep the number of special requests to a minimum and to maintain cross-organizational equity in assignment of awards. For similar reasons, the CEO has to approve adjustments in corporations A (diversified luxury goods), H (high tech), and L (specialty chemicals), and senior corporate executives have to approve them in corporations B (electronic equipment) and F (hospitality). The benefits of these extra, multiple-approval administrative procedures must be balanced against the costs of the management time involved.

The second exception occurs where a bonus pool is created on the basis of overall corporate performance. In such cases, decisions about overriding the predetermined calculation of the size of the pool because of uncontrollable influences are made at a high level, generally the compensation committee of the board of directors. This is the way contracts are designed in corporations D, E, J, and K, but adjustments in these corporations tend to be quite rare.

Corporation E's (diversified chemicals) approach is representative. Its contract allows the CEO to recommend to the compensation committee that adjustments be made to the target award fund on the basis of "performance in light of competition, the economy, the quality of our performance, or the motivational impact of the award." Senior managers observed that every year some unforeseen economic factors, such as demand changes, currency devaluations, or changes in significant raw materials (particularly oil), affect net income performance, and these factors often come up for discussion in the compensation committee meetings. The committee, however, often decides to ignore these factors. In the words of one manager, "They don't bend very much."

The other firms' practices are similar. In corporation D (diversified industrial products) the compensation committee can add up to 10% of the standard pool if conditions warrant. In corporation J (consumer products), the compensation committee can allocate up to 15% of the target bonus pool to profit centers that make their targets even if the corporation does not make its target. These adjustments affect the variation of the profit center managers' bonuses, but they do not limit the specific business risk felt at the profit center level.

Uncontrollables for Which Adjustments Are Made

Some firms do make adjustments for uncontrollables, but their practices vary considerably depending on the type of uncontrollable. The uncontrollable factors for which some firms sometimes adjust can be classified into four basic types: (1) decisions made (or approved) by personnel at higher organization levels, (2) economic factors, (3) competitive factors, and (4) unexpected, nonrecurring events that I call acts of nature.

Decisions Made (or Approved) by Personnel at Higher Organizational Levels

A common form of adjustment for uncontrollables occurs where executives decide that profit centers should not bear certain costs because the decision to incur them was made at a higher organization level (the profit center was "ordered to do something") or because the profit center manager received permission to make the decision. I found evidence of adjustments for the effects of these decisions in all 11 firms where any types of adjustments for uncontrollables were made for bonus purposes.

There are two ways of adjusting for this type of uncontrollable. One is to charge the costs, which invariably are not included in the budget, to a corporate-level account. The other, which is feasible only in corporations that use operating income measures of profit center performance, is to move the costs "below the [operating income] line."

An Example

Managers in corporation B (electronic equipment), which uses an operating income measure of profit center performance, described an example that involved both methods of adjustment. A new profit center manager decided to close two of his remote locations and consolidate operations at a central site. He moved some employees and laid off the rest and abandoned the buildings in which they worked. The largest building, however, could not be sublet even at half the rate and with the offer of a significant finder's fee because of a real estate glut in its geographical area, and its lease had another four years to run.

The profit center controller argued that the expenses associated with this restructuring were caused by poor decisions made in past years by a different management team and that they were nonoperating in nature. She asked that a reserve be taken in nonoperating expense to cover all the restructuring expenses, which were expected to total almost $7 million, a significant amount for a profit center with revenues slightly over $20 million. The group and corporate controllers agreed with her logic, and they approved her accounting entry that placed the restructuring expenses below the operating income line.

Unfortunately for the profit center, the corporation was filing a shelf registration with the SEC for some debt financing, and in the course of their audit, the firm's external auditors found the restructuring expense entry. They objected to it because a recent SEC staff bulletin required that such costs be charged to operating income, so the costs were put back above the profit center's operating income line.

Financial staff at profit center and group levels then resorted to a motivation argument, claiming that this accounting treatment would demoralize profit center personnel because of the size of the expenses and the fact that they were not included in the unit's annual plan. They proposed that for internal reporting purposes the expenses be held at corporate and not reported on the profit center's books.

The issue was taken to the CFO for a decision. His initial preference was not to make an exception, but after considerable discussion, he concurred with the finance staff proposal. He explained:

> Intelligent people can make different judgments. Moving expenses for employees are clearly operating expenses. But if we shut down a regional office and move the people to corporate, there is definitely a bias in our system to call those nonoperating expenses. I wanted to call them operating expense, but I ended up calling them nonoperating because I was concerned that [without this accounting treatment] the

> people [in the profit center] would not discharge their responsibility. It had nothing to do with the merits of their arguments.

He was, however, also concerned that including the expenses in the current year would distort the profit center's performance trends.

Other Examples

I found many similarly controversial examples. For example, a profit center controller in corporation C (distribution) said, "[The corporation] is pushing us to participate in an insurance program with very high deductibles (around $50 million). If we were a stand-alone business, we couldn't afford to do that. If we take a $50 million hit, I would expect some forgiveness. It wasn't our decision."

And in corporation J (consumer products) an adjustment was made for a decision that was taken out of the manager's hands: "A few years ago we decided to close a factory in Germany that was working at 30% of capacity. The expenses were deducted at the corporate level. It was not the decision of the manager in Germany, so we couldn't penalize him."

Some profit center managers actively lobby for such an adjustment before they make decisions they consider desirable in the long run but that will have adverse effects on the short-term results measures. They attempt to have their superiors concur with the decision, and in essence share responsibility for it, to increase the possibility that a performance adjustment will be made. For example, a profit center manager in corporation E (diversified chemicals) said, "As things happen, I inform [my boss] and get him to buy into the decision to go over [my expense] budget. Then he will have a tendency to be compassionate when I don't make my profit target."

Although I found examples of adjustments for the effects of decisions made by higher-level managers in 11 firms, not all such decisions qualify for adjustments. The decisions for which adjustments are made tend to have very large effects. Common examples are acquisitions, divestments, and restructurings. It is in such cases that the benefits of eliminating the distorting effects of the uncontrollables are sufficiently large to offset the costs of analyzing the situation.

Economic Factors

Although most firms adjust for the effects of decisions made at higher organization levels, adjustments for the effects of economic factors such as changing economic conditions (an unplanned business downturn for example), unexpected cost increases, foreign currency fluctuations, or an uncontrollable loss of supply (caused, for example, by a strike in a supplier's plant) are rare. Only three of the 12 firms will even consider such adjustments, and in these three firms, few such adjustments are made.

Corporation D (diversified industrial products) does make complete adjustments for two types of uncontrollable economic factors—industry volume and foreign currency fluctuations. To adjust for industry volume, this firm uses a formal flexible planning system. Profit center personnel identify each of their income-statement accounts as fixed or variable, and the performance standard against which their performance is evaluated is a "flex plan" based on actual industry volume. The industry volume variance is considered uncontrollable. Similarly, an uncontrollable foreign exchange variance is calculated by including actual translation rates in the flexible plan.

While corporation D's group vice presidents assign bonuses to profit center managers subjectively, the flex plan-versus-actual comparison affects their judgments significantly. The controller explained:

> The managers are generally not held accountable for a volume variance. We don't want to penalize them for changes in total industry volume. Some businesses have only three customers, and if something goes wrong with one of them, there's no way to make it up. But if they are losing market share relative to everyone else, they are held accountable.

A group vice president agreed with this explanation: "If someone misses plan continually, I judge that he is not in control of his operation, and if he's not managing his programs well, that's a problem. On the other hand, if the misses are caused by changes in the industry, then it's not their concern."

Another group president said:

> The managers know they're held accountable for the profit plan. That's basically the plan at the beginning of the year. But if market conditions fall apart, we'll focus instead on the flex plan.
>
> [In other words] if the market is there, we expect them to make the profit plan. If the market falls to seven million units from a forecast of nine million, we can't expect them to make the plan.

Corporation D does not make adjustments for any other type of uncontrollable economic factor. Similarly, in the other firms that are willing to consider adjustments for economic factors, the adjustments are rare. Even in corporation C (distribution), the firm described above as being particularly amenable to making adjustments for uncontrollables, a group executive explained: "We don't want to make an adjustment for every uncontrollable event that comes along. We say that if the economy turns sour, it's too bad. If you owned your own company, who could you turn to? Nobody was complaining last year when the economy was better than forecast."

Competitive Factors

Adjustments for competitive factors, such as price, are even rarer than those for economic factors. Adjustments for uncontrollable competitive factors are considered in three corporations—C (distribution), E (diversified chemicals), and F (hospitality). Even in these firms, such adjustments are made only in exceptional cases where the factors are deemed to be totally uncontrollable and the effects are huge.

In corporation C, for example, the firm described above as generally the most tolerant of adjustments, top-level managers considered but decided not to adjust for an event that was expected to cost a profit center manager all of his 1986 bonus. This example involved a liquor-distribution profit center that faced a major price war beginning in February 1986. The war caused the margins on a case of product to decline from a normal level of $6–7 per case to $1.50. The margin decline made every sale unprofitable because distribution costs were approximately $4.20 per case. The war was particularly costly because it affected sales volumes, as well as margins, and it was impossible for the manager to reduce fixed expenses as quickly as the revenues were decreasing.

When he was preparing his plan for 1986, the profit center manager knew a price war was possible: he saw a non-full-service wholesaler making market share gains at the expense of a full-service company. But he noted, "There is no way to include such things in the forecast. Such blips occur on the upside as well as on the downside. For example, we have experienced tremendous sales growth of wine coolers, which no one forecast."

Because the decision was made not to adjust for the effects of this uncontrollable competitive factor, this manager knew that his chances of earning a bonus for 1986 were "nil to none." He felt he could have met his plan if the price war had not occurred until the second or third quarter. But while he was not happy about losing his annual bonus, he saw such possibility as part of being a general manager.

A profit center manager in corporation E (diversified chemicals) expressed a similar feeling:

> My boss is a compassionate guy, but if I face tougher competition than I forecast, he would say that is too bad, that I had gotten us into the business. I can't argue with that. I try to run this [profit center] as if it were my own business, and I have to accept the good with the bad. If it turns out to be a fiasco, somebody has to suffer.

The risk profit center managers bear for uncontrollable competitive (and economic) factors is not unlimited, however; they bear it only until the performance standards (typically budget) are revised to reflect the new reality. This risk limitation was illustrated in another profit center in corporation C, a distributor of gift- and glassware, which faced a major uncontrollable event with effects so significant that upper-level managers probably would have made an adjustment. In this case, however, enough lead time was given so that the manager could incorporate the event in his budget before any adverse effects were felt.

In November 1984, the supplier of this profit center's largest and most profitable product line announced that it was taking away its exclusive franchise and source of supply. This product line accounted for 50% of the profit center's revenues and an even greater proportion of its earnings. This loss of supply was seen by profit center, group, and corporate managers as being totally outside the profit center manager's control. It was caused by legal problems the supplier was having, not by poor service from the profit center.

The upper-level managers were not faced with an adjustment decision, however, because the supplier was required contractually to give one year's notice before withdrawing the supply. Thus the profit center manager was able to incorporate the loss of this business in his budget for 1986. Since the short-term bonus contract calibrates performance to the degree to which budget plans are met, this manager's bonus was not affected by this uncontrollable event.

Acts of Nature

The fourth category of uncontrollable influences includes large, one-time disasters such as fires, earthquakes, tornadoes, floods, and accidents judged not to be caused by negligence. Five firms tend to make adjustments for acts of nature if they meet both of two conditions. First, the effects must be large; the profit centers are expected to be able to cope with small problems. And second, it must be determined that the disasters were truly uncontrollable. This means that the adjusting decision maker must believe that personnel in the profit center did not contribute to the likelihood that the disaster would occur, such as by neglecting safety regulations. The comment by an executive in corporation C (distribution), who was asked if he would make an adjustment if a fire occurred in a warehouse, was typical:

> I would start with the assumption that this couldn't be foreseen. You can't say that there is a 20% chance of fire in the forecast or the plan would be a disaster plan. Then I would look at the causes. Was the fire caused by a breach of security or a lackadaisical attitude toward safety? If the fire was outside the manager's control, I would make the adjustment.

Method of Adjustment

Firms that choose to make adjustments for any of the preceding types of uncontrollables can do so using objective or subjective methods. The objective methods require calculations to adjust either the actual performance measures (or the standards) for the effects of the uncontrollable factors. These calculations tend to yield a *complete* adjustment for the uncontrollable, whereas the subjective judgments typically provide only a *partial* adjustment.

Objective Adjustments

As is shown in Table 6-1, most adjustments stem from subjective judgments made by the profit center manager's immediate superior. The objective adjustment methods, which involve either evaluating performance in relation to similar organizations facing similar economic conditions or calculating variances that are isolated as being uncontrollable, are quite rare. None of the firms makes explicit use of relative performance evaluation.[2] Corporation C (distribution) sometimes calculates some variances on an ad hoc basis; several instances were described at the beginning of this chapter.

Corporation D's (diversified industrial products) use of flexible budgeting to remove the effects of industry volume and foreign currency fluctuations was also described above. Corporation D is able to use flexible planning because it has good data on the actual conditions in its primary markets. For example, one of its primary markets is the automotive industry, and when the vice president of the automotive group evaluates the profit center managers' performance, he knows with great precision the number of vehicles of each type produced and the components of each profit center going into each type. In some of the other groups, however, the flex plan does not work as well. The controller of a profit center in another operating group explained, "We have a current controversy as to whether market share can be measured. The market data do not mirror our mix of products very well, and what we make are substitutes for products in other segments."

Some of the other corporations have considered flexible budgeting but have not been able (or willing) to implement it. Corporation A (diversified luxury goods) also had trouble finding accurate industry data. The controller explained, "Maybe [flexible planning] would be a good idea if we could identify what our industry sales are, but that's tough. We just don't have good industry numbers. The figures we have are not totally reliable because they come from industry associations. The submissions are voluntary [and unaudited], and they also tend to be late."

Some groups in corporation A also found that separating fixed and variable expenses was difficult. A profit center manager explained:

> We're moving toward flexible budgeting, but we're not there yet. We haven't identified the core of expenses below which a prudent businessman wouldn't go. For example, 3,000 dealers sell our products. As long as our business is not in a depression, we must service the dealers on at least a minimum basis with some technical people in the field. Determining what that minimum is is not easy. The people who work for me will always consider more to be in the core than I will.

Another problem is a concern that the system will be too complex to administer and understand. The same profit center manager in corporation A observed, "The plan must be simple. It must be something that the people in the organization can understand. There are 300–400 people in my division alone on the plan. Adding industry variables to it would complicate it."

A final consideration is whether it is desirable to consider industry volume changes uncontrollable. Some corporations want profit center managers who are faced with lower industry volume to find other actions that will generate the budgeted level of profits. The controller of corporation A made this point: "Why do we not have a flexible plan? One reason is that many of our [profit centers] are marketing-oriented. There is no reason to reward them if sales are down. We don't want to accept a lower profit number, and we don't want to give [profit center managers] the idea that we do."

Subjective Adjustments

The alternative to variance analyses or flexible planning is to use subjective judgments to make allowances for uncontrollable factors. Here is a typical example of a subjective bonus award given in 1985 to the manager of a large ($600 million annual sales) profit center in corporation E (diversified chemicals), even though his profit center's results did not warrant one. This manager, John, described his goals as being 30% quantitative and 70% qualitative. Quantitative targets were set for cash flow, net income, and return on capital. The weighting among these factors was not explicit, but John said that group management had indicated that cash flow was his most important goal because his profit center's products were in the mature phase of the product life cycle. The qualitative targets were a list of concerns, including personnel outplacement and meeting information system development milestones.

In 1985 the corporation suffered significant losses. Sales were flat, and top management took strong steps to reorient the company toward faster growing markets. It liquidated some businesses, laid off a significant number of people, and implemented an early retirement program. According to the incentive compensation plan formula, which included a limited bonus based on corporate net income (as a percentage of budget), no bonuses should have been paid. However, bonuses were paid on a subjective basis to about 25% of the personnel participating in the plan. These bonuses were called special payments.

John received a special payment. He said he was not told why he received the award, but he thought it was because management recognized that he handled the restructuring of his business, including a plant closing, well. It was not because of his profit center's financial results, because his profit center experienced a loss in 1985.

Subjective adjustments for uncontrollables can also be made in less obvious ways. For example, although it appears that few adjustments are made for uncontrollables, in many corporations executives make an "interperiod adjustment." That is, they allow the profit center manager's bonus to suffer in the current year, but they allow a slightly easier budget target in the subsequent year.

A less common, but equally subtle, adjustment method occurs in corporations F (consumer products) and L (specialty chemicals). Sometimes when the financial performance measures are adversely affected by uncontrollable influences, executives compensate in part for the effect on the bonus award by being more lenient in their ratings in the largely subjective personal objectives performance areas.

Direction of Adjustments

Where adjustments for uncontrollables are made, their effects are almost invariably in the profit center managers' favor. Corporate managers give two related reasons for this choice. One is that they find it difficult to take bonuses away from profit center managers when the shareholders have done well. A typical comment, by the CEO of corporation A (diversified luxury goods), who uses considerable subjectivity in making his evaluations: "I would not judge performance down even if the manager was lucky because the shareholders benefited." The other reason for the asymmetry in the adjustments for uncontrollables is that the evaluators face little pressure to make downward adjustments; the profit center managers do not raise the issues.

When Should Adjustments Be Made for the Effects of Uncontrollables?

The preceding sections described the primary sources of the less than totally controllable effects that distort profit center results measures, alternatives for removing these effects, and the choices firms make about whether to remove them. Like the other contract design choices, these decisions involve trade-offs. The benefits from removing these effects must be balanced against the costs of removal.

BENEFITS AND COSTS

The benefits derived from eliminating the effects of the uncontrollable influences stem from the rationale for the controllability principle.[3] If adjustments are made, managers will not bear the risk caused by factors they cannot control, and evaluations of their performance will be more reliable. The managers' frustrations with unfair evaluations will decrease; they will be less motivated to engage in unproductive earnings-management activities to achieve performance targets that uncontrollables have made impossible to achieve with normal business practices; and the firms' compensation costs will decrease because the managers will not have to be compensated for bearing the extra risk. The universality of the benefits of eliminating the effects of uncontrollable influences leads some compensation consultants to make unequivocal prescriptions such as: "Specific incentive formulas of all kinds must be avoided."[4]

The potential benefits of adjusting for uncontrollable influences increase with the size of the distorting effects of the uncontrollable factors. These factors include both unpredictable exogenous factors and the dependence of profit centers on other entities in the corporation.

The costs of adjusting for the effects of the uncontrollable influences come in several forms. One form results from inferior decisions stemming from reduced goal congruence if the adjustments buffer the managers from the effects of partially controllable influences to which they are expected to react.[5] Administrative costs typically increase, since mechanisms such as flexible planning systems and variance analyses require time and resources to implement, maintain, and use. And some costs often stem from reduced measurement objectivity, since the choice of adjustments and their size are usually significantly affected by subjective judgments. In many situations, the costs stemming from reduced measurement objectivity dominate the other costs. That is, many firms' successes and failures in making adjustments for uncontrollables vary directly with the profit center managers' reactions to those subjective judgments. The importance of this subjectivity/cost relationship is described in the following sections.

Tolerance of Subjectivity in Performance Evaluations

In most cases firms find it impossible to describe in advance the formulas and procedures they will use to remove the effects of uncontrollables from performance measures. Thus if managers want to remove the effects of the uncontrollables, they must generally do so subjectively. To a large extent, the variation in the firms' treatment of uncontrollables is directly related to their taste for allowing subjectivity in the administration of the motivating contracts. I judged that most of the managers in only five corporations—A, C, E, J, and M—out of the sample of 12 are comfortable with subjectivity. Allowing subjectivity in evaluating performance and awarding bonuses has both advantages and dangers.

The Advantages of Subjectivity

Most managers recognize that formal (explicit) control systems, which include measures, processes, and rewards, are not perfect. They know that strict adherence to predetermined formulas will probably mean paying profit center managers for windfalls and penalizing them for bad luck. These reward vagaries will, in turn, induce managers to take defensive and deceptive actions to lower their risk. The limitations of the explicit contract elements are particularly salient in situations where the performance measures are not reliable indicators of true performance or where good performance standards are not available, perhaps because of an inability to predict the future accurately. Subjective judgments, which form the important implicit parts of the contracts, are used to fill in the gaps and to provide evaluation flexibility so as to make the contracts more nearly perfect.

Corporation A (diversified luxury goods) is one of the firms that has had good experience with the subjective elements of its motivating contracts. The CEO is allowed considerable subjectivity in setting performance standards and in making adjustments for uncontrollables. He values this subjectivity:

> I believe discretion in the plan is important. Without it, you can lose people and create some unfairness that is not warranted . . . .
>
> For every rule, there is an exception. If a [profit center] did not make its target but I feel the managers have done an exceptional job, I may give them a modest bonus.

The subjective awards he grants must be approved by the compensation committee of the board of directors, but the committee generally concurs with his recommendations.

Operating managers in corporation A like the subjective elements of the firm's compensation contract. A typical profit center manager attitude was expressed as follows:

> Subjectivity is good. If the industry is down but we did a good job, we would still get something. [The CEO] can also take something away by comparing our results with [those of our one main competitor]. It's tougher for him to do that with [several other divisions] that have no direct competitors . . .
>
> We like and trust [the CEO]. Our plans depend on his judgment, and each is different. He knows our businesses; we report directly to him, so he has a personal relationship with the division presidents, and he works at it. He challenges us.

These positive feelings are not solely dependent on the managers' trust of the CEO. Even most of corporation A's managers who do not report to the CEO are comfortable with subjectivity because the corporate emphasis on fairness has permeated the organization. For example, a profit center manager who reported to a group vice president actually wanted more subjectivity in his evaluations: "A totally subjective evaluation by [the group vice president] would be better than what we've got. [The group VP] is fair in dealing with his people. I trust him." But he reserved the right to change his opinion because "we could get some screwball in there . . . ."

Managers in other corporations who are comfortable with subjectivity have similar reactions. For example, some managers in corporation L (specialty chemicals) noted that allowing the CEO to exercise subjectivity in establishing performance standards provides fairer targets for the profit centers than the minimum 20% ROA and targeted 35% ROA hurdles that are explicitly written into the contract. A group vice president in corporation L said: "Evaluation has to be subjective. I know the business. I can see it in their eyes. I would choose to base my judgments on different performance indicators depending on the circumstances." And a senior corporate staff vice president commented: "[The CEO] likes to play King Solomon. He knows we can't put everything in writing."

A group vice president in corporation D (diversified industrial products) was also favorably disposed to subjectivity:

> I would hate to see us get to a real numbers-oriented plan. There is too much you can't measure in dollars and cents. Evaluating is my job, and that of [the CEO and controller]. Performance ratings should result from an accumulation of knowledge. Accomplishing plan should be a part of the evaluation, but a lot of other things must enter in.

THE COSTS OF ALLOWING SUBJECTIVITY IN PERFORMANCE EVALUATIONS

Most managers, however, are not comfortable with subjectivity in decisions about what uncontrollable influences should be adjusted for.[6] They are concerned about uncertainty in the standards used in performance evaluations, possible favoritism, and creation of an "excuse culture."

Concern about uncertainty of evaluation standards and possible favoritism. Managers in corporation K (electronic systems) were almost unanimously opposed to allowing subjectivity for purposes of assigning bonuses because they had had a bad experience with an almost totally subjective plan. This plan created uncertainty about what was being rewarded and whether the evaluations were fair. A personnel vice president described the old plan as follows: "We had a bonus plan based on how one or two people felt about a person. That's no system at all."

A group controller elaborated:

> With our old plan the reward was half for effort and half for corporate results. It forced a ranking of everybody, and no feedback was provided to the individuals being evaluated. The rankings tended to be done the same way as for the annual performance reviews but with a six-month time difference. It was good when we were a small company because everybody knew what everybody else was doing, but our new system is a far better system for a corporation our size that plans to be even larger.

And a typical profit center manager comment: "Most good people like to be measured on whether they meet their goals. [Evaluations] should not be dependent on whether someone likes them or not."

Corporation K abandoned its highly subjective short-term incentive compensation plan in 1986 and implemented a new plan that provides awards based on the achievement of corporate, profit center, and individual performance targets, with subjective adjustments of the awards expected to be rare. The consultant who participated in the design of the new plan explained its philosophy:

> Subjectivity is bad. It is based on an individual's judgments, and it leads to partiality in the ways people get treated and feelings of unfairness. If completely uncontrolled, it leads to an unwise use of corporate resources [rewards paid when not deserved] . . .
>
> I think there is general agreement [in corporation K] that there is room for one [subjective adjustment] per year. It might come in mid-year, as the board may decide the original plan is not meaningful because of an inability to forecast unforeseen events (for example a collapse in oil prices or a change in

> accounting rules). The board has reserved the right to make such an adjustment, but this is not a compassionate board, and I support that. They are supposed to represent the shareholders. Most boards are not like that. They sit back and watch the presentations and generally side with management . . . .
>
> Subjectivity is demotivating. People strive to make goals. Subjectivity is bad because it is not consistent from year to year. People don't know how they're going to be evaluated.

Some managers in corporation L (specialty chemicals) also expressed distaste for their firm's highly subjective method of dealing with uncontrollables. Most claimed not to understand the standards being used for evaluations because they felt that the CEO's subjective judgments were not consistent. As one staff manager put it, the CEO's judgments are "liable to come out 180 degrees different from year to year. He can raise the target within the year. He can even decide in February after the year is over what the hurdle was. More often than not, he rules in favor of the division, but they remember [more clearly] the times he takes money out of their pockets."

Many corporation L managers also felt that their short-term incentive contract was difficult to understand, especially for new profit center managers, because the terms of the contract were not written. The CEO, however, did not want the contract elements written down. He felt that if the managers figured out the rules, they would play games designed to improve their short-term performance measures.

In summary, the unwritten contracts with subjective performance evaluation used in corporations K and L were intended to lower the profit center managers' risk. For many managers, however, the perceived effect was exactly the opposite. Their perceived risk actually increased because they faced high uncertainty about how their performance would be evaluated and feared that the evaluations would be biased against them.

Creating an excuse culture. Corporate managers in most of the corporations worried that even allowing consideration of adjustments would encourage the profit center managers to make excuses for not meeting their performance targets.

Here is a typical comment from a group executive in corporation C (distribution), a firm that makes some adjustments for uncontrollable factors:

> I frequently receive calls from [profit center managers] claiming that they are suffering costs that are uncontrollable and that, therefore, should be adjusted for. I have to explain to them that while these things might be unexpected from their point of view, most of them are just part of running their business.
>
> For instance, it is common for managers to ask me for allowances toward the extra costs they have incurred to support an unexpected increase in sales volume, such as to build a new warehouse. I explain to them that the profit calculations are designed to test whether these incremental expenditures should have been made.

In corporation L (specialty chemicals), the group presidents and the CEO, especially, were allowed considerable latitude in tailoring performance targets to the profit centers' capabilities and in deciding whether the profit centers would get relief on elements they submitted for consideration (such as a large foreign exchange translation loss). The subjectivity became particularly controversial several years ago when the corporation created a $20 million "provision for restructuring the business." The expenditures to be covered by this provision were not clearly spelled out because the corporate accounting manual included no definition of restructuring costs. Corporate finance staff relied on the Accounting Principles Board Statement #30 definition of an "unusual item," as being infrequent, material, and out of the ordinary.

The ambiguity in this definition led to a significant number of requests from profit centers for a piece of the reserve. The controller said these were among the requests he had received:

> "I need to shut down my warehouse in [a Midwest city]. Maybe you can come up with $500,000 to cover me on that."
>
> "I have to relocate six guys to a new location. Maybe the corporation can cover their relocation cost."

"We're going to hire a consulting firm to study the productivity of our sales force. This is a major program that could change the way we do business."

Such requests concerned the controller because "We can't take everything that doesn't happen every quarter and call it unusual. Our usual answer is that we don't have excess reserves, plus if you want to do that, you have to pay for it yourself. But we did cover some things, and the word gets around because the managers talk."

In the final analysis, most of the requests were approved. Senior management felt that including the expenses in cost of goods sold or discretionary expense would distort the profit centers' financial trends and ratios. It also felt that covering the expenses might encourage the profit centers to take the necessary painful steps because doing so would not obliterate their incentive compensation. Thus management felt the choice to use the restructuring reserves to cover these profit center expenses would be good for the shareholders. The CFO also noted that the CEO's leniency in making these adjustments might be good for retention purposes: "Maybe he had no choice because people would have gotten no incentive compensation at all."

Some managers, however, felt that the lenient allocation of the provision for restructuring had induced profit center managers to look for excuses rather than be committed to making their performance targets. A group vice president said: "The excuse culture has crept into [the corporation]. There are too many ways to beat the system."

Most managers in corporation L were expecting major changes in the corporation's incentive compensation contract when the CEO retired in the near future. They predicted that the new incentive contract would allow less subjectivity.

Deemphasizing Earnings Measures When Significant Uncontrollable Factors Are Present

In some profit centers, contract designers lessen the weight given to earnings measures that are unreliable indicators of performance because they are buffeted by significant uncontrollable influences that cannot be excluded either before or after the measurement period. I even found an extreme example where a profit center manager is not held accountable for earnings at all because the distortions caused by uncontrollable factors are considered too serious. If adjustments were made for the effects of uncontrollable influences in this profit center, their effects could be larger than the residual accounting figures.

Ellen is the manager of this small profit center in corporation F (hospitality) that provides meals for a single institutional client. Most of the meals are served at lunchtime, but Ellen's personnel also cater some of the client's meetings and parties and service the vending machines on the premises. The profit center has nine employees, and total revenue is approximately $500,000 per year.

Ellen's management authority is sharply limited by corporation F and the client. She is responsible for communicating with the client and for preparing the budget. She trains and supervises the employees and has authority to hire (and fire) them. She ensures that corporation F's many procedures are followed. On any given day she decides what entrees to offer, but her choices are taken mostly from a list of eight options on a centrally prepared menu. She can deviate from the list somewhat by offering some specials, and she is encouraged to do so if she feels the specials will boost sales. All food is prepared using standard recipe cards. Ellen orders through central corporation F warehouses or from preapproved purveyors who have contracted with group headquarters to provide items of a specified quality and at preset prices. The client owns the facilities and capital equipment, and includes Ellen's employees on its payroll.

The profit center is run on a cost-plus contract between corporation F and the client. Price increases are limited by contract.[7] Corporation F earns its profit by charging a management fee as a percentage of sales. If the profit contribution for the profit center (after the allocation of the management fee) is negative, as typically occurs, the client covers the loss. Ellen has pressure to minimize this loss, however, because, as her immediate superior (a district manager) noted, "Fee accounts are almost like profit and loss accounts. The client wants you to come in at [the planned subsidy], no more."[8]

The effect of this cost-plus contract is that the operating risk is shared between corporation F and the client. For example, if a sale is not rung on the cash register, the lost sale contributes to the loss the client will have to cover. If, on the other hand, cash is stolen from the cash register, corporation F has to cover the loss because this is cash that should have been turned in.

Ellen is held accountable for controlling the costs of labor (including overtime), food (portion control, waste), and expendable items (china, glass, silverware, supplies), and managing the cash. The controller of the group of which Ellen's profit center is a part noted: "We try to keep the financial statements as pure as possible. [The profit centers] are charged only those costs and revenues the managers have direct control over. That way you strip away part of the problem when you try to explain variances." As is true of many profit center managers, the key trade-off Ellen has to worry about is between the quality and cost of services provided.

Accounting earnings measures do not provide a good indication of Ellen's performance because, in the words of her immediate superior, "She does not control all the marbles." Her profit center's profit is affected by many decisions made by the client, including changes in the population served, the hours of operation, the hours the employees are allowed to work, the design of the cafeteria or kitchen, and the number and type of special requests, such as requirements to provide box lunches or to serve dinner for a small (uneconomical) number of people. It is also affected by changes in food costs combined with a client reluctance to allow price increases.

Because these uncontrollable influences add significant noise to the profit center earnings measures as an indicator of Ellen's performance, she is evaluated only on a series of specific performance measures. These measures include the level of service provided (food taste and presentation, employee coverage, sanitation) as judged by her superiors during weekly visits, control of the costs of food, labor, and controllable operating expenses, employee relations, and customer relations. Ellen's superiors use the overall profit measure only as a signal that a problem may exist and that they should investigate.

Ellen's profit center is an extreme case.[9] In the other 53 profit centers studied, the managers are evaluated at least partly on profit (and its derivatives) and are promised incentive compensation for profit performance. In all these cases, the contract designers are convinced that the earnings measures provide useful indications of performance after all the adjustments for uncontrollable influences that are justified (which may be none) are made.

NOTES

1. For most other reward/punishment purposes, including raises and promotions, the firms' treatment of uncontrollables generally falls somewhere between their treatment for job retention and bonus purposes.

For recognition awards, however, the controllability practices may be anywhere on the continuum. Corporation C (distribution), for example, gives profit center managers awards for such accomplishments as being among the top "earnings producers" or the top "growth businesses." For such quantified awards, generally no adjustments are made for uncontrollables. Some corporations also recognize intangible contributions in ways explicitly intended to take uncontrollables into account. In corporation C, for example, an award is given for "efforts above the call of duty."

2. Similarly, Maher (1987), in a field study of six firms, finds no examples of explicit inclusion of relative performance evaluation in division management incentive contracts.

3. These benefits are described in Magee (1986, pp. 268–269), Merchant (1985, pp. 21–24), and Maciarello (1984, pp. 135–136).

4. Sibson (1981), p. 249.

5. Other researchers make similar observations. For example, Antle and Smith (1986) suggest that it is not in the shareholders' best interest to protect managers from industry risk when those managers are responsible for selecting the firm's industry.

6. These findings are consistent with psychological research showing that ability to challenge evaluations and consistent application of standards are two of the primary factors contributing to perceived fairness of performance evaluations [Greenberg (1986); Leventhal et al. (1980)]. Subjectivity interferes with both of these factors. Longenecker and Gioia (1988) provide evidence that executives fear

that the subjective elements of their performance appraisals will be affected by politics or their appraiser's dishonesty or incompetence.

7. The client has the final price-setting authority, and prices need not be based on costs. For example, the client can (and usually does) choose to sell Christmas dinner for $1.

8. This shows a subtle distinction between a cost center and a profit center.

9. It is not a unique example, however. Simons (1987) finds that bonuses for managers at Johnson & Johnson are subjectively determined and not based on meeting performance targets. He reports that the managers are rewarded for their actions and efforts, rather than their results. He concludes that this approach is desirable because high environmental uncertainty and changing commitments make it impossible to set reasonable goals in advance.

CHAPTER 7

Using Motivational Contract Elements for Nonmotivational Purposes

The preceding chapters have discussed the trade-offs caused by two major design constraints: the short-term bias in accounting earnings measures of performance and the inability to isolate in the results measures managers' individual contributions. When contract designers address these two problems by making the correct trade-offs, they produce contracts that are close to optimal in the sense that they motivate profit center managers effectively and produce minimum side effects, as shown in the middle box in Figure 2-1.

The characteristics of these near optimal contracts can be summarized briefly: they promise profit center managers meaningful rewards for achieving preset, challenging targets in areas they can influence; they place the profit center managers under consistent short-term performance pressure, but they balance the short-term pressure with incentives that cause the managers to maintain a long-term focus; and they protect the managers from the distorting effects of significant, substantially uncontrollable factors when either the eliminations can be done objectively or the managers are tolerant of subjectivity.

Despite the motivational advantages of the features listed above, however, it is rare that all of them and no others are found in firms' rewards-for-results contracts, because corporate managers often alter some of the contracts to further corporate aims other than motivation. Such alterations create much of the contract variation across firms.

Four important contract features used in a substantial proportion of the firms to serve aims other than motivation are discussed in this chapter. They are: (1) limiting the range of profit center performance within which rewards are linked to results, (2) linking reward payouts to corporate performance to reduce corporate and managers' risks, (3) using long-term incentives with golden handcuff provisions to reduce management turnover, and (4) allowing profit centers to have budget targets that seem less than fully challenging.

Limiting the Performance Range Within Which Rewards Are Linked to Results

For ideal motivation, rewards should be directly linked to profit center results. Greater rewards should be provided for better results.

Most firms, however, do not follow this simple rule in designing their short-term incentive contracts. Their contracts have a direct results/rewards link, but they limit the range of performance within which results are promised. Below a predetermined performance level, no rewards are given, and no additional rewards are given for performance above a predetermined upper limit.

As Table 2-4 (line 8) illustrated, nine of the 12 firms have a lower cutoff level; no bonuses are provided for performance below this level. Six of these cutoffs are set at a fraction of the targeted annual performance (which is typically the budgeted level). These fractions are commonly around 80%, but they seem to vary with perceptions of the predictability of the performance target (they are lower if predictability is lower). One corporation (C—distribution) sets the lower cutoff at the prior year's actual performance, and one (corporation L—specialty chemicals) has a timeless minimum performance standard (20% ROA, although this level is sometimes altered by the CEO, depending on the circumstances of individual profit centers).

Firms define these *lower cutoffs* because they do not want to provide extra pay for results they consider mediocre. A typical comment, by the consultant involved in the design of corporation K's (electronic systems) plan: "We don't want to pay any bonus if the manager can't perform at the 80% level."[1]

Nine firms (not the same nine) define an *upper cutoff* level of performance. Seven of these maximum performance levels are defined as a percentage of the annual target. The range is broad: from 105% to 150% of the target. The other two firms (H—high tech and L—specialty chemicals) define a timeless performance maximum. For corporation L, it is 35% ROA (but again the CEO sometimes chooses a different level for some profit centers in some years). For corporation H, a maximum is defined for each of the performance factors on which bonuses are based: 50% ROS, 100% ROA, and 100% profit growth.

The firms use any of five reasons for including these upper cutoffs in their contracts. One is that managers usually do not deserve bonuses for reported results that exceed the defined maximum. Corporate managers have observed that the most common causes of extremely high performance are: (1) a windfall gain due to uncontrollable circumstances, not the profit center manager's efforts; (2) shortsighted behavior by a manager who has maximized profit in the short run at the probable expense of the long run, such as by failing to make investments that will pay off in the future or by charging dangerously high prices that may attract competitors; or (3) particularly with a new plan, a faulty plan design. For example, in the words of the consultant who assisted in the design of the corporation K plan that included an upper cutoff at 150% of budgeted profit: "The likelihood of doing more than 150% of plan is small. If it occurs, it is the result of a windfall or a poor compensation system design . . . and the board always has a worry about managers who are out for themselves and who screw the company." Similarly, the CFO of corporation H (high tech) said: "We think that if they overachieved by more than 25%, it's because they were lucky, and it doesn't make sense to compensate them for that. If they can't carry the extra over for the next year, then they won't have an incentive to shoot income up just for the short term."

A second reason for having an upper cutoff on short-term incentive compensation is to deliver a message that the corporation values stability rather than the generation of unsustainably high growth and profitability. For example, corporation H (high tech) had what its chairman considered excessively rapid growth two years ago, so maximums were set for bonus purposes for each of its three results factors—growth in profits, return on assets, and return on sales. The chairman explained:

> Our optimum long-term growth rate is 40%. We need stability. Name one company that has grown at 100% [for any period of time] and not ended up on the beach. If we doubled every two years, we wouldn't know half the people who are employed here . . . .
>
> With our high growth rate, we need to have a high ROE to fund the growth. It is bad to keep going to the banks for funding. We are self-financing—we have had no public offerings . . . .
>
> I value stability. I don't want the managers to give me all their profits. I want them to reinvest in their future.

Similarly, in corporation J (consumer products), the vice president of administration noted, "The pool cuts off at 8% growth because we want to encourage the long-term strength of the business. We want to show steady, long-term growth."

A third reason for having an upper cutoff is to maintain vertical compensation equity within the firm. As corporation K's consultant noted: "There will be chaos if a division manager makes more than the president." The chaos would result from negative reactions to the perceptions of reward inequity. Most managers believe that jobs higher in the managerial hierarchy are more complex and demanding and, therefore, that higher-level managers should earn larger rewards than lower-level managers. The managers recognize that when certain profit centers are performing well but the corporation is not, there may be periods where a profit center manager earns more than the corporate CEO. But they believe that it is destructive for this situation to persist for more than a year or two at most.

Interestingly, most managers are willing to tolerate situations in which nonmanagement employees, particularly salespeople, earn more than the general managers of their operating entities and sometimes even the CEO. The difference in feelings is caused by the perceived reliability of the short-term performance indicators. The managers feel that the salespeople's short-term performance measures (such as volume generated) indicate their performance quite reliably, whereas short-term profit (and the other measures used) are not totally reliable indicators of managers' performance.

A fourth reason for having upper reward cutoffs is to maintain compensation consistency over time. Some managers believe that very high compensation in one period may be dysfunctional. The CFO of corporation H (high tech) said, "Someone shouldn't earn bonuses of 300% or 400% of salary. They would have a reduction of expectations in subsequent years." In essence, the upper cutoffs protect the profit center managers from developing a life style that their position will not allow them to sustain.

Corporate executives in corporation D (diversified industrial products), whose business is highly cyclical, had a similar concern. They wanted to reduce the volatility of compensation because they did not trust the measures on which the awards were based. The president said, "It's damn hard to tell that people are doing a good job just because the business is doing well." To reduce compensation volatility, corporate executives made a bargain with the compensation committee of the board. They rolled part of the incentive compensation into salary and accepted an upper constraint on the bonus awards in exchange for a lower minimum level. The corporate controller explained, "The maximum has to do with what the board is comfortable with. Agreeing to a maximum makes it easier to get a lower minimum, and that is worthwhile because this is a highly cyclical business."

A fifth reason for having an upper cutoff is to adhere to standard corporate and industry practices. For example, in designing its new incentive compensation contract, the compensation committee of corporation K (electronic systems) proposed an upper cutoff. The consultant who worked with the committee explained, "They did not want to pay more than a certain amount of bonuses no matter what. They knew that 90% of the plans in the United States have a cap, and they saw no reason to deviate from the norm. That's the way corporate managers think." The managers' argument is that it is best to follow industry practices in the absence of good, specific reasons for deviating from them.

Linking Incentive Payments to Corporate (or Group) Performance to Reduce Corporate and Managers' Risks

Some motivational contracts have features intended to force profit center managers to share the overall corporate risk and to share risk with each other. They can also provide a message that the corporation values cross-profit center teamwork.

Actually, all performance-related incentive contracts reduce corporate risk because employees who expect to derive compensation from the contracts tend to accept lower fixed salaries.[2] They are willing to do so because each manager's total compensation package, which equals salary plus expected bonuses, is roughly fixed, at a level equal to the managers' alternate employment possibilities. Thus promising managers higher expected bonuses allows the firm to promise lower fixed salaries.[3]

When firms use rewards-for-results contracts, therefore, compensation becomes more highly variable with firm performance, and corporate risk is reduced. The firm pays its employees higher bonuses when it is better able to do so, and earnings are smoother because salary expenses are higher when profits are higher. The size of the risk-sharing effect varies, of course, with the proportion of total costs that is compensation costs.

When performance is measured in terms of factors employees can influence, rewards-for-results contracts have a positive motivational effect. But some corporations purposely base some rewards-for-results contracts for profit center managers partly or totally on corporate (or group) performance, on which the managers' actions have virtually no impact.

The Practices

Corporate risk-sharing features are added to motivational contracts in either of two basic ways. The most direct way is to include one or more measures of corporate (or group) performance directly in the measurement function. As was shown in Table 2-5, six of the 12 firms (B, E, F, K, L, and M) base a percentage of the short-term incentive award directly on corporate or group performance, typically measured in earnings, ROI, or sales. Thirty percent of the bonuses in corporation K (electronic systems), for example, are based on corporate earnings per share and return on investment. The weighting given to the corporate or group performance measures ranges across the corporations, and in some cases across the profit centers in them, from zero to 50%.

The second method of getting managers to share the shareholders' risk is to calculate, or limit the size of, the bonus pool to be allocated to profit centers on the basis of corporate performance. As was shown in Table 2-4, five of the 12 firms limit their short-term incentive awards on the basis of corporate financial performance. Three firms (D, E, and J) make incentive payments to profit center managers out of a bonus pool whose size is based on corporate earnings or return on capital. Two firms (A and K) define an upper constraint on the total awards to be made in terms of corporate performance.

Many of the firms' long-term incentive contracts also reduce corporate risk. As was shown in Table 2-5, ten of the 12 firms provide rewards in the form of stock grants or options. Managers benefit only when the corporation's stock performs well. Six firms base either their cash or stock awards directly on long-term corporate financial performance.

Corporate Risk-Sharing

One purpose of these contracts (or contract features) is to force profit center managers to share the corporate "pain" in bad times. For example, a group vice president in corporation B (electronic equipment) described his firm's incentive plan as "a variable salary program, not a bonus program." Similarly, a group vice president in D (diversified industrial products) described his corporation's plan as "a profit-sharing plan, more than an incentive plan." The contracts used in both of these corporations are based to a relatively large extent on corporate performance.

Some firms use risk-sharing contract features because of a concern about funding bonuses. These firms do not want to have to pay bonuses when cash is short because of poor operating results. For example, the vice president-administration of corporation B (electronic equipment) said, "A plan of this sort must be self-funding. We can't pay resources that we don't have. It must be funded with real money. We don't want to borrow . . . . At some point all a company can do is pay for results. We don't want to pay for trying hard; we want to pay for results."

The actual proportion of the corporate risk that is shared with the managers is small, because managerial compensation is usually not a significant proportion of total corporate costs. Nevertheless, some risk-sharing is achieved. Furthermore, the contract feature provides a useful political message to shareholders that their risk is being shared with the managers; in other words, their interests and the managers' interests are aligned. When the corporation is not reporting good profits, the shareholders are presumably not earning good returns, and the managers are not earning high levels of compensation.

DIVERSIFYING MANAGERS' RISKS

Another advantage of basing rewards at least partly on corporate or group performance is that it diversifies the profit center managers' risk. It causes the managers to share risk with each other and makes the variable portion of compensation less volatile, particularly for managers of cyclical businesses. As one profit center manager in corporation K (electronic systems) expressed it, "Sometimes I'm pulling them; sometimes they're pulling me." If the same profit centers consistently pull or trail the rest of the corporation, however, this benefit becomes nonexistent, and the actual effect can be destructive to the morale of the personnel in the better-performing profit centers.

DIRECTING MANAGERS' ATTENTION

A third advantage of providing rewards based on corporate or group performance is that it directs profit center managers' attention in a beneficial way. Shared rewards help deliver a cultural message that "we're all in this together." In corporation K (electronic systems), for example, the group vice presidents' incentives are based 80% on corporate performance and 20% on group performance; the division managers' incentives are based 30% on corporate performance and 70% on division performance. The compensation consultant explained:

> The purpose [of basing a portion of bonus awards on the performance of higher-level entities] was to build a consensus that everyone is working toward the corporate targets. They are being sent the message that the corporation wants them to worry about what is going on above them.
>
> Division managers are being sent a different message. Their awards are based primarily on division performance, but we wanted to make everybody feel (in their paycheck) that they are part of [the corporation].

This attention-directing benefit varies directly with the value of the message. This value is especially high in five corporations—A (diversified luxury goods), B (electronic equipment), J (consumer products), K (electronic systems), and M (consumer durables)—because organizational interdependence—either shared resources or transfers of goods or services—is relatively high, and corporate management wants to encourage organizational cooperation. Thus it is not surprising that in each of these corporations some portion of the profit center managers' incentive awards is based on corporate or group performance.

Personnel in the operating entities generally confirm that these risk-sharing contract features have attention-directing effects that can strengthen teamwork. A profit center controller in corporation K, for example, noted that a purpose of his firm's short-term incentive plan, in which 30% of rewards is based on corporate financial performance, was to bring the two major operating groups, one of them recently acquired, closer together: "The only way you can achieve camaraderie is to suffer together and share together. Differences in incentives encourage an 'us-them' mentality . . . . We envision at some point we will work toward centralized purchasing, inventory systems, a shared manufacturing facility, and other things."

Each reason provides a good rationale for basing profit center managers' rewards partially on corporate or group performance. These risk-sharing features, however, as well as the upper performance cutoff features, can undercut the motivational effects of the contracts. This issue is discussed further in Chapter 9.

Managerial Retention

Most of the firms' written long-term contracts are designed to encourage managerial retention.[4] Typically the cash or stock payments are made to the profit center managers long after the managers have learned they have earned them, and if the managers leave the corporation before the measurement or vesting period is complete, they forfeit all the awards they were due. If the awards are significant, they give the managers a strong incentive to stay with the corporation.

One of the long-term contracts used in corporation A (diversified luxury goods) is typical. This contract is a restricted stock plan designed for about 500 of the top managers in the corporation. Each participant is allowed to buy a specified number of shares at 10% of the market price on the date of the grant. The plan was originally designed so that the number of shares each participant was allowed to buy would be related to performance, but over time the link with performance disappeared. The corporate secretary said, "Most of the time the number of shares is assigned by position. There is also a belief that once you are in the plan, you're always in the plan."

The participants pay for the shares immediately, and the shares become unrestricted at the rate of 20% a year over five years. The corporate secretary described the plan's purpose as: ". . . 'silver handcuffs.' If they leave before the five years are up, they must sell back the stock that has not been released."

In some corporations, these compensation and retention purposes are considered far more important than motivation. For example, the president of corporation G (electrical connectors) explained his concern about the failure of his firm's stock option plan to provide profit center managers with significant rewards in terms of compensation and retention, not motivation:

> What we're missing is a way to have our [profit center] managers accumulate long-term wealth. A [profit center] manager should have the ability to make a reasonable amount of money over his lifetime to accumulate good wealth. If they don't believe this, they will leave. [Because we are] a public company, a big portion of the wealth has to be accumulated through stock, through devices such as performance shares and restricted stock. But [the awards] must be tied to performance.
>
> We have a stock option plan, but the stock is valued at less than half what most of the options are written at. With most [stock option] plans, you can't get enough options in their hands to amount to much.
>
> We also want golden handcuffs. If you've got someone you want, why not try to keep him?

Highly Achievable Budget Targets

As I have mentioned, budgeted earnings targets are the most important performance standards for profit center managers in most corporations. The "make-the-budget-or-else" and short-term incentive contracts promise profit center managers rewards for achieving budgeted profit targets. In most profit centers, these targets are less than fully challenging because the managers are almost certain to achieve them with reasonable effort. Thus they may not stretch the profit center managers to find creative operating alternatives or induce them to take personally difficult actions (such as laying off employees). Contract designers allow the profit center managers to have these highly achievable targets, however, for reasons other than motivation.

Managers' Incentives for Highly Achievable Budget Targets

Profit center managers obviously have strong incentives to negotiate for highly achievable budget targets. They can, in particular, increase their potential rewards (in the current year), augment their operating flexibility, and protect their autonomy.[5]

It might be expected that top management, knowing of these incentives to negotiate for highly achievable targets and the potential motivational cost of less than fully challenging targets, would try to raise the targets. I found, however, the profit center managers' superiors are aware that the targets are highly achievable.[6] They have a tendency to accept the profit center managers' conservative budget submissions with, perhaps, minor upward modifications, and sometimes they actually lower targets that they believe are optimistic.

As was discussed in Chapter 4, highly achievable targets reduce short-term pressure and thus can alter the balance between short-term and long-term incentives in a desirable way. But in most firms, the corporate managers have other, more important, nonmotivational reasons for allowing profit centers to operate with highly achievable budget targets.

They include improvements in corporate financial reporting, in resource planning, in control, and in compensation,[7] as well as positive effects on morale and on the managers' business creativity.

Why Corporations Allow Highly Achievable Targets

To Improve the Predictability of Corporate Financial Reporting

Improving corporate financial reporting is one of the reasons corporate managers allow highly achievable budget targets. The managers feel such targets increase the corporation's ability to report predictable and, it is hoped, steadily increasing earnings and sales. Not only can the profit centers be relied upon to achieve the targets in their annual plans, they will be able, on average, to exceed them.

Corporate managers believe that predictable financial reporting, in turn, has an important positive influence on the performance of corporation's stock. As a group president in corporation L (specialty chemicals) expressed it, "Corporate managers can't deal with surprises in reporting results that are either too good or too bad. It's too tough to explain to the security analysts (although it's easier to explain good results)."

This perceived need for predictable earnings provides an important motivation for corporate managers to allow profit centers to have highly achievable budget targets and then to treat the targets as commitments to the corporation. This philosophy is evident in a comment from the CFO of corporation H (high tech): "Our philosophy is that once you've put it in terms of numbers, it becomes a fact. You've got to follow your budget."

The commitment philosophy is also evident in corporation J (consumer products). One profit center manager said, "We submit numbers that we think we can deliver. An independent observer would say we are conservative, but we have to deliver. The company depends on [this division] to turn in profits."[8] This manager's controller expressed the same idea in these terms: "The budget is more than a forecast. It describes what we are going to do."

The top-level managers of corporation G (electrical connectors) came to realize the importance of predictable plans only recently, and this realization caused them to change their philosophy about budget achievability. Before 1987, the company had a philosophy of "stretch" budgets because it believed that setting very aggressive targets would push its managers to do their best. Bonuses were promised for profit performance greater than or equal to 60% of budget. This philosophy was abandoned because, as the president explained:

> The problem is that if you're forecasting for stretch targets, you must be thinking optimistically. But in the meantime, the corporation misses its plans. For four years now, we have had some [profit centers] do well and some do poorly, but the corporation never achieved its targets. As a public company, we need [to achieve the targets consistently].

Under the new philosophy, budget targets are set at a level intended to be a "minimum performance standard" with a 100% probability of achievement, assuming consistent effort by an effective management team. Corporate managers now feel that the consolidated corporate budget targets provide a good indication of forthcoming corporate performance.

Treating the budget targets as commitments provides top management with peace of mind. The consolidated profit center budgets represent a highly probable lower bound for reported annual corporate earnings. When the highly achievable targets are allowed to persist, the profit center managers will build up cushions of unreported profits, in such forms as conservatively set reserves or undervalued inventories. Top management generally knows about these cushions, and they can call for them if necessary.

To Improve Resource Planning

The chance to improve resource planning gives corporate managers another reason to allow highly achievable profit center budget targets. Such targets provide more reliable numbers for internal corporate planning purposes, such as financing, because they are highly likely to be achieved.[9] A profit center manager in corporation D (diversified industrial products), who knew his budget became a firm commitment when top management lowered his targets, expressed this idea:

> I just got a request from my group president to downgrade the numbers in my strategic plan. He got uneasy that the numbers are too high. We are the only organization that has a solid hold on its market and [as we are the largest and most profitable division in our group], the corporation depends on our cash. If I promise $60 million cash, I should work toward that.

Most top executives also feel that "optimistic" budget targets, with improbably high forecasts of sales and profits, are dangerous for resource planning purposes. For example, the vice president-administration, of corporation B (electronic equipment) expressed this concern as follows: "Like most companies in [our industry], we used to think that 22–25% growth was our God-given right. We staffed up for that level of growth, but eventually it stopped happening. It became important to not overplan sales, to be conservative. We're now more worried about overforecasts than sandbagging." The president of the same corporation added, "I think we ought to have a semiaggressive plan, but one that is achievable. We want to make it every year. It's too hard to adjust on the downside, to slough off commitments of expenses, or not launch something you have a psychological commitment to."

These comments illustrate two conclusions that most corporate managers come to. First, they worry that optimistic budgets (with high forecasts of sales and profits) give profit center managers a sense that extra expense is affordable. This will in turn encourage them to, for example, staff up for activity that may not be forthcoming. Second, most corporate managers believe that the cost of shedding excess resources (particularly labor) quickly is far greater than the cost of acquiring them on short notice.

To Reduce the Cost of Control

Most managers of divisionalized corporations have found that it is efficient to control their operating entities with a management-by-exception philosophy. That means that negative variances from budget signal that intervention, or at least investigation, is called for. For example, one profit center manager in corporation H (high tech) noted, "The purposes of the budget are to give management a feel for where the profit center is going, to give them a standard against which to compare actual performance, and to give them a basis for tweaking people who are not performing well."

In such settings, highly achievable budget targets provide an advantage in that negative variances are relatively rare. Thus the number of interventions, or at least investigations, is minimized, and top management attention is directed to the few situations in which problems are most probable and most acute.

To Provide a Competitive Total Compensation Package

In some corporations there is a compensation reason for having highly achievable profit center budget targets. In two of the firms studied, corporation L (specialty chemicals) and until recently, one group in corporation K (electronic systems), most managers' budget targets were set to be easily achievable to ensure that they would earn some performance-dependent bonuses. This was important because base salaries were below the average in the industry, and bonuses were necessary to make the total compensation package competitive.[10]

Neither of these corporations' plans was designed to operate this way. Both corporations found themselves in this situation because top management had instituted a salary freeze during difficult operating times, and when the freeze was removed, salaries were below competitive levels. But top management was reluctant to increase the corporation's fixed costs sharply through an immediate salary boost. Instead, both corporations began using variable compensation (bonuses) to make the managers' total compensation packages competitive with industry and local averages.[11] After a series of good years, everybody in the corporation became accustomed to receiving bonuses, which reinforced the practice. As the bonus became expected, budget targets became easily achievable to ensure that the bonus became part of regular compensation.

To Make Managers Feel Like Winners

Even without corporation-provided rewards, most profit center managers would negotiate for achievable targets because the achievement is its own reward. It makes the managers (and the people who work for them) feel like winners. Winners are people who feel good about themselves and their performance. For example, a profit center manager in corporation G (electrical connectors) said, "If I were to miss my budget, I would feel like a failure. When I exceed my budget, I feel proud." He has these feelings even though he knows, deep inside, that his targets are set to be achievable. Budget achievement defines managerial success.

Conversely, having highly achievable budget targets can reduce the chances that managers will give up in the face of goals perceived to be unattainable. I asked profit center managers what would happen if they were given a budget they judged highly unlikely to be achieved, and most said they would either position themselves for the subsequent year, such as by forcing as many expenses as possible into the current year, or find another job where they could be successful. As one profit center manager described it, being forced to operate with unattainable targets would "[cause me to] move to an environment that will give me more control."

To Stimulate Business Creativity

Highly achievable targets also create budgetary slack that can provide the operating freedom necessary to stimulate creative ideas for business development. These ideas are distinct from the creative cost-cutting ideas stimulated by short-term budget pressure.

Budgetary slack allows profit center managers to make discretionary investments without having to request either corporate approval for the investment or permission to exceed budgeted expenses. Some corporate executives recognize that certain profit center managers are in the best position to determine how to develop their own business units, and their "skunkworks" (unauthorized projects) often give the corporation excellent returns.

For any and all of these reasons, most firms base their budget- and short-term incentive compensation contracts on budget targets that effective, hard-working managers will achieve, at least much more often than not. At least some of the potential benefits are present in virtually every profit center.

NOTES

1. A compensation consultant who was interviewed noted that sometimes the lower cutoffs are set for survival reasons. For example, the corporation may be in bankruptcy court, and if it fails to make the plan, the company will not survive. These so-called "cliff" plans were not used by any of the corporations participating in this study.

2. Kanter (1987) is among those who have noticed the importance of this purpose of incentive compensation plans. She concludes, "Much of the ferment in pay reflects attempts by employers to improve organizational performance while controlling fixed payroll costs." A new pay-incentive plan introduced by Du Pont is partially designed to serve this purpose (Hays, 1988).

3. Total monetary compensation is only roughly equal because all nonpecuniary job benefits must be taken into consideration.

4. Eaton and Rosen (1983) provide evidence that various types of "delayed compensation" are used to bond executives to their firms.

5. These incentives are described in Sharfman et al. (1988).

6. This can be seen in Table 2-2. In the 21 profit centers for which subjective-probability estimates were collected from both the profit center managers and the immediate superiors, the mean responses were 80% for the profit center managers and 78% for the superiors.

7. This section elaborates on themes presented in Barrett and Fraser (1977).

8. In the last several years, this division has accounted for approximately 30–35% of the corporation's total profits.

9. Donaldson (1984, p. 150) makes a similar observation by distinguishing between what he calls the disciplinary and predictive functions of goals. Disciplinary goals have a motivational function because they are meant to elicit superior performance. Predictive goals provide realistic measures of management's expectations.

10. Analyses of the motivational effects of varying sizes of the results-dependent rewards are complicated by these calibration differences. Virtually guaranteed results-dependent compensation is not really incentive compensation—it is essentially salary.

11. Corporation K's management is making major cultural changes brought about by the acquisition of a firm about its own size. Some changes involve increasing salaries to the level of previous total compensation and promising bonuses for attaining more challenging, but still achievable, financial targets. Corporation L's management still has not increased its managers' salaries to competitive levels.

CHAPTER 8

Evaluating Contract Effectiveness, Part I: The Incidence of Myopia and Earnings Management

> "When the budget is approved, there is no question in my mind that we're going to make it. The only question is how we're going to make it and how much damage we're going to do to the future."

An important part of contract design is analyzing the outcomes of contracts that have been implemented and modifying the contracts to reduce the costs of dysfunctional outcomes. This analysis is not easy, however, because, as I have discussed, the design choices at profit center organization levels involve unavoidable trade-offs that make some dysfunctional outcomes inevitable. Evaluation, then, requires studying the situations carefully to distinguish the dysfunctional outcomes stemming from design trade-offs that have been knowingly and correctly made from those that indicate contract flaws stemming from either ignorance of the alternatives available, ignorance of the various cause-and-effect relationships that form the bases for the trade-offs, or a failure to fit the various contracts and contract elements into a cohesive package.

This chapter discusses the incidence and causes of two important, related dysfunctional outcomes—investment myopia and earnings management. Corporate managers are aware that the short-term performance pressures they put on their profit center managers increase the incidence of these dysfunctional outcomes, and most of them are not greatly concerned because they have concluded that the benefits of the short-term pressure exceed the costs. The evidence I gathered, however, convinced me that the incidence of these costly practices is higher than it should be in some corporations because the corporate managers overestimate the benefits of high predictability in corporate financial reporting and underestimate the costs of creating a culture of deception within the company.

Evidence of Investment Myopia and Earnings Management

In Chapter 3, I described the importance of maintaining consistent short-term performance pressure to ensure that the profit center managers do not allow their operations to become sloppy or wasteful. I also described the importance of offsetting the short-term bias inherent in accounting earnings-based measures of performance so as to balance the long-term incentives with the short-term pressures. I concluded that it is possible to express a proper short-term/long-term balance in the motivational contracts used at profit center organization levels. During my study, however, I discovered that a proper balance probably has not been struck in some profit centers.

Two forms of evidence point to this conclusion. First, many operating managers complained that their corporations placed them under excessive short-term performance pressure. Second, most of them described dysfunctional, myopic actions that the pressure forced them to take. Some of these actions stemmed from investment myopia and resulted in decisions they felt were detrimental to the long-term success of the profit center even though they had positive effects on reported short-term earnings. Others were actions taken to "manage" reported earnings to evade short-term performance pressures, which were dysfunctional because, at a minimum, they distracted the managers from their efforts to increase shareholder value. Some of them also diminished or destroyed profit center good will.

Operating Managers' Criticisms of Their Firm's Motivational Contracts

To help me evaluate the corporations' motivational contracts, I asked the operating managers (general managers and controllers at the profit center and group organization levels) directly for their criticisms. My question was: "If you had the power to change one aspect of your firm's planning, budgeting, measurement, evaluation, and reward systems, what would you change?"

Table 8-1 summarizes the responses to this question, using categories that reflect the terms most of the operating managers used. One conclusion from this table is that most managers are satisfied with their firm's motivational contracts, as only 45 of a total of the 142 operating managers (32%) voiced even a single criticism.[1] In no firm did the number of managers voicing a contract criticism exceed those who mentioned no such criticisms.

The lack of criticism is not surprising. The contracts are so important to the operating managers that they either adapt to them, knowing that perfect contracts are not feasible, voice their criticisms loudly enough that the designers change the contracts, or, if the unresolved problems are important to them, leave the firm. Thus the contracts evolve over time as the designers react to problems with which they become familiar. The managers, themselves, also evolve. Those who work for their corporation for some period and intend to stay with it reach an equilibrium of satisfaction with, or at least resignation to, the motivational contracts under which they are asked to operate.[2]

Of the operating managers expressing a criticism, however, the most common complaint by far, expressed by 20 of the 45 managers (44%), was that there was too much pressure for short-term performance. This criticism was expressed by at least one manager in ten of the 12 firms. The

Table 8-1
Profit Center and Group Managers' Primary Criticisms of Motivational Contracts

	A *Diversified Luxury Goods*	*B* *Electronic Equipment*	*C* *Distribution*	*D* *Diversified Industrial Products*	*E* *Diversified Chemicals*	*F* *Hospitality*	*G* *Electrical Connectors*	*H* *High Tech*	*J* *Consumer Products*	*K* *Electronic Systems*	*L* *Specialty Chemicals*	*M* *Consumer Durables*	*Total*
Criticisms													
Too much pressure for short-term performance	1	2		3	4	1		2	3	2	1	1	20
Evaluations are unfair	2	1	1			2		1	2		2		11
Results-related incentives are inadequate		1	1	1			1			1	3	1	9
Performance standards sometimes not realistic	1	1				1	1			1			5
Number of managers with criticisms	4	5	2	4	4	4	2	3	5	4	6	2	45
Number of managers with no criticism, or criticism not related to motivational contracts	12	6	10	8	13	13	3	6	9	7	6	4	97
Total number of operating managers interviewed	16	11	12	12	17	17	5	9	14	11	12	6	142

managers went on to explain that the pressure created considerable personal stress and forced them to take actions they felt were not in the best long-term interest of their profit center.

Evidence of Myopic Actions

Finding definitive proof of investment myopia is quite difficult. Without detailed knowledge of the investment alternatives and prospects, it is usually impossible to conclude that managers have let short-term incentives dominate long-term objectives. For example, does the following comment by a profit center manager in corporate E (diversified chemicals) indicate myopia?

> The only concern I have today [with our control system] is that the current environment makes us manage too much for the short term. The financial targets have been very difficult. They have caused us to operate on a very tight shoestring. We have had to delay plans that would have been good for us to accelerate. We're paying our own way, and we're funding some of the other SBUs [strategic business units]. If I were on my own, I could have grown the business faster, but [my boss] has a different perspective.

Many profit center managers, such as the one quoted above and many of those who criticized their firms' motivational contracts, complain about not being able to get their "good" ideas funded. But such criticisms do not necessarily indicate investment myopia. People have a natural bias in favor of their ideas, but other, more objective managers may conclude that the ideas are not worth funding. Jensen's free cash flow theory and the evidence he provides to support it suggest that without consistent pressure to return cash to shareholders or debtors, managers sometimes overinvest. They make unwise investments (with negative net present values) because of the easy availability of funds and their natural desire to expand their firms.[3] In other situations corporations force their managers to have a short-term orientation out of necessity—at the extreme, to survive. In such cases, profit center managers may have legitimately good investment ideas that do not get funded.

Because of the uncertainty surrounding most investment alternatives, most firms are able to identify only a wide "acceptability zone" around the point where the long-term/short-term balance is ideal. For example, managers in a profit center in corporation E (diversified chemicals) that had recently sharply cut expenses felt their business would probably have been better off in the long run without the cuts, but they recognized that some good may have come from them. At the time of the interviews in this profit center, eight months into the 1987 fiscal year, the profit center manager felt he would achieve his profit target of $33.5 million, even though sales were running well below budgeted levels, because the profit center was aided significantly by lower oil prices and favorable foreign currency translation gains. But, he noted, "I can assure you we would not have made $33.5 million if our budget was the number I preferred—$26 million. We might have made $31 million, but I would have spent more on manufacturing programs, technology . . . I might have bought a new airplane to help our marketing effort." The controller added:

> Maybe the tough goal caused us to work harder. Maybe it caused us to focus more on profit. It's tough to tell. But I hope we don't have to go through it again because we don't want to be put on a post and whipped if we miss [a tough target] . . . . Morale depends on the size of the cuts we would have had to take. The cuts at the top and the bottom were very demoralizing. They went very deep.

In answer to the question whether the short-term emphasis has been detrimental the controller responded, "We're still spending a big chunk on research. Should we spend more? What would it be on? I haven't seen any program that was cut to the detriment of the company. What level is right? We have cut advertising, but maybe we'd have overadvertised if we were doing well."

Managers in corporation J (consumer products), in which profit centers were put under considerable short-term performance pressure, were particularly philosophical, as this quotation illustrates: "There's no question there is a short-term bias in this corporation. Is it overwhelming? That's not clear. Any of us could spend a trillion dollars to develop the long-term business. But that's obviously too much to spend, and we don't know what the right amount is."

Another profit center manager in corporation J who had recently been forced into some major cost-cutting made similar comments:

> It's not possible to say whether I've hurt the long-term business. The maximum-growth strategy is to spend the maximum on promotion, but the realistic question is where to limit the spending. I can see businesses I have where I think more spending would be good, but the investors look at EPS [corporate earnings per share]. Maybe *they* are short-term-oriented.

Despite the philosophical observations about the difficulty of knowing when enough long-term investment is being made, the weight of the evidence indicated that corporation J's motivational contracts probably did create investment myopia. All of the profit center managers interviewed felt they had been forced to reduce or eliminate worthwhile long-term investments because of the corporation's demand for short-term performance. And, perhaps more important, personnel at higher organization levels agreed with them. The group vice president said:

> [The president] likes profit. His mission is to make a profit, and he will stop there. He is constantly, absolutely preoccupied with the bottom line . . .
>
> We all feel a responsibility to help [the chairman] achieve his public commitments. He is driven by Wall Street, and he has made the stock of this company behave beautifully. But it makes me antsy that we react so strongly to the stock market. That's a problem with American business. [The chairman] drives us toward quarter-by-quarter improvement. That's a great objective, but we should be investing in market share.

A pattern of comments such as the following suggested that at least some profit centers in other corporations suffer from myopia as well:

> Return-on-operations (ROO) measures have always focused on short-term financial performance. They discourage investment even though we try to plan for long-term growth. I can make my ROO targets by letting my plant go to hell because then I only have to make $1 million profit. But it will eventually put me out of business. We are competing with cultures that think long-term (a profit center manager in corporation B—electronic equipment).

> We have tremendous pressure on short-term results. If we had not had them, I would have made different decisions on product and market development. On the other hand, we are constantly being reminded that the company will support all growth possibilities. It sounds good on paper, but in corporate meetings, it tends to be forgotten even though something has been previously approved. Our corporate memory is awfully short. I see us losing some ability to go with out intuition (a profit center manager in corporation H—high tech).

> We spend 4% of sales on R&D. This is above the industry average. But we have considerable difficulty getting corporate to spend a lot of money on a high-risk project. There is more and more emphasis on acquisitions because they feel we can better measure the cash flows. It is certainly easier to ask for money for an acquisition than to ask for funding for a new "gee-whiz" product (the manager of planning in one group of corporation D—diversified industrial products).

> The operating managers won't bet on a horse unless the race is three-quarters over and a horse is far in the lead. Why? Their previous successes in life have occurred from not taking risks, by saying no, by not doing something new. Doing new things is absolutely counter cultural. The problem is that the operating managers are faced with the necessity of meeting a budget target. They cut their R&D expenditures. You can't do that. You can't keep laying people off and hiring them back (manager of corporate technology at corporation E—diversified chemicals).

Evidence of Earnings Management Actions

Many profit center managers also engage in deceptive earnings management practices because of high pressure for short-term performance.[4] When profit center managers manage earnings, they take actions that have the desired effect on reported earnings even though they know they have no real positive economic benefits and may actually be quite costly to the profit center in the long run.[5]

Methods of Managing Earnings

In all 54 profit centers studied, the managers admitted to having one or more methods of managing short-term earnings.[6] The methods can be classified into two basic categories—accounting and operating methods.[7]

Accounting methods of managing earnings. Accounting methods of managing earnings involve having the profit center controller merely "sharpen his pencil" and make the entries that produce the desired level of earnings. Many of these actions are legal and consistent with generally accepted accounting principles (GAAP), although these are the "cooking-the-books" actions about which many critics have written.[8]

At profit center organization levels, the accounting methods of managing earnings involve taking advantage of the flexibility allowed in many accounting rules, not of the flexibility allowed in the choice of accounting rules.[9] Some managers base their judgments about the size of needed reserves (such as for inventory obsolescence and bad debts) and expense accruals (such as for bad debts, vacations, social functions, and inventory shrinkage) on whether additional profit is needed. For example, a profit center controller in corporation J (consumer products) noted, "Reserves are certainly not a black-and-white matter. Our judgments are certainly shaded by how the [profit center] is doing. If we're having a good year, I'll build our reserves, and when we need them I'll reduce them." Similarly, a group controller in corporation M (consumer durables) said, "Reserves can be justified within a very large range. It's OK to borrow from them when you need to as long as you are still within that acceptable range. Don't get into the black, but it's OK to take advantage of the gray. By their nature, accounting standards are gray."

Some flexibility is also allowed in accounting for sales. Managers may base their judgments about the key factors that determine whether a sale should be recorded, such as the uncertainty of product performance or customer collection, on whether they wish to recognize the profits from the sale during the current accounting period. A profit center controller in corporation C (distribution) explained his use of these earnings management methods in the following terms: "Accounting is gray. Very little about it is absolute, so where you put the debits and credits is largely up to you. You can help your company by doing things in sales and expenses, and if it's legal, then you are justified in doing it."

Similarly, some managers classify expenditures as expense or capital with an eye to the bottom line. For example, a profit center controller in corporation D (diversified industrial products) mentioned several examples where he considered the accounting largely "discretionary." One was as follows: "From time to time we have to rebrick a furnace, and that costs around $20,000 to $30,000. The accounting rules say that if the expenditure is adding life to the furnace, we should capitalize it. If not, we should expense it. But it is not clear that the rebricking is adding life." If in doing his accounting he considers whether or not his profit center needs additional profit, this controller can be said to be managing earnings.

Finally, in corporations that use an operating income measure of performance, managers (or their controllers) can sometimes use flexibility in the accounting rules to increase income by moving an expenditure below the operating income line. (I described several examples of this type of action in Chapter 6.)

Operating methods of managing earnings. Operating methods of managing earnings usually have direct effects on cash flows, as well as on earnings. They involve changing actual operating decisions to push sales, expenses, or the recognition of gains and losses into the accounting period in which their effects will provide the most benefit (or do the least harm).[10] Some managers alter shipment schedules depending on whether their profit center needs more (or less) revenue and profit. In most cases, sales accelerations do not result in permanent sales boosts; the practice merely involves borrowing sales from the future. For example, a profit center controller in corporation E (diversified chemicals) admitted that his profit center had engaged in this practice: "We could call our customers and have them accept early delivery. We may have to offer them extended terms. We have done this, but not often. We could boost our operating profit by maybe $3 million [approximately 5%]. It would affect shifts of only one to three weeks. It would not cause customers to take product they don't need."

The recording of sales can also be postponed by delaying shipments or customer approvals past the end of the accounting period. One manager in a government business said that if he is having a good year, he will tell his people not to be aggressive in pursuing the government contracting officers' signatures on the approval forms. He noted that eventually the officers will want to sign the form to conclude the project, but he estimated that he could delay the recording of the sale for up to four months.

Most managers can also shift discretionary expenditures between periods. In one group of corporation A (diversified luxury goods), this type of action, which is common, is called "the roller coastering problem." In their endeavors to achieve budget targets, some profit center managers in the group have deferred repairs, liquidated inventories of supplies and repair parts, and delayed the hiring of needed personnel.

Finally, some managers place the recognition of unrealized gains (or losses) in the period where they will do the most good (or least harm). Some managers capture unrealized gains by selling assets with a below-market book value when they need additional profit. Losses are generally more difficult to time, because accounting rules require recording losses when they are first recognized. There is no one fixed point at which a loss is certain enough to book, however, and some managers alter their business judgments to recognize the losses when they will do the least harm.[11]

With the operating methods of managing earnings, the accounting can be said to "fairly present" what actually happened, but the changes in the operating decisions have the same effect as the accounting methods; they either boost or "save" reported income, but have no real, positive economic effects, and their effects may be quite harmful. In some of their destructive forms, operating methods of managing earnings are prime examples of operating-decision myopia.

The Incidence of Earnings Management

Although all 54 profit center managers interviewed described one or more methods they could use to manage earnings, not all of them choose to do so. Table 8-2 shows the proportion of profit center managers in each corporation that has managed earnings within the past two years. In three of the firms, all of the managers interviewed have managed earnings, using either accounting or operating methods, but across all the firms less than two-thirds of the managers have done so.

Two major factors explain why the types and extent of earnings management vary across corporations and profit centers: feasibility and performance pressure.

Earnings management feasibility. Earnings management feasibility has three determinants: authority to affect the earnings management decisions, business flexibility, and constraints imposed by the corporate control system.

Authority to take the actions is an important factor explaining why almost twice as many profit center managers use operating methods of managing earnings as use accounting methods. Nineteen of the 54 profit center managers reported that they were unable to use any accounting methods of managing earnings. Most of these managers have limited authority in accounting areas because they do not have their own controller. On the other hand, all the profit center managers reported that their authority afforded them opportunities to use at least one of the operating methods of managing earnings.

Business flexibility is the major determinant of the dollar amounts (in relation to the size of the profit center) by which profit center managers can manage earnings. The managers' ability to move profits between accounting periods varies

TABLE 8-2
Incidence of Earnings Management Practices

		Proportion of Profit Center Managers Admitting to Having Managed Short-Term Earnings Using:		
Corporation	*Number of Profit Centers Studied*	*Accounting Methods*	*Operating Methods*	*Either Accounting or Operating Methods*
A (Diversified luxury goods)	5	60%	60%	100%
B (Electronic equipment)	3	0	33	33
C (Distribution)	6	50	33	50
D (Diversified industrial products)	4	50	25	50
E (Diversified chemicals)	6	33	83	83
F (Hospitality)	6	0	33	33
G (Electrical connectors)	4	0	50	50
H (High tech)	5	20	60	60
J (Consumer products)	5	100	100	100
K (Electronic systems)	3	67	67	67
L (Specialty chemicals)	5	20	60	60
M (Consumer durables)	2	100	100	100
Average		37%	64%	66%

widely because of differences in the extent to which they can move sales and expenses between periods.[12] For example, a profit center manager in corporation G (electrical connectors) with sales of $10 million felt he could move less than $50,000 in profit between periods, because he was committed to fixed product delivery dates and because few of his expenses were discretionary. Most profit center managers in corporation F (hospitality) have even less flexibility.

Profit center managers in some corporations, on the other hand, talked about their ability to affect reported profits by many millions of dollars. One profit center manager in corporation J (consumer products), admittedly an extreme, said, "In the short run we have the ability to manage to any profit number you want." He explained that he could go on a "sales blitz" that, because of his products' high profit margins, would provide a significant boost to short-term profits by pulling future-period sales into the current period. The sales blitz could be (and has been) implemented by offering distributors special deals (for example, promotional monies, such as 2% cooperative advertising if delivery is taken sooner), by providing extra and earlier promotion to stimulate demand, by offering delayed payment terms, and by making direct shipments to retailers earlier. In addition, this manager noted that "In good years [as he had had], we try to keep our reserves topped up," and he felt that he could develop the rationale for turning in some of those reserves if they were needed. Changing judgments about reserves could affect profit significantly because the profit center had large reserves for coupon redemptions and inventory and machinery obsolescence. Finally, this manager knew he could identify some expenditures (particularly advertising and hiring) that could be delayed until the following year if extra profits were needed.

Corporate control processes, implemented by line management, control personnel, and auditors limit the profit center managers' ability to engage in some methods of managing earnings. Most profit center managers felt that their earnings management actions were limited primarily by controls within the corporation, not by external auditors. The comment of a group controller in corporation M (consumer durables) was typical: "You can get almost anything past a public auditor." The ability of the external auditors to control earnings management activities is limited because their tests are designed to detect material deceptions, and almost nothing in a single profit center's financial statements is material to the corporation's consolidated financial statements.

Corporate controls generally limit the managers' ability to use the accounting methods of managing earnings more than they limit the operating methods. Detecting accounting manipulations is easier, because the accounting rules are written, and accounting judgments are expected to be made consistently and conservatively. When major differences are observed, such as in the size of an accounting reserve, corporate managers or personnel on their control staffs ask questions. Furthermore, the organizational control function tends to be accounting-oriented, and operating decisions are usually considered to be within the discretion of the profit center managers.

Corporate control systems do place limits on the use of some operating methods of managing earnings. For example, a profit center manager in corporation K (electronic systems) reported that he was unable to move discretionary expenditures between periods. This profit center's products were in the development phase, so virtually all discretionary expenditures were for R&D. The profit center manager knew he could not make cuts in R&D to achieve his budget targets because those expenditures had high corporate visibility: "The only thing I could do is cut R&D drastically. I would have to get corporate approval to do that." (This manager did have some ability to manage earnings, however, because he had some unrealized gains that he could choose to recognize when it was to his advantage to do so.)

Most profit center managers, however, are not significantly constrained by control processes in their use of operating methods of managing earnings. It is not easy to detect some of the operating forms of earnings management. In addition, sometimes corporate managers actually want the profit center managers to manage earnings, and they can use the operating methods without worrying that external auditors will object.

Some of the operating methods of managing earnings deviate only slightly from practices that most firms consider to be acceptable and clearly within the profit center managers' discretion. For example, a group vice president in corporation M (consumer durables) discussed the earnings management method that generally has the most significant effects in consumer-product firms: an end-of-period promotion to induce distributors to buy in the current accounting period, rather than the subsequent period. He drew a curve showing the pattern of sales over the period of a typical promotion (see Figure 8-1). Sales (and profits) increase sharply and almost immediately when the promotion is announced. When the promotion expires, or when the distribution channels are full of product, sales usually fall back to a level below where they would have been without the promotion. Thus if a promotion is timed just before the end of an accounting period when a boost in earnings is needed, the action can be construed as earnings management because the sales and profits are merely being borrowed from the subsequent period.

In some cases, however, the profit center managers hope that because the dealers are stocked heavily they will establish their own promotions to move the product. If that happens, the manufacturer's promotion will result in higher sales (and presumably profits) cumulatively over the two accounting periods. A profit center controller in corporation B (electronic equipment) described such an example in which an earnings management activity was felt to have costs, but also a positive economic effect:

> Last year we called our customers and asked if they would take early delivery. We generated an extra $300,000 in sales at the last minute. We were scratching for everything. We made plan, but we cleaned out our backlog and we started in the hole this year. We missed our first quarter sales plan. We will catch

FIGURE 8-1
The Pattern of Sales and Profits Over the Period of a Typical Promotion

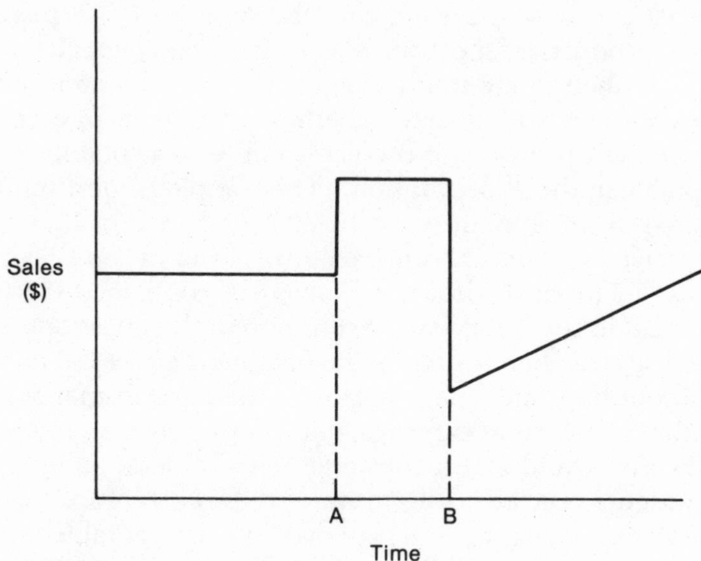

A = time at which promotion is announced.

B = time at which promotion expires.

> up by the end of the second quarter. Sure, this mode of operating is costly, but it has a positive effect too; we cut our lead time to the customer.

He expects that the reduced lead time will produce higher sales in subsequent periods.

In this and similar cases, upper-level managers are usually not able to distinguish the good management decisions from the manipulative decisions. Most of them follow the spirit of decentralization and do not evaluate the timing of most of the profit center managers' promotion and expenditure decisions. Except in obvious cases, they are unwilling to intervene in the profit centers' operating affairs.

Most corporate managers tend to be quite tolerant of actions profit center managers may be taking to manage earnings, but they are conservative about allowing accounting methods of earnings management. To confirm this impression, I included in the questionnaire I sent to the senior financial executives in each corporation a list of 13 possibly counterproductive short-term earnings management practices described to me in interviews. The questionnaire asked the executives to indicate whether or not each earnings management practice on the list would be acceptable or unacceptable in their corporation. (The complete questionnaire is shown in the appendix.)

I received responses from executives in 11 of the 12 corporations.[13] The data, shown in Table 8-3, confirmed the feelings I had in the interviews. Even though the questions were written so that there would be no obvious difference between the accounting and operating manipulations in materiality, direction of effect on earnings, manager motive, or any other factors that could affect the judgments of acceptability, the respondents reacted to them quite differently. In total, the various accounting methods received 63 unacceptable ratings from the 11 respondents and only 4 acceptable ratings,

TABLE 8-3
Senior Financial Executives' Judgments of Acceptability of 13 Hypothetical Earnings Management Practices (n = 11)
Hypothetical setting:
A division that accounts for 10% of corporate earnings

	Acceptable	*Questionable*	*Unacceptable*
Accounting Methods of Managing Earnings:			
1. On December 15, a clerk in the division placed an order for $3,000 worth of office supplies and the supplies were delivered on December 29. The order was a mistake because the division general manager (GM) had ordered that no discretionary expenses be incurred for the remainder of the fiscal year, and the supplies were not urgently needed. The company's accounting policy manual states that office supplies are to be recorded as an expense when delivered. The division GM learned what had happened, however, and to correct the mistake, he instructed the accounting department not to record the invoice until February		1	10

	Acceptable	*Questionable*	*Unacceptable*
2. At the beginning of December 1986, the GM realized that the division would exceed its budgeted profit targets for the year			
a. He ordered his controller to prepay some expenses (e.g., hotel rooms, exhibit expense) for a major trade show to be held in March 1987 and to book them as 1986 expense. Amount: 0.5% of annual division PBT (profit before tax)	1	1	9
b. He ordered his controller to develop the rationale for increasing the reserve for inventory obsolescence. By taking a pessimistic view of future market prospects, the controller was able to identify some finished goods (worth 5% of annual division PBT) that conservative accounting would say should be fully reserved (i.e., written off), even though the GM was fairly confident the inventory would still be sold at a later date at close to full price	3	3	5
3. The next year, the division described in question 2b sold 70% of the written-off inventory, and a customer had indicated some interest in buying the rest of the inventory the following year. The GM ordered his controller to prepare the rationale for reducing the reserve for obsolescence by 1.5% of annual division PBT (i.e., writing up the remaining 30% of the previously written-off goods to full cost). The GM's motivation for recapturing the profit was:			
a. to be able to continue working on some important product development projects that might have had to be delayed because of budget constraints		2	9
b. to make budgeted profit targets		1	10
4. In November 1986, the division was straining to meet budget. The GM called the engagement partner of a consulting firm that was doing some work for the division and asked that the firm delay sending an invoice for work done until next year. The partner agreed. Estimated work done but not invoiced in 1986:			
a. 0.2% of annual division PBT		1	10
b. 5% of annual division PBT			11

TABLE 8-3 (*Continued*)

	Acceptable	*Questionable*	*Unacceptable*
Operating Methods of Managing Earnings:			
1. The division's buildings were scheduled to be painted in 1988. Since the division's earnings were way ahead of budget in 1987, however, the GM decided to have the work done in 1987. Amount: 1% of annual division PBT	9	2	
2. The GM ordered his employees to defer all discretionary expenditures (e.g., travel, advertising, hiring, maintenance) into the next accounting period so that his division could make its budgeted profit targets. Expected amount of deferral: 1% of division PBT			
a. The expenses were postponed from February and March until April in order to make the first-quarter target	8	2	1
b. The expenses were postponed from November and December until January in order to make the annual target	7	3	1
3. In September, the GM realized that the division would need strong performances in the last quarter of the year in order to reach its budget targets.			
a. He decided to implement a sales program offering liberal payment terms to pull some sales that would normally occur next year into the current year; customers accepting delivery in the fourth quarter would not have to pay the invoice for 120 days	1	4	6
b. He ordered manufacturing to work overtime in December so that everything possible could be shipped by the end of the year	10	1	
c. He sold some excess assets and realized profit of 0.5% of annual division PBT	8	2	1

whereas the operating manipulations received 9 unacceptable ratings and 43 acceptable ratings. Thus, although the senior financial managers' opinions do differ in some areas, most of them consider the accounting methods of manipulation unacceptable but the operating methods acceptable.[14]

Pressure to manage earnings. The other major factor that explains differences in the incidence of earnings management across the profit centers is the severity of the short-term performance pressure the profit center managers feel. This pressure stems from several sources. One often powerful source is direct period-end requests from upper-level managers to "turn in" more profit. For example, a profit center manager in corporation J (consumer products) reported that he managed earnings at quarter- and year-end, but he went on to note: "[My boss] is usually driving [the practices], asking what I can do [in delivering extra profit]." Similarly, a profit center manager in corporation A (diversified luxury goods) explained that he maintained excess reserves that he could "turn in" when he received the requests for more profit:

> They nibble at me all year long. They take my cushion away from me by asking me to turn it in. I'd rather reinvest it, but I keep it all in anticipation of their requests. I try to keep around $1 million [in unreported profits, in a profit center with $50 million in annual sales]. I'd get fired if I buried $10 million. I can carry it over year-end, but I must have my arguments ready for the auditors . . . .
>
> It's a game. [My boss] is always trying to figure out what I've got. He called me last year in the third quarter and asked me "the absolute maximum [earnings] I could do" for the year. I said $10 million. (My latest forecast [for the year] was at $9 million.) Then he wanted to know where the other $1 million was.

Profit center managers in seven of the 12 corporations mentioned receiving at least one such direct request to turn in more profit. Table 8-4 identifies the corporations and shows the highest frequency of requests found in each. In some corporations the requests were rare, but in others some profit center managers were asked for more profit nearly every quarter. A profit center manager in corporation J (consumer products) was faced with this situation: "Last year we made $60 million in profit. The budget was $54 million. [Top management] wanted the extra profit. They called us [at the end of] every quarter and said, 'We want x.' The request last quarter was for an extra $2 million. We gave it to them."

Although these requests create a powerful motivation for

TABLE 8-4
Period-End Requests for More Profit

Corporation	*Are Some Profit Center Managers Asked to Turn In More Profits?* Yes	No	*Greatest Frequency of Requests*
A (Diversified luxury goods)	x		Almost every quarter
B (Electronic equipment)		x	
C (Distribution)		x	
D (Diversified industrial products)	x		Some quarters, as needed
E (Diversified chemicals)		x	
F (Hospitality)		x	
G (Electrical connectors)	x		Had happened only once in four years
H (High tech)		x	
J (Consumer products)	x		Nearly every quarter
K (Electronic systems)	x		Every quarter
L (Specialty chemicals)	x		Once or twice a year
M (Consumer durables)	x		Once or twice a year

boosting short-term performance reports, they do not automatically lead profit center managers to criticize their firm's motivational contracts. Some managers consider the requests a normal, though annoying, part of being a general manager in a publicly held firm. The comments of a profit center manager in corporation D (diversified industrial products) were representative:

> I get the phone calls near the end of a quarter. Somebody from corporate calls me and asks for more profit. They need something to report to the press. Corporate wants to maintain stability of earnings because the security analysts think that's important.
>
> If they need it, I'll come up with it. This is the only [profit center] in the corporation that has a solid enough hold on its market that it is in a position to provide, and we will continue to provide for many years. I am a team player, and I'll give them what they want by borrowing from an accrual. That's what I mean about the numbers not being a good measure of my performance . . . . They've never asked me to bury anything. I wish they would.

These requests do, however, create short-term performance pressure that is significantly related to the earnings management activities, as the data in Tables 8-2 and 8-4 suggest. In the seven firms in which requests for more profits are made, the average proportion of managers managing earnings is 75%; in the five firms in which no such requests are made, it is only 52%.

The requests for additional profits tend to create a vicious circle in which the deceptive behavior is reinforced. Profit center managers learn that they may be asked for more profits, and they want to be able to satisfy those requests. They are thus prone to negotiate forcefully for easier performance targets and to create pockets of unreported profits.[15] Upper-level managers, of course, get a feel for their managers' conservative tendencies, and these feelings fuel more frequent calls for additional profits because they know they can rely on the profit to be there when they need it. Furthermore, asking for it is one way to squeeze some of the slack out of the organization. But the more frequent calls for additional profits just increase the profit center managers' incentives to manage earnings. The result is the creation of a culture of deception that obscures the true earnings trends and, consequently, strips much of the information content from the earnings reports.

Some short-term performance pressures also stem from one or both of the short-term motivating contracts—pressure to meet budget or to improve expected bonuses. Some top executives make their requests for more profit at the beginning of the measurement period rather than at the end—they ask for more profit at budget target-setting time. For example, a profit center controller in corporation H (high tech) told of pressure that caused the manager of his profit center to search for methods of increasing profits:

> Our original budget was 16.6% profit. They rejected it. That was the only time that ever happened. It forced a layoff. We cut our hiring, expenses, payroll increases. He had to go back to the bottom to get all the cuts broken out by department, but our real problem was sales, not expenses. In R&D, we needed to hire people to get back into business. This will hurt our product development effort. We argued that the corporation was being very shortsighted. Our plan was for 16.6% this year and 24.3% next year. That averages over 20%. What's wrong with that? They are either shortsighted or they feel they can make us do both.
>
> Based on what they did this year to our budget, I would hesitate to report more than 20% profit. I'll put some money away, although I won't hide it where they can't find it. It irritated me that we did things the way we should and our performance has been good. We got an award for being one of the best [corporation H profit centers] just a couple of years ago. How quickly they forget.

Similarly, a profit center manager in corporation D (diversified industrial products) reported that his budget targets sometimes caused him to scramble at year-end for more profit:

> If I'm short at year-end, I can eke out more sales. I will pour on the coal and get more deliveries. I will call in a favor (or ask for one) from a procurement contracting officer for a sign-off

> "in place." We'll get them to inspect it in our plant. We have close relationships with most of the government employees with whom we deal. When the approval form is signed, it's only a paperwork war from then on [to receive payment]. It's a small risk. On the cost side, I may defer software purchases and any G&A. I can eke out an extra $1 million [approximately 10% of annual profit center profit]. We did it this year.

And a profit center manager in corporation J (consumer products) said:

> We used to have $10 million in reserves for brand expansion [cooperative advertising], coupons, obsolescence, bad debts, and the like (versus sales of $450 million and profits of $62 million); it's easy to build up reserves in this business. But there's only about $3 million left. We used the rest.
>
> If we had a fantastic year, I'd like to build the reserves back to $15 million. Top management would be aware of this, of course.

Finally, some pressure also stems from the reward cutoffs included in most of the firms' short-term bonus contracts. For example, a profit center manager in corporation H (high tech) described how he would react if earnings promised to be above his firm's upper cutoff level:

> If I am [above the upper cutoff level for bonus purposes], I will create some new reserves. We have reserves for warranties and other contingencies, and we have a better feel for these than anyone else. I will also not ship product at year-end, and I will probably write off some excess inventory. Holding the shipments alone can move about $500,000 in profits [between years], and I can move about $200,000 in reserves and $50,000 in inventory. [These numbers compare with annual profit of approximately $6 million.] These actions would not attract management attention. [The CFO] would only be upset if he felt we had misallocated our effort.

The lower cutoffs can also cause earnings management. Some profit center managers who are having a poor operating period take actions to lower current-period earnings to put the profit center in a better position for the subsequent accounting period. A group vice president in corporation B (electronic equipment) had encountered this type of problem: "I have had a problem with some people knowing in the first quarter of the year that they are out of the running for [an incentive compensation award]. It creates a morale problem and they just plan for the following year by loading all their expenses into the current year. It is the 'take the bath' phenomenon."

Why Don't Corporate Managers Offset the Short-Term Performance Pressures?

The evidence presented above suggests that many of the profit center managers feel intense short-term performance pressure and that this pressure induces some dysfunctional responses: investment myopia and earnings management. In most cases, corporate managers are aware of these dysfunctional outcomes, even though the profit center managers usually do not make their dysfunctional responses obvious. For example, with respect to earnings management, the president of corporation L (specialty chemicals) said, "[Division personnel] will hide more if they feel they will be punished for their [poor results]. They have the ability [to hide things] because so much of accounting is judgment."

The corporate managers' awareness of the risk of inducing earnings management raises the question why they do not reduce the short-term pressures or offset them with long-term incentives. The answer is that many of them believe the benefits of the short-term pressures outweigh the costs.

The Benefits of Short-Term Performance Pressure

One benefit of short-term performance pressure is the motivational advantage I described in Chapter 3. Consistent pressure keeps everyone cost-conscious and working hard. It provides real benefits in virtually all profit centers.

There is an additional corporate benefit—the positive effect of smooth and, it is hoped, steadily increasing corporate earnings on stock prices. Most corporate managers feel they can best serve their shareholders by reporting a smooth earnings pattern because they believe the stock market responds forcefully to short-term reported-earnings swings. The comment of the chief financial officer of corporation H (high tech) is typical: "I feel very strongly that [corporation H] stock responds very strongly to quarterly earnings per share and the continuation of the earnings pattern. It determines our PE [price-earnings] ratio."

To explore how widely the belief in the value of smoothing earnings is held, I included the following item in the questionnaire sent to the senior financial executives: "The stock market favors companies with a steady pattern of growth as compared to those with an irregular pattern of growth even if the long-term growth rates are the same." All 11 respondents agreed with this statement, and six agreed "strongly."[16] Where the executives work under the threat of a takeover, as was true in corporation J (consumer products), the perceived benefits of smooth and, it is hoped, higher short-term earnings are especially great.[17]

Because they believe smooth short-term earnings reports benefit stock price, corporate managers put considerable pressure on operating managers to cut their long-term investments in difficult times. Where I heard the loudest complaints from profit center managers who felt they were not able to fund what they considered good long-term investments, I also heard comments about the "insidious effect" of the stock market. Here is an example of such statements, from a group vice president in corporation M (consumer durables): "We're more short-term oriented than the Japanese. They don't even talk one year. But [the U.S.] financial community focuses on quarters. It's that simple. The reality is that we have those pressures. People who don't believe that are naive."

When times are good and it is easy to report steady increases in corporate earnings, the short-term pressure on the profit center managers subsides. In the responses to the questionnaire, only four of the 11 financial executives disagreed with the statement, "In good business times, top management is willing to accept a reasonable amount of slack in the operating budgets."

In good times, the profit center managers are still promised larger bonuses for larger short-term earnings, but the desire for marginally higher bonuses does not create strong pressures for short-term performance. For most managers the incentive to earn short-term bonuses seems to be generally smaller than their desire to invest in the future growth of their businesses. The comment of a group vice president in corporation H (high tech) was typical: "There is a point where you want to stop R&D expenditures, but I don't apply a brake. [The profit center managers] make that election. We have the luxury that we're running 24% PBT [in my group]. The extra R&D we're spending comes out of my and their pockets."

Thus much short-term performance pressure is based on corporate managers' belief that the corporation is better off with the pressure than without it, even if pressure induces investment myopia and earnings management. Even though motivational contracts can be adapted to give profit center managers incentives to develop long-term business potential, corporate managers who want to emphasize the short term are not greatly interested in encouraging the long-term focus if it comes at the expense of short-term earnings.

The Costs of Short-Term Performance Pressure

The costs of the investment myopia and earnings management induced by short-term performance pressure are subtle and difficult to estimate. The value of the returns to be earned on most investments is quite uncertain, so the benefits foregone when profit center managers act myopically are similarly uncertain. By assuming conservative projections of the returns to be earned or a high discount rate for risk, corporate managers often can easily justify reducing or delaying investments until "they can be afforded."

The costs of earnings management come in many forms, and most of them are also generally difficult to estimate. The most obvious costs are the out-of-pocket expenses caused by some operating forms of earnings management, such as the overtime incurred to accelerate shipments or the costs of reworking hastily shipped product, and the adverse effects the practices can have on the employees who may be forced to work the overtime, the customers who must return the product, and the suppliers whose delivery schedules are disrupted. In addition, these manipulative activities distract managers from their primary mission—creation of value.

A less obvious cost of the earnings management activities is that profit centers that have to "borrow" future earnings to satisfy current-period reporting obligations run considerable risk of getting into a cycle of escalating earnings management. In addition to meeting their future targets, they must repay what they have borrowed, and in a business downturn, the debt grows.

In one declining profit center in corporation K (electronic systems), for example, the manager asked his sales and production personnel each quarter to accelerate as many sales and shipments as they could so that quarterly targets could be met. These people worked at greater than normal capacity in the third month of each quarter and cleaned out the order pipelines, but they had a natural letdown at the beginning of the subsequent quarter. As a result, the sales in each quarter became distributed between the months in an extreme pattern: 5% of the quarterly total in the first month, 10% in the second, and 85% in the third.

Another serious, but less obvious, problem is that the manipulations distort the corporations' and profit centers' financial trends and can delay managerial recognition of problems. As a profit center manager in corporation E (diversified chemicals) expressed it: "We're only kidding ourselves. [These manipulations] are only cosmetic." Unless the managers incur the expense to keep two sets of books, they can be fooled by their own numbers.

Finally, both the operating and accounting manipulations can undercut corporations' attempts to set a high moral tone. It is easy for operating managers to become cynical when the corporation publicizes codes of conduct and then encourages quarter-to-quarter earnings games.[18] A corporate spirit of gamesmanship may eventually manifest itself in fraudulent activities.

Are the Dysfunctional Outcomes Evidence of Contract Flaws?

The investment myopia and earnings management described in this chapter are dysfunctional outcomes caused by the firms' motivational contracts, but they are not necessarily evidence of contract flaws. As I mentioned earlier, virtually all of the corporate managers are aware of the relationship between short-term performance pressure and these dysfunctional outcomes, yet many of them still apply pressure. Thus, to conclude that myopia and earnings management are evidence of flawed contracts, we must conclude that the corporate managers' judgments are based on an incomplete understanding of the alternatives available or on incorrect beliefs about cause-and-effect relationships. My conclusion is that in many cases either or both of these judgment problems exist.

The primary problem arises because when corporate managers press for short-term earnings to signal good performance to the stock market, they seem to spend little time thinking about or estimating the costs of the dysfunctional outcomes. Many of them seem to simplify the decision problem by assuming that the benefits of the additional reported earnings are obviously greater than the costs, except in extreme cases where the managers cut or delay a program of major strategic importance or act illegally or inconsistently with generally accepted accounting principles. This one-sided, benefit-focused evaluation sometimes leads to contract flaws because the managers' assumptions about the benefits of steady growth in quarterly earnings seem to be based on a mechanical, and probably generally incorrect, model of how the stock market works.

Many (probably even most) managers believe that the investors who drive the market merely extrapolate from the most recent quarters' results. This model was expressed by a profit center manager in corporation E (diversified chemicals):

> We play games only because of Wall Street. The analysts are mostly very lazy. They don't do their homework. Their planning horizon is six months, and they don't understand the key questions that govern the business. It's obvious that when companies can't cover the short-term swings and have a bad quarter, their [price-earnings] multiple declines. It's totally a [short-term] numbers game.

Most research evidence suggests, however, that the mechanical model of market behavior is not correct; analysts base their forecasts on much more than just recent earnings reports. For example, many analysts report that they focus more on cash flows than earnings.[19] Frederick Taylor, the chairman of the investment policy committee at U.S. Trust Co., recently said: "Earnings are very important, but if cash flow is improving, we will buy a stock where earnings have been going nowhere."

Because analysts base their forecasts on cash flows and a broad range of nonfinancial information that is useful for predicting future cash flows, in addition to earnings, the correlation between earnings and stock prices is significantly less than 1.0. There are many examples of a firm's earnings having increased while its stock price declined, even in relation to the overall market movements. Studies have shown that the correlation between *annual* percentage changes in accounting earnings and annual percentage changes in market prices is in the range of .38.[20] The correlation between *quarterly* accounting earnings and market price changes is undoubtedly much lower. Moreover, this correlation proves no causation—changes in earnings may not be causing stock price changes; earnings and stock prices may merely be changing concurrently.

Research has also shown that the vast majority of market analysts are not short-term-oriented; they use a multiyear forecasting horizon. A relatively recent study by Brown et al. summarizes the previous research evidence and provides new evidence to this effect.[21] These authors conclude:

> The results in this monograph are inconsistent with the capital market having a myopic focus, or short-run fixation, on the current quarter's or the current year's reported income. . . . At a minimum our results place an increased onus on management to provide support of the allegation that short-run decision making is "necessary" because of the short time horizon used by the capital market.[22]

The corporate managers' assumptions about the importance of quarterly earnings disclosures are certainly not completely incorrect, as the market clearly does respond to them, as it does to all relevant public disclosures.[23] It may respond even more forcefully to sharp earnings changes in firms that have a strong reputation for managing short-term earnings because, in such cases, a sharp change signals a change in business fortune: the profit trend has shifted despite the managers' efforts to smooth it.[24]

Overall, however, the market appears to keep the short-term disclosures in perspective. In corporations that are making numerous long-term investments, sophisticated market analysts are likely to place a higher value on the likely successes of those investments than on this quarter's earnings.[25] Thus, the quarterly earnings disclosures have the least value in precisely those firms that are most vulnerable to investment myopia.

Corporate managers in firms subject to investment myopia and the negative effects of earnings management face two challenges. First, they should examine the evidence suggesting that the stock market is not excessively short-term oriented and revise their beliefs as necessary.[26] Second, they should improve public disclosures about investments made and their prospects.[27] The extent and quality of the information disclosed about a firm's prospects are directly and negatively associated with the importance the market attaches to short-term earnings. Effective disclosures therefore reduce the benefits of smooth but possibly misleading earnings patterns, and they make it easier for corporate managers to reduce the pressures the profit center managers feel for short-term performance. If the firms' disclosures can be improved, as is probable, the assumptions many corporate managers appear to make about the benefits of smooth short-term earnings patterns are overstated.

If managers' perceptions of the benefits of short-term earnings pressure can be changed so that the perceived benefits do not dominate the costs of investment myopia and earnings management, the managers may spend more time analyzing the hard-to-estimate costs. They might conclude that some of these costs are actually quite significant. In particular, they might look at the costs of the spirit of gamesmanship that pervades many corporations. The gaming activities are deceptive and distracting, and they create an environment that is conducive to more serious, illegal forms of behavior.

NOTES

1. Some of the 97 managers did express criticisms about one or more of these system elements that were not related directly to motivational contracts. Common were criticisms that corporate paperwork requirements for planning and reporting were excessive.
2. For similar arguments, see Hirschman (1970).
3. Jensen (1986).
4. Profit center managers can also manage some other performance measures. Because of the primary importance placed on accounting measures of performance, however, the discussion in this chapter is on managing earnings.
5. Earnings can be managed only in the short run because over the long run cumulative earnings closely approximate cumulative cash flows.
6. This finding was not surprising, as prior studies also show high frequencies of earnings-management actions by middle-level managers. For example, Mihalek et al. (1987) find that over half of the 326 division-manager respondents to their survey report pressure to manage net income or return on investment materially. The manipulative responses are significantly higher in publicly held firms. Merchant (1989) finds that 91% of a sample of 54 profit center managers in a large, publicly held, well-regarded firm pull profits from the following year into the current year to achieve their budget targets.
7. To assess the extent to which the profit center managers (and controllers) engaged in earnings management practices. I listened to managers' stories about their efforts to make budget or, if they were having a good year, to save income to improve their prospects for achieving next year's budget. I also asked hypothetical

questions as to what they would do if they needed a last-minute earnings boost or if they were having an exceptionally good year, and how much income they thought they could move between periods. And I tried to learn their motives for their actions and how they felt about their earnings management activities.

8. The "Numbers Game" section included in most issues of *Forbes* magazine provides frequent criticism of companies' accounting practices. See, for example, Chakravarty (1987) and Jereski (1987).

9. Corporate managers can sometimes manage income by changing accounting methods with an eye on the bottom line. A change from accelerated to straight-line depreciation for financial reporting (but not tax) purposes, for example, often produces an immediate boost in earnings, but has no associated cash flow effect. Healy (1985) provides evidence that short-term bonus plans provide one motivation for such changes.

Profit center managers, however, rarely have authority to make changes in accounting methods without corporate approval. Thus, they generally are not able to use these methods of managing earnings.

10. Baber and Haggard (1987) find that managers are prone to defer R&D expenditures to "manipulate" accounting earnings to meet objectives.

11. A study by Fried et al. (1986) finds that over half (52%) of the 1,354 write-offs reported on the Dow Jones News Service during the period 1980–1985 occurred in the fourth quarter of the year, and another 23% were disclosed in the third quarter. Elliott and Shaw (1988) find that 63% of large discretionary write-offs are recognized during the fourth quarter. One factor undoubtedly contributing to this pattern is that corporate managers wait until late in the year, when they can determine whether the corporation can "afford" the write-off. Many corporate managers, however, look at accounting as an annual cycle, so they do not take a close look at their asset values and the adequacy of their reserves until near year-end.

12. Bart (1988) provides evidence that budget games, involving the addition of "cushions and hedges" to performance standards, similarly vary across businesses. In particular, he notes that the opportunity to engage in budget games varies directly with the size of the businesses' promotional budgets and growth objectives and the extent to which the expected financial ratios are in line with earlier figures.

13. One CFO said he was too busy to complete the questionnaire.

14. The other findings were generally as expected. For example, where they were judged unacceptable, large manipulations were judged more serious infractions than small manipulations. For a discussion of these other findings, see Bruns and Merchant (1988).

15. Bart (1988) provides evidence that operating managers are prompted to build hedges into their budgets to protect themselves from arbitrary budget cuts by senior management during the year.

16. This finding is consistent with those of a recent interview survey, conducted by *Business Month* (Wattenberg, 1988), of the chief executives of a sample of 609 U.S. corporations with annual revenues of at least $50 million. Almost 90% (89.2%) of these executives feel American businesses are too short-term-oriented. A typical explanation, in the words of one respondent: "Everyone is working for the benefit of financial analysts—short term instead of looking ahead" (p. 29).

17. DeAngelo (1988) provides evidence that dissident stockholders who wage a proxy contest for board seats typically cite poor earnings rather than poor stock

price performance as the motivation for their action. Also see Jensen (1988), Stein (1988), and Palepu (1986).

18. In an earlier, related study, I conclude that in the vast majority of cases of fraudulent financial reporting, the problems start with small manipulations. Honest people are trapped because their corporation's culture either encourages the manipulations directly or indirectly by providing easy rationalizations, or offers temptations to which they eventually succumb. See Merchant (1987).

The report of the National Commission on Fraudulent Financial Reporting (1987) (the Treadway Commission) also emphasizes the importance of setting what it calls the proper "tone at the top."

19. See Dreyfus (1988) and Kaplan (1985).

20. Beaver (1981).

21. Brown et al. (1985).

22. Ibid., p. 5.

23. For example, Hand (1988) finds that the market does not respond mechanistically to paper gain in income caused by debt-equity swaps. However, it does not totally unscramble the firms' financial statement data to arrive at unbiased inferences about the probability distribution of future cash flows.

24. Mendenhall and Nichols (1988) present evidence that the stock market reacts more strongly to bad news announced in earlier quarters than in the fourth quarter. (Bad news is defined as involving announcements where the actual earnings are less than predicted.) They suggest that bad news is more meaningful in earlier quarters because managers have greater discretion to delay releasing the bad news.

25. Analyses show that far less than half of the value of the stocks of the 20 largest publicly traded U.S. corporations is derived from "prospects that are more than five years distant" (Hector, 1988), p. 68.

26. In a *Fortune* article, Hector (1988, p. 64) notes the argument that the stock market is short-term-oriented is "widely accepted as gospel," but he also writes that "It isn't valid." He goes on to present some of the evidence and describes examples of managers who feel that "the best way to *prevent* a takeover is to manage for the long term" (p. 74).

27. Hill et al. (1988) make a similar argument.

CHAPTER 9

Evaluating Contract Effectiveness, Part II: Foregone Motivation and Excessive Compensation

Contract effectiveness can be impaired by problems other than overestimation of the benefits of smooth reported earnings and underestimation of the costs of a culture of deception. Some corporate managers also underestimate the cost of the motivation foregone when corporate risk-sharing and reward-cutoff features are added to incentive compensation contracts. And some managers pay profit center managers too much because they incorrectly calibrate the target rewards or make asymmetric adjustments for the effects of uncontrollable events. Both of these potential problems result from one or more communication breakdowns or barriers to learning that prevent or delay managers' recognition of the contract deficiencies.

Foregone Motivation

The main purpose of motivational contracts is to increase motivation. Profit center managers are motivated to generate higher results only when they earn extra personal rewards for that performance. Some corporations, however, sever the results/reward connection by forcing profit center managers to bear some of the corporate risk or by limiting the maximum rewards the managers can earn. Both of these features are costly in foregone motivation, and I concluded that some corporate managers underestimate these costs.

The Motivational Costs of the Corporate Risk-Sharing Features

In Chapter 7, I described two types of features that some firms add to motivational contracts primarily to make managerial compensation more variable and thus to reduce corporate risk. These features are including corporate performance in the incentive compensation calculation and limiting the bonus pool on the basis of corporate performance. Underlying these features is a belief that managers should not be earning much (or any) incentive compensation unless shareholders are also reaping rewards.

The comments of a majority of the profit center managers I interviewed convinced me, however, that these corporate risk-sharing features are often inimical to motivation. Risk-sharing underlies the operating managers' second and third most frequent criticisms of their firms' motivational contracts (shown in Table 8-1)—that the evaluations were unfair and that the results-related incentives were inadequate.

When firms base profit center managers' rewards on corporate performance, they are holding the profit center managers accountable for the results of entities over which they have little or no control. Individual profit center managers almost invariably have only an infinitesimal effect on corporate performance. Thus, when risk-sharing features are used, profit centers performing better than average are, in essence, being penalized for the relatively poor performance of other profit centers. These penalties cause frustration and reduce motivation.[1]

Frustration was expressed by most of the profit center managers whose rewards were so affected.[2] For example, in the words of a profit center manager in corporation L (specialty chemicals): "Profit-sharing plans are demotivating. They cause good performers to be paid the same as poor performers. Why do we implement these plans and pay money to demotivate people?" Similarly, before a recent contract change, corporation J (consumer products) provided no short-term bonuses if the company did not make its target. A profit center manager remembered the frustration he felt when this limit cost him: "The first two years I was the manager of [an international profit center], we performed well but [the corporation] did not do well. We earned no bonus. It was very frustrating. Somewhere in the world something had gone wrong, but it had nothing to do with me. It was very difficult to swallow."

Stimulation of teamwork is one of the purported benefits of risk-sharing features, but managers in some firms thought they might actually have the opposite effect. Where rewards are being reduced by a poorly performing group, the risk-sharing features can be destructive. The managers of subpar profit centers get a "free ride" on the good performance of other units, but these managers are not necessarily happy about receiving the unearned rewards. They may be subjected to intense peer pressure, and teamwork may actually be discouraged.

Some firms use risk-sharing contract elements out of a belief that bonuses should not be paid if the corporation is not earning profits. Explaining to shareholders why managers are earning bonuses when the corporation is not doing well certainly is politically sensitive. The performance of an individual profit center, however, often has little to do with how the corporation is performing, and holding profit center managers accountable for something that is clearly beyond their control is not functional. It is almost certain to evoke feelings of unfairness, which may lead to decreased motivation and higher management turnover. Most corporate managers who include these risk-sharing elements in their firms' motivational contracts seem to underestimate such costs significantly.

I suggest that corporate risk-sharing elements be used sparingly. Poor corporate performance is not a good reason to abrogate the all-important profit center motivating contracts. If corporate managers want to use risk-sharing contract features, either to encourage cooperation or to show shareholders and their representatives (the board) that managers' fortunes are tied to their fortunes, I suggest they do so only in a token sense. They can limit the proportion of the managers' incentive compensation based on corporate performance to, say, 10% or less. In this way, they can capture some benefits of the uncontrollable risk-sharing features but minimize the damage to profit center manager motivation.

The Motivational Costs of the Reward Cutoffs

I also came to question some of the reward cutoffs many firms include in their short-term incentive compensation plans. Firms use lower bounds so as not to reward managers for mediocre performance. They use upper cutoffs for several purposes: to reduce the possibility of paying high bonuses for reasons not stemming from the profit center managers' efforts, to induce the managers to expand their businesses at a sustainable (not maximum) rate, to protect the corporation's sense of vertical equity in total compensation, to maintain consistency in compensation over time, or to match competitors' compensation practices.

These cutoffs have drawbacks, however. They can cause either loss of motivation or displaced motivation in ways that some contract designers appear to overlook or underestimate.

With the lower cutoffs, the main risk is that managers will incur large losses ("take a bath") to prepare the entity for the next period. Some contract designers are ignorant of this risk or downplay it. For example, the consultant primarily responsible for the design of corporation K's (electronic systems) new short-term incentive compensation plan admitted that the inclusion of a lower cutoff places an extra demand on the corporation's control system. But, he said, "We have to assume the corporation's management and control systems are tight enough to prevent managers from 'taking a bath.' We tend to walk away from that."

Corporation K's systems, however, are probably not up to this control challenge. Corporation K is a relatively young, rapidly growing firm that has recently acquired a firm about its own size. Control personnel admitted that because of the growth and instability, some of the firm's control systems are inadequate, yet control people were not part of the motivational contract design team. The lower bonus cutoff has created an incentive that will probably lead to dysfunctional behavior that the company's systems cannot detect and control.

Upper cutoffs can also have dysfunctional results, including an adverse effect on motivation in good periods. A group vice president in corporation D (diversified industrial products), a firm with no limits on individual awards, understood this problem:

> I believe the top salesman, research engineer, or division manager should be able to make more than the chairman of the board. They can earn you a lot of money, and they need incentives for working hard through periods when they might not earn bonuses because their efforts haven't paid off yet. The best thing you can have is to have someone blow the top off the incentive plan. Caps take some of the thrill out of business.

The president of corporation G (electrical connectors) had a similar concern: "I never cut off anybody's opportunity. I've never understood that philosophy. The leverage for the company is so powerful."

The effects of these cutoffs would not be large if actual performance always fell below the cutoff level. In the firms that used them, however, the cutoffs usually affected the bonuses of at least some profit center managers.

Like the lower cutoffs, the upper cutoffs can stimulate short-term earnings management, as managers may "save" earnings until they can be used in a period where they can be converted into bonuses. Some corporate managers recognize this potential problem. For example, a group vice president in corporation H (high tech) said, "The maximums on the plan are a deficiency. It leads to gamesmanship."

The costs and risks of these dysfunctional consequences of bonus cutoffs are difficult to estimate. Even in firms whose managers recognize all the risks, there is no unanimity of opinion about the net benefits. For example, the manager of executive compensation in corporation B (electronic equipment), a firm that used an upper incentive cutoff, felt his firm had made the incorrect choice: "We have a maximum because we don't want to pay for a 'bluebird' [windfall] coming in. I don't buy into that concept. If the shareholders are getting wealthy, we should share the wealth with the managers."

I listened to many profit center managers express frustration about the cutoffs and describe earnings management activities to avoid their effects. My conclusion is that award cutoffs should generally be avoided. Managers should be made to feel they are earning extra rewards for better results (or paying penalties for worse results) at all times.

The cutoffs cause potentially high costs of foregone motivation and high risks of earnings management. Most profit center managers are given incentives *not* to take risks because they face often severe penalties if their risky ventures are unsuccessful. If corporations want profit center managers to take risks, they should provide compensating incentives, the most obvious of which is the opportunity to reap high rewards for success. Placing upper cutoffs on bonus potential curtails the managers' propensity to take risks.

Generally the most important benefit of the upper cutoffs is to protect the firm from paying bonuses that are unnecessarily high because they are undeserved. But firms can protect themselves against this possibility by allowing top management or the compensation committee to make adjustments for large uncontrollable factors.

The one unusual circumstance in which upper cutoffs are warranted temporarily occurs when a new plan is implemented. Upper cutoffs do protect the firm from the risk of a poorly designed plan. But this benefit decreases over time. Thus, perhaps an upper cutoff is warranted in a plan's early years, but it should be abandoned after the plan has been in place for several years. Even in this exceptional case, corporate managers should decide to use the risk-sharing contract features and upper reward cutoffs only with full awareness of the motivational costs that these contract elements will involve.

The Provision of Excessive Incentive Compensation

Firms may overpay their profit center managers if the rewards for meeting targets are calibrated incorrectly or if a policy of making asymmetric adjustments for uncontrollable factors causes unanticipated rewards with no motivational effects.

Incorrect Calibration of Target Awards

Corporation K's (electronic systems) new short-term incentive plan provides perhaps the best example of a contract based on faulty calibration. The corporation hired a consulting firm to help it redesign its plan. The primary consultant explained that he set the target bonuses to provide a competitive compensation package. These bonuses were based on achievement of budgeted profit targets, which he assumed were the expected performance level. I asked him what he thought the probability was that a typical profit center manager in corporation K would at least achieve budget. He replied:

> That's a tough question, but it's an important one because performance expectations are at the heart and soul of every incentive plan. If the board [of directors] is comfortable with the [annual] plan as reasonable, I take that as evidence that it's a good plan . . . .
>
> I think that a plan with a 50% probability of achievement is a comfortable position. That [type of plan] ought to be difficult but achievable. If the probability of achieving plan is 90%, that would make the target levels much easier. That was not our aim—this plan is not intended to provide "breathing" pay. If that is true, it certainly would make the compensation plan suspect.

From conversations with profit center managers in corporation K (which, incidentally, the consultant did not have), I estimate the achievability of the profit center budgets is around 80%. This is considerably higher than the fifty percent probability assumption on which the plan was based.

Corporate managers were not aware of the achievability assumption the consultant built into the new incentive plan. Under the plan, they will probably be paying profit center managers more than they want to without realizing it. The plan is in its first year, and corporate managers may realize over time what they have done, but that realization is hampered by considerable noise in the performance measures and in the data about competitors' compensation practices.

Asymmetric Adjustments for Uncontrollables

Another calibration problem may be caused by the common practice of adjusting for uncontrollable factors only when the adjustments are in the managers' favor. As was shown on line 3 of Table 6-1, these adjustments are made asymmetrically for short-term incentive compensation purposes (with only minor exceptions) in 11 of the 12 firms.

It is easy for the evaluators to rationalize this practice. The rationale is that managers should be protected against uncontrollable bad luck. And when the managers benefit from good luck, the shareholders also benefit. So who is to complain?

What often goes unnoticed, however, is that this asymmetry in adjustments raises the firm's compensation costs with little or no motivational benefit. The practice raises the question who is representing the shareholders' interests. When no adjustments are made for uncontrollable good luck, profit center managers are rewarded for events over which they had no control. No control means the rewards have no motivational effect, and the costs of the incentive awards are incurred for naught.

Most profit center managers who are tolerant of subjectivity in performance evaluations will accept a symmetrical adjustment process if it is communicated well and applied fairly. I base this conclusion on evidence that profit center managers accept such processes in corporations where they are used, and many profit center managers who were rewarded for being "lucky" spoke of their uneasiness about earning rewards that they did not deserve. Here are examples of each of these types of evidence.

Adjustment for the Effects of Favorable Uncontrollables

In corporation A (diversified luxury goods), the CEO rarely makes adjustments to the current year's results, but he sometimes makes interyear adjustments for uncontrollable events that affect profit center results favorably by adjusting the budget targets on which the bonuses for the next year are based. He recently made such an adjustment in one profit center that operates in an industry that is very sensitive to economic conditions.

For four years in a row (before 1987), economists had been predicting an economic downturn in this industry, and the manager had incorporated these predictions in his budget projections. But in all four years the economy was strong and bonuses were large.

For 1987, the profit center manager again incorporated a pessimistic economic forecast in his planning, and submitted a budget target he felt he had a 90% chance of achieving. But the CEO decided to make an interyear fairness adjustment to compensate for the years of good luck. He increased the profit goal by 30%. The profit center manager accepted the new target. He pledged to do what he could to achieve it, even though he believed his chances were virtually nil. He also informed the employees in his organization that they had been given a new budget target to shoot for.

Uneasiness about "Undeserved" Rewards

Some profit center managers are actually uncomfortable when they earn rewards they feel they do not deserve. One such manager, of a profit center in corporation L (specialty chemicals), described his concern. In his profit center, approximately 60% of the product costs are for materials, and the prices of many of the most important ones, such as oil and agricultural products, fluctuate widely. The profit center is also affected heavily by foreign currency fluctuations, since many of its materials and 30% of its sales come from overseas.

In 1987, material prices were relatively low and the dollar was strong, so the profit center's financial results were excellent; profits were 50% higher than in 1986. Some of this performance improvement came from the closing of a money-losing plant and the implementation of a highly visible operations-improvement program profit center management had initiated, but profit center management worried that top management did not understand that a large portion of the improvement was due to uncontrollable factors. The profit center controller observed:

> In 1988 when prices turn around, we're going to get bashed. Nobody has asked me to quantify how much of our good results stem from our own doing. We're getting overpraised now for things beyond our control. I'm not complaining about that, but we've raised [top management's] expectations to a level that cannot be repeated. I don't want corporate spoiled by things we can't control.

The profit center manager's response was to have his controller perform the necessary variance analyses and to bring them to the attention of the corporate executives. His purpose was "to tell corporate what our real running rate is, what they can expect. These [adjusted] numbers are reality. They are what the [profit center] can be expected to deliver."

With both causes of probable excessive compensation—incorrect calibration of target awards and asymmetric adjustments for uncontrollables—corporations could lower their contract costs with little or no adverse effect on incentives. If the profit center managers learn that they can expect to earn total compensation that is more than competitive, the excessive costs may have some benefit in reducing management turnover. Even so, the additional costs could be better spent by promising rewards that provide additional motivation.

NOTES

1. The authors of a major study of American society (Bellah et al., 1985) conclude that "individualism lies at the very core of American culture" (p. 142). Like most Americans, managers value freedom and autonomy highly, and they wish to be judged on their own successes (and failures).

Weiss (1987) presents business-specific evidence that managers want their rewards to be based on their own successes. When an electronics manufacturer switched from individual to group incentives, its most able workers left to work for other firms that rewarded high individual performance.

2. This belief appears to conflict with the finding of many studies that group financial incentives have generally favorable effects on productivity [see summary by Kendrick (1987)]. Most of the studies, however, track the effects of lower-level employees on short-term productivity, and their findings probably cannot be generalized to profit center organization levels. Furthermore, the studies have been criticized for several significant methodological weaknesses (Florkowski, 1987).

CHAPTER 10

Designing and Managing Good Motivational Contracts

The preceding chapters have described the importance of motivating profit center managers properly, the many choices that must be made in designing motivational contracts, and the three categories of trade-offs that complicate contract design. They also described some design mistakes some firms may be making because they do not understand fully the design alternatives or the alternatives' benefits and costs.

It should be obvious that the contract design choices are complex and difficult. Much of the complexity is portrayed in Figure 10-1, which shows that a broad range of factors affects either the severity of one or more of the design trade-offs or the corporation's ability to cope with the trade-offs. These factors are descriptive of the corporation, the profit center manager's evaluator, the profit center itself, and the profit center manager. Managers address the trade-offs by choosing the number of contracts to use and the specific features to include in each.

Because of this complexity, it is impossible to provide simple advice to managers charged with designing and managing good motivational contracts. No single set of contracts serves the contract aims—effective motivation with minimal dysfunctional side effects—equally well in all profit center situations because the situations are different.

Designing effective motivational contracts requires knowledge of the full range of the feasible contract alternatives and

FIGURE 10-1
Factors Affecting Contract Design Choices

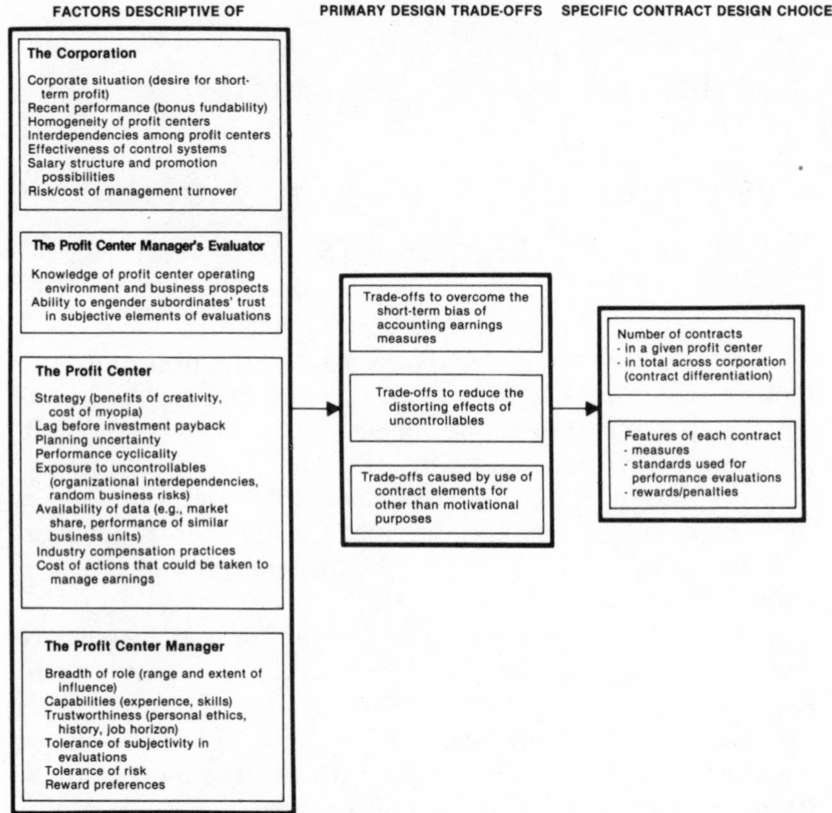

the factors that affect the costs and benefits of each design trade-off. Typically, however, only some of the factors listed in Figure 10-1 are of prime importance; their effects dominate those of the other factors. Thus, an important part of the design task involves discovering which factors are particularly relevant.

To tie together and summarize much of the discussion in the earlier chapters and to illustrate the varying importance of the situational factors in different corporations (and profit centers), this chapter describes briefly the contract-design choices made in two corporations—H (high tech) and A (diversified luxury goods)—and the reasons for those choices. These two corporations are chosen for illustration because differences in their situations cause some sharp differences in their motivational contract choices.

The chapter concludes with some observations about the processes needed to design effective motivational contracts and, equally important, to ensure that the contracts are refined over time and adapted to changing conditions. As the relevant design factors change, so too must the motivational contracts.

Corporation H: High Risk, High Reward

The Corporation

Corporation H (high tech) was founded 30 years ago as a research and development firm. Over the years it has expanded and diversified by acquiring a number of small, high-tech, manufacturing companies. Total annual revenues are now several hundred million dollars.

Performance has been excellent. Corporation H's ten-year compound growth rate is approximately 40% in both sales and net income, and over 20% in earnings per share. Growth has been generated both internally and through acquisition.

The corporation is highly decentralized. The 24 business-unit profit center managers report to four group vice presidents who report to the corporate president, but group and corporate managers try not to become involved in the profit centers' businesses unless problems arise. When they make an acquisition, corporate managers promise the selling owner/entrepreneur that he or she can continue to run the business with minimal interference, assuming good performance. For example, one profit center manager noted:

> If this was just my own company, I probably wouldn't be doing things much differently. Sometimes I feel like we're strangers to [the people at corporate]. They have kept exactly the same team here [since the acquisition four years ago], no additions or reductions. We feel responsible for everything here. Of course they have the right to interfere with our deci-

> sions, but if they did, then we would be able to blame them for things that went wrong . . . .
>
> I realize that we're different from most other firms. Maybe we have the strength to be different because we've been so successful.

The profit center managers are not even tied to their own businesses. If their markets falter, they are expected to develop other products or make acquisitions that will enable them to reach the desired levels of performance.

Each profit center is nearly self-contained. The profit centers include their own product development, control, administration, marketing, and sales staffs, and they have their own bank accounts. There is little interdependence among the companies, and corporate management puts virtually no pressure on the profit center managers to source materials internally or to create inter-profit-center synergies.

Most of corporation H's profit centers serve small, but fast-growing, niches in large markets, including telecommunications, specialty electronics, video communications, and scientific instruments, by selling products that use electronics and microprocessor-based technologies. Their success depends largely on development of new, innovative, high-margin products and, to a lesser extent, improvement of manufacturing efficiencies. Thus, the profit center managers are asked to be creative and to make product-development investments.

Corporate and group staffs are small. The main services provided centrally are cash management, tax, external reporting, employee benefits, and acquisitions. Few corporatewide procedures are enforced; the only manual in the organization is the accounting manual, and it is written in broad terms that allow the profit centers considerable flexibility in financial record-keeping.

Contracts Used

Corporation H uses a combination of three contracts to motivate its profit center managers. These contracts promise:

(1) high autonomy for managers who are able to meet an annual minimum performance standard, (2) cash awards for annual results, and (3) stock-option awards for profit growth measured over three years.

The minimum performance standard is timeless; it does not vary from year to year. It is 25% growth in sales and 20% profit before tax (as a percentage of sales). The managers of the few profit centers where the plans do not forecast this level of performance or where the results fall short of these targets are required to "get help." They must appear before a Profit and Growth Committee comprised of four members of top management to discuss their business prospects and plans.

The annual bonus contract is based on an aggregate performance measure weighted 50% on growth in profit before tax, 35% on return on sales, and 15% on return on assets. The cash payments promised under this contract are large in comparison with those promised in the other corporations. The maximum bonus possible for a profit center manager is 140% of salary, and bonuses of 80–100% of salary are common.

The third contract promises awards of stock options to profit center managers based on three-year growth in profits in relation to other profit centers in the corporation. (This contract was described in detail in Chapter 4.)

The promises embodied in all three contracts are absolute and fixed over time. They subject the profit center managers to considerable risk because none of the contracts includes provisions for adjustments for uncontrollables; the managers' rewards are affected by the full range of business risk factors, including economic conditions, interest rates, and customers' successes and failures. And except for the long-term contract, which uses a form of relative performance evaluation, the performance standards do not vary: the payoffs are calibrated by timeless performance standards, not annual budget targets that could vary with changing economic conditions.

SITUATIONAL FACTORS AFFECTING CORPORATION H'S DESIGN TRADE-OFFS

Corporate managers' contract choices are related to the presence of several important situational factors. One is the growth orientation of their profit centers' businesses. Most of the profit center managers are making investments that will not provide returns for several years, so it would be counterproductive to evaluate the managers' performance solely in terms of annual earnings. This factor makes the first category of design trade-offs—those aimed at overcoming the short-term bias of accounting earnings measures—important in corporation H.

Unfortunately, corporate managers' ability to cope with the short-term bias problem is hampered by their lack of knowledge of the details of the profit centers' operations and businesses prospects—they are unable to tailor leading-indicator measures to individual profit centers. Their lack of detailed knowledge stems from:

1. Their decision to operate a highly decentralized corporation and remain aloof from most decisions except in cases of potential management problems.
2. The fast-moving and highly technical developments in the industries in which their profit centers are operating. Even if it wanted to, top management could not stay well informed about all these developments.
3. The short time that many of the profit centers have been part of the corporation. Even if it were feasible to learn the details of the profit centers' businesses, there would be a lag before the learning could take place.
4. The difficulty of communicating with the profit centers, which are highly dispersed geographically.

Corporation H's top managers are also limited in their ability to administer unwritten long-term contracts. Managers of profit centers that are reporting good results are already promised high autonomy, and the other major form of reward typically promised in unwritten contracts—improved promotion prospects—is not of great interest to many of the profit center managers. Many of the former entrepreneur/managers purport to know only their profit centers' products; they want to remain in the business they founded to ensure its continued success; and they are not interested in becoming cogs in a corporate bureaucracy.

Corporate managers' ability to cope with the short-term bias problem is strengthened, however, by the relative homogeneity among the profit centers' operations and strategies. Corporate managers are able to address the problem somewhat by using a uniform set of motivational contracts for all profit center managers. This set of contracts:

- places the greatest weight (50%) on the growth factor in the profit center managers' annual bonus contract;
- relaxes the pressure for short-term performance in profit centers that are performing well—those that are well above the timeless minimum performance standard; and
- promises rewards for long-term (three-year) profit growth.

Corporate managers have some concern that their combination of contracts may still be too short-term-oriented, however. They realize that the profit growth factor is a short-term (annual) measure, and they are not yet convinced that the new (one-year-old) long-term contract will significantly lengthen the profit center managers' decision-making horizons, particularly since the company's stock price has been declining the past few years. But without specific knowledge of the profit centers' products and industries, their contract options are limited.

The high planning uncertainty faced by most of the profit centers is another important factor influencing motivational contract choices in corporation H. High uncertainty means a high risk of unforeseen, distorting influences. It increases the importance of the second category of design trade-offs—the trade-offs designed to reduce the distorting effects on the results measures of uncontrollable influences.

Here again, corporation H's managers' abilities to cope with a design trade-off are hampered by their lack of detailed knowledge of the profit centers' operations and business prospects. They do not want to design their measurement system to buffer the profit center managers from the environmental forces to which they want the managers to respond, and their lack of knowledge makes them generally unable to make informed adjustments for uncontrollables. As a result, they have implemented inflexible contracts that promise rewards for reported results, with no adjustments allowed for uncontrollable influences.

The only contract flexibility occurs where profit centers are unable to achieve the minimum acceptable performance level. In such cases, corporate managers seek more information, by requiring a presentation to the Profit and Growth Committee, to protect themselves from firing effective managers who are burdened by bad luck.

Fortunately, however, corporation H's managers have found they can use rigid contracts because most of the profit center managers have a high tolerance for risk. As former entrepreneurs, they are accustomed to bearing the full business risk, and because most of them became wealthy when they sold their companies to corporation H, their need for a steady income is lessened.

The high risk the profit center managers are asked to bear, in turn, provides the primary explanation for the high cash reward potential promised in the annual bonus contract. Managers who are asked to bear high risk must be compensated for bearing that risk if they are successful, and the former entrepreneur/managers are accustomed to earning high rewards.

Finally, corporate managers' fear that the corporation might grow faster than it is able to handle leads them to make a nonmotivational design trade-off. They implemented the upper cutoff on the reward potential (at 140% of base salary) to temper the profit center managers' growth ambitions.

Corporation A: Highly Flexible Contracts

The Corporation

Corporation A (diversified luxury goods) is in some ways quite different from corporation H. It is a much larger and older manufacturing company. The bulk of its revenues comes from the sale of luxury goods, the demand for which is highly cyclical, but over the years the corporation has diversified into a broad range of products and services. Total annual revenues are several billion dollars.

Performance has been excellent since the 1980 oil shortage and recession because of the healthy U.S. economy, reasonably low and stable interest rates, and, arguably, good management. In the last four years alone earnings have more than tripled.

Corporation A is organized into nine divisions whose managers report directly to the corporate CEO. The flat organization is intended to shorten decision response times; "everything comes to the top quickly." The divisions range widely in size, from less than $100 million in annual sales to more than $1 billion. Some comprise multiple profit centers whose managers are responsible for specific products or geographic regions.

Each division is nearly self-contained. It creates wealth by designing, building, selling, and servicing its products. The divisions' strategies, however, vary widely. Product and service quality is a fundamental value throughout the corporation. But some divisions compete by developing a succession of increasingly superior products. Others, particularly those facing foreign competition, compete by maintaining quality while lowering price, and generate profits by maintaining stringent cost controls.

The responsibilities of corporate staff are to preserve the wealth the divisions create and to provide services, such as taxes and legal, that are more economically provided on a centralized basis. To reverse a trend of increasing centralization and bureaucracy, the CEO has cut corporate staff sharply (by over two-thirds) over the past six years.

Contracts Used

Corporation A uses three primary motivational contracts for its profit center managers. These contracts promise: (1) high autonomy and increased promotion possibilities for managers who are able to reach annual profit-after-tax targets, (2) cash awards for exceeding the annual targets and for achieving other favorable results, and (3) restricted stock awards based partly on meeting three-year financial and nonfinancial goals.

The annual profit-after-tax targets the profit center managers are asked to reach are negotiated between the profit center manager and the CEO and are set to be reachable approximately 80–90% of the time. Profit center managers who fail to reach the targets are subject to loss of autonomy and reputation, and in extreme circumstances loss of job.

The annual bonus contract is based on an aggregate performance measure weighted 35% on profit after tax, 35% on cash flow, and 30% on two personal objectives. Profit center managers start earning bonuses at 80% of the targeted performance levels; they earn bonuses of 20% of salary for reaching the targets; and they earn a maximum bonus of 60% of salary for reporting results at 110% of target.

The first two contracts are flexible in that the performance targets vary from year to year. The targets depend on each profit center's business prospects, so the profit center managers bear business risk only until the factor can be incorporated in the new year's target.

The contracts are also flexible because the CEO (and other evaluators of profit center managers) are allowed to exercise subjectivity in administering the minimum performance standard and annual bonus contracts. The CEO can "forgive" profit center managers whose entities fail to meet their minimum performance standards if he decides that extenuating circumstances caused the shortfall. He can also adjust for the effects of uncontrollables for bonus purposes: on relatively rare occasions, he assigns modest bonuses to managers who are working hard but "can't see the light at the end of the tunnel." More often, however, he makes bonus adjustments across periods for the effects of uncontrollables; he makes profit centers' performance targets more (or less) challenging, depending on whether they were positively (or negatively) affected by uncontrollable influences in prior periods (as was illustrated by a specific example described in Chapter 9). The latter practice shows interdependence between the two contracts because when the performance targets are made more challenging, the negative signal provided when managers fail to reach them is weakened.

Corporation A's third contract promises restricted stock awards to profit center managers. Although the awards are based primarily on corporate performance—three-year return on equity—the contract has a direct motivational effect on profit center managers because the awards are affected plus or minus 20% by achievement of profit center earnings targets and two quantitative, personal goals, which can be financial or nonfinancial. (This contract was described in detail in Chapter 4.)

SITUATIONAL FACTORS AFFECTING CORPORATION A'S DESIGN TRADE-OFFS

Corporate managers' choices of these specific contracts and contract elements are directly related to several of the corporation's situational factors. As in corporation H, corporation A's profit center managers are asked to make investments that will provide payoffs years in the future. Thus the trade-offs aimed at reducing the short-term bias problem are important.

Corporation A's managers made two choices to address the short-term bias problem. They based a significant proportion (30%) of the profit center managers' annual bonus awards on leading indicators of forthcoming profits, such as completion of an acquisition, winning of a new contract, or implementation of a new, improved management system, and they implemented the long-term-oriented restricted stock plan.

The use of leading performance indicators requires top management to know the profit centers' operations and businesses. The profit centers' strategies and business prospects are quite disparate, so the leading indicators have to be tailored to the profit centers' situations. The CEO is able to judge the fairness of this tailoring because he understands the profit centers' businesses quite well. He has worked for the corporation for over 30 years and had assignments in several of the divisions. He knows the profit center managers and their idiosyncracies well because most of the corporation's managers have also been with the company a long time. And his task is made somewhat easier because corporation A's businesses are less technically sophisticated than the businesses in corporation H.

The second major contract design trade-off—the reduction of the distorting effects of uncontrollable influences—is also important in corporation A because the profit centers' markets are volatile and uncertain. This trade-off is made easier to address because of the CEO's knowledge of the profit centers' businesses and the profit center managers' willingness to allow subjectivity to enter into performance evaluations. Because they have not had bad experiences in the past, the managers generally feel that subjective evaluations will be made fairly.

Limiting the profit center managers' annual bonuses to 60% of salary is a result of a nonmotivational trade-off. The CEO is generally reluctant to make downward adjustments for the effects of favorable uncontrollable influences because "the shareholders benefited." The upper bonus cutoff is used as an alternative method of protecting the corporation against the possibility of paying huge, undeserved bonuses.

A final unique feature of corporation A's annual bonus contract is the inclusion of a cash flow measure of performance. The feature stems from a temporarily strong corporate desire to reduce the level of debt, which had risen because of several large acquisitions.

Comparing and Contrasting the Two Corporations' Motivational Contracts

The similarities and differences between the sets of contracts used in corporations H and A provide some useful illustrations both of generally dominant contract choices and of the importance of specific situational factors.

Contract Similarities

The corporations' contracts are similar in that all of them include accounting earnings measures of performance, which are weighted heavily. This choice is made for the reasons discussed in Chapter 3—earnings is the single best performance measure available:

- Earnings measures are at least partially congruent with changes in shareholder value;
- Earnings measures are bottom-line, summary performance measures that can be used to provide motivation in an unobtrusive way that is consistent with the spirit of decentralization. Decentralization is preserved because the profit center managers are allowed considerable operating autonomy to make many of the important business trade-offs;
- Earnings measures are significantly more objective and verifiable and less costly than other, potentially more congruent alternatives, such as inflation-adjusted earnings or direct measures of changes in shareholder value;
- Earnings measures are inexpensive to prepare and report because they must already be produced for other purposes, such as corporate financial reporting; and
- The most serious weaknesses of the earnings measures, particularly the short-term bias, can be ameliorated by adding other contract features.

The two corporations' contracts are also similar in that profit center success or failure is defined as reaching or failing to reach an annual performance standard that top management feels will be reached by an effective, hard working management team. The achievable performance standards make most managers feel successful, and in so doing, energize them and make them more willing to take prudent risks. They provide consistent, but reasonable, short-term performance pressure. The consistent pressure helps prevent profit center managers from being wasteful or from allowing their operations to become sloppy, and the reasonable nature of the pressure limits the managers' incentives to act myopically or deceptively. The achievable targets reduce the potential for discouragement in managers who face targets they feel are unachievable, but at the same time they help identify the managers who are not able to perform at an acceptable performance level. They protect against the likelihood that optimistic plans will lead managers to acquire unneeded resources that are difficult to divest (such as additional employees). And they improve the predictability of corporate financial reporting; the summation of the profit centers' targets sets a highly probable lower bound on the total performance the corporation will be able to report.

A third similarity between the two corporations' contracts is that a sizable portion of the rewards is provided in cash. Even in corporation H, where the former entrepreneur/managers are already reasonably wealthy, cash awards are felt to provide effective motivation because, as one profit center manager put it: "The bonus is not important for the money. It's the way to keep score."[1]

Fourth, both corporations include an upper cutoff on the profit center managers' reward potential. The limit is 140% of salary for managers in corporation H and 60% of salary for managers in corporation A. This similarity is somewhat coincidental because corporate managers had different reasons for including the cutoff. In corporation H, the rewards were limited to smooth the corporation's pattern of growth. In corporation A, the cutoff was included to protect the corporation from paying large but undeserved bonuses due mainly to a windfall gain—favorable uncontrollable influences.

Finally, both corporations promise rewards for long-term (three-year) performance. This contract similarity stems from a situational characteristic the two corporations share: their desire to have their profit center managers make investments that promise returns in subsequent accounting periods.

Contract Differences

There are four major differences between the two corporations' combinations of contracts. First, corporation A's contracts are much less uniform. The contract measures, their weighting, and the performance standards vary across profit centers and between periods. Second, corporation A is much more likely to make adjustments for the effects of uncontrollable influences. Third, the potential cash rewards are much larger in corporation H. And fourth, corporation A rewards profit center managers for generating cash flow, as well as earnings.

The following five situational factors are the primary causes of these differences:

1. Depth of evaluators' knowledge of the profit centers' operations and business prospects.
2. Degree of homogeneity of profit centers' strategies.
3. Profit center managers' trust in evaluators to exercise subjectivity in performance evaluations.
4. Profit center managers' tolerance for risk.
5. Corporate desire for short-term cash flow.

Although these situational factors largely explain the contract differences between corporations H and A, different sets of factors account for other choices made in other corporations. For example, managers of corporation C (distribution) have not implemented a long-term incentive contract because they are unconcerned about management myopia; their profit center managers make few long-term investments. Managers in corporation K (electronic systems) allow no adjustments for the effects of uncontrollable influences because they are unable to make the adjustments objectively and their profit center managers have little tolerance for subjectivity. And managers of corporation L (specialty chemicals) virtually guarantee their profit center managers some bonuses because the corporation's base salaries are below competitive levels.

The list of potentially relevant situational factors is long. Each of the factors listed in Figure 10-1 helps explain why at least one contract feature is included in the contract packages used in one or more of the 12 corporations studied.

Effective Contract Design Processes

Because the design of effective motivational contracts for profit center managers requires consideration of many factors, several parties should be involved in the process. Generally top management, profit center managers, the profit center managers' evaluators, personnel staff or compensation consultants, control staff, and the audit committee of the board of directors should contribute their expertise and ideas. Top management knows about the corporate risks and desire for short-term performance, the homogeneity of profit centers, and the cost of management turnover. Profit center managers know about their profit centers' strategies and critical success factors, their ability to achieve their performance targets, their taste for subjectivity in performance evaluations, their tolerance of risk, and their reward preferences. The profit center managers' evaluators know the breadth of the profit center managers' roles, and they know how much or how little they understand about the profit centers' business prospects and operating environment. Personnel staff or compensation consultants know how to make the contracts competitive with industry and regional competitors for labor resources, and they are most likely to be aware of other firms' innovative practices that the firm would be wise to consider. Control staff (including auditors) know how able they are to detect and prevent dysfunctional earnings management behavior. And the compensation committee should represent the shareholders' interests and ensure that the rewards promised the managers are not excessive.

An effective motivational contract design process requires bringing all of this specialized knowledge together, along with knowledge of the full range of design alternatives and their trade-offs. Corporate managers should recognize that they cannot delegate the contract design tasks. They should be personally involved in the design process, and they should ensure that each of the parties listed above is also involved. If any of the important knowledge is lacking or if the contracts are designed in a piecemeal fashion because the knowledge is not well communicated and integrated, design mistakes will be made.

Managing Sets of Motivational Contracts

The initial design and implementation of the set of motivational contracts is only the start of contract management, however. Contract change is the norm in most corporations and industries. For example, even though most of the 12 firms participating in this study have used short-term incentive compensation agreements for many years, major changes in these contracts have been made in over half of the firms within the last four years. Other studies present evidence of similar patterns of widespread changes.[2]

Some of these changes stem from corporate managers' learning about the contract alternatives and the effects of various contract features. The managers monitor the favorable and unfavorable outcomes of their contracts and make changes in anticipation of improvements.

Corporate managers' efforts to monitor contract outcomes, particularly dysfunctional outcomes, are, however, hindered by some potentially significant barriers to learning. Profit center managers whose motivation is weakened by the corporate risk-sharing features of their firms' incentive contracts, for example, are not always likely to publicize their dissatisfaction. Some of them are reluctant to speak out, while others are not informed about incentive contract design alternatives and trade-offs and just assume that these features are warranted. Thus, it can be many years before corporate managers are able to detect the deleterious effects of these features on motivation. They may eventually detect them only by noticing an audit report of questionable accounting practices, higher management turnover, or somewhat lower performance.

Similarly, profit center managers who are induced to manage earnings to avoid the harmful effects of the performance cutoffs on their bonuses are not likely to disclose their activities or the reasons for them.[3] And managers who feel they are being given excessive compensation are certainly not likely to complain about their good fortune, while shareholders and their representatives are not likely to be aware of the problem.

Improving contract evaluation by reducing these barriers to learning is a continuing challenge. To help ensure that their firms' motivational contracts evolve effectively and promptly in response to the real and changing conditions faced in the profit centers, corporate managers should be aware of these barriers and try to avoid them when they can. They should also monitor the contract outcomes frequently, using devices such as opinion surveys and exit interviews, to refine their understanding of the effects the various contract features produce. They should make a greater effort to understand other companies' experiences, particularly where innovative approaches have been attempted, and relevant research findings; they should conduct within-company experiments when they are not confident of their knowledge base; and they should encourage managers to be candid about their criticisms and ideas.

Not all contract changes are positive evolutionary refinements, however. Some are reactions to changes in the situational factors shown in Figure 10-1. In changing environments, failure to adapt contracts to new situational factors may mean that the contracts being used are becoming less and less appropriate. To respond appropriately, corporate managers must recognize changes in relevant factors and know about the contract alternatives and their effects.

Because so many factors are potentially relevant, important knowledge is dispersed among many parties, and the trade-offs are complex, the tasks of designing and managing sets of motivational contracts for profit center managers are challenging. But the stakes are high. Little is more important in divisionalized corporations than properly motivating profit center managers.

NOTES

1. This belief in the universal appeal of cash awards is not unusual; it is prevalent in much of the incentive compensation literature. See, for example, Speck (1987), Balkin and Gomez-Mejia (1987), Swinford (1987), Sears (1985), Kerr (1982), and Opsahl and Dunnette (1979). A major sociological study by Bellah et al. (1985) supports this belief by finding that managers use monetary rewards as a standard by which to judge self-esteem (p. 66).

2. For example, Mason (1988) reports that in the 1975–1983 period, the compensation incentive plans of the 200 largest U.S. industrial corporations had an average life span of less than 18 months. Donaldson (1984, p. 134) finds in the 12 firms he studies that the compensation systems are undergoing periodic review and change as the managements "change direction or seek fresh stimuli."

3. Chris Argyris has written much about organizational factors that create defensive reasoning and deceptive actions. See, for example, Argyris (1985) and Argyris and Schon (1988).

APPENDIX

Research Method

The findings reported in this book are based on a field research study. This appendix reviews the purpose and evolution of the study and the methods used in the research.

Purpose of the Study

The general topic of control of profit centers in divisionalized corporations has been of central interest to me since the early 1970s, when I worked as a staff planning process designer and then as a profit center controller at Texas Instruments, Inc. These business experiences, and others I had later as a consultant, convinced me that a wide range of organizational devices that can be called controls affect the behavior of profit center personnel in both positive and negative ways and that understanding these effects is one of the keys to bringing about and judging management effectiveness.

I was also drawn to this subject because of a knowledge void—few researchers have chosen to study control systems at the profit center level of analysis. Study of profit centers is difficult: obtaining access to field sites is frustrating and often impossible; assembling data bases large enough to provide the statistical significance most academic journals look for is time-consuming and expensive; and controlling for all but a few variables of particular interest is virtually impossible because profit centers and the settings in which they operate are so varied. Despite these impediments, I concluded that the potential payoffs warranted the research difficulties and risks, and I decided to proceed into the field. However, this research would not have been possible without the luxury of several years in which to conduct it and generous financial support from the Division of Research at Harvard Business School.

I designed this project as a broadly conceived study of how profit centers are controlled in divisionalized corporations. My intent was to obtain an understanding of problems, practices, and issues that I could write in a form that would be useful to both managers and researchers. In the interviews, I asked questions about many behavior-influencing devices. These included planning and budgeting processes, definitions of managerial authorities and responsibilities, approvals needed for spending money and hiring people, incentive compensation agreements, and coverage by internal and external auditors.

Gradually I narrowed my focus of investigation. I chose the motivating-contract theme because I found I could explain most of my most important findings under this rubric. The rewards-for-results contracts exist in all the corporations I studied, and they are interesting because they vary—sometimes markedly—across the corporations and profit centers. Managers are almost invariably interested in talking about their firms' motivational contracts. Many corporate managers were uneasy about their contract choices; virtually all the profit center managers reported that the contracts had significant effects on their behavior, and many of them had complaints about how they were being motivated.

Research Design

My original plan was to study 48 profit centers—four in each of 12 corporations. I chose the corporate sample size of 12 because it was small enough to allow me to complete an intensive investigation in the time I had available (three years), yet large enough to ensure that the findings would not depend on the unique experiences of a few corporations. I chose to study four profit centers in each corporation so I could focus on two levels of analysis: corporate and profit center. I wanted to determine the extent to which the control practices varied across the profit centers within each corporation as well as how they varied across corporations.

My selection of corporations was somewhat purposive and somewhat opportunistic. It was purposive in that I approached a diverse set of divisionalized corporations. Diversity was important because I was developing theory grounded in the lived experiences of those making the decisions.[1] To make this theory as rich as possible and to increase the possibility that it could be widely applied, I wanted to observe as full a range of contract alternatives and relevant relationships as possible. The sample selection was somewhat opportunistic in that I used personal contacts and those of my colleagues to elicit the corporations' interest.

I did not consider approaching just any corporation, however. I requested participation only from arguably well-run, publicly held corporations headquartered in the United States. I approached only corporations that were arguably well run because the managers of corporations that have recently enjoyed at least several years of good economic health are more likely to have thought through the issues involved in motivating profit center managers, and more likely to be able to explain them. I focused on publicly held corporations because they were more likely to face stock-market pressures that, critics have maintained, lead to management myopia. And I limited the study to U.S.-based corporations to minimize travel expenses and to control for a broad range of legal and cultural factors that would have limited my ability to synthesize my observations.

I began the project in the summer of 1985 by requesting research access to several corporations through a letter to a senior corporate officer, generally the CFO or CEO. This letter (shown in Figure A-1) explained the broad questions I was investigating, described the cooperation I was request-

FIGURE A-1
Letter Requesting Research Access

HARVARD UNIVERSITY

GRADUATE SCHOOL OF BUSINESS ADMINISTRATION

GEORGE F. BAKER FOUNDATION

KENNETH A. MERCHANT
Associate Professor of Business Administration

SOLDIERS FIELD
BOSTON, MASSACHUSETTS 02163
617-495-6791
FAX: 617-495-6001

December 1, 1986

(Name)
Corporation name
Address

Dear (Name):

I am writing to ask you if you would be willing to have (Corporation name) participate in my research study on control of profit centers in divisionalized corporations. (Corporation name) is a very appealing company for me to include in my study because ...

Here are some of the general questions I am exploring:

1. How do upper-level managers endeavor to maintain good control over lower-level profit centers? How much emphasis is placed on each of the various forms of controls (for example, measurement/reward, policies and procedures, reviews/approvals of planned actions, internal audits)? Does the emphasis differ in profit centers of different types (for example, depending on business, mission)?

2. How is the control vs. autonomy tradeoff addressed?

3. How are performance targets set? How is the balance struck between top-down and bottom-up planning? Do the performance targets reflect the most likely outcomes, or are they set to be especially challenging or relatively easy to achieve?

4. To what extent are profit center managers held accountable for performance areas over which they do not have complete control?

5. What, if anything, is done to protect against managers' overemphasizing short-term results?

6. How do the profit center managers react to the controls placed on them? Do they feel a positive team spirit? Or do they have a potentially harmful spirit, evidenced, for example, by circumvention of controls or biasing of performance indicators and targets: Do they have negative feelings, such as frustration?

FIGURE A-1 (*Continued*)

In each firm I am studying, I focus my attention on four lower-level profit centers chosen from different parts of the company. In order to understand how these profit centers are controlled and with what effects, I need to conduct interviews with the profit center managers, their immediate superiors, and personnel at corporate headquarters who are knowledgeable about the corporation's overall control system and processes. I also need to review written company records, including planning and budgeting manuals, descriptions of information systems and administrative processes, and relevant interoffice memos and reports. It would be useful also to have access to actual plans, operating reports, and compensation agreements. If these interviews provide some interesting findings, I might like to test the generality of the findings by sending some short questionnaires to a broader sample of managers.

I have chosen this design because I think it is the most efficient for me and least burdensome for you. I expect that I would be on-site at various (Corporation name) locations for a total of about a week. I have research funding to cover all my expenses.

If you participate in the study, I will promise you the following:

- My ideas as to how your control system choices are similar and different from other companies I am studying and with what effects.

- A copy of my final research report which I expect will be published in book form. The working title is "Profit Centers: Performance Measurement and Control."

In all of the writings, the identities of the firms studied will be completely disguised unless I receive permission to remove the disguise. All information will be treated with utmost care and confidentiality. I have no plans to use any (Corporation name) material for preparation of a teaching case, although it is possible that such a case might at a later date be seen by both of us as useful byproduct.

My schedule is very flexible, and the interviews could be conducted anytime in the winter or spring that is convenient for you. I will call you in a couple of weeks to see how to proceed. Thank you for your consideration.

Sincerely,

Kenneth A. Merchant

KAM/d

ing, and listed my promises of anonymity and descriptions of the findings. I followed up this letter several weeks later with a telephone call.

Approximately half of the corporations whose cooperation I solicited agreed to participate. Most of those that declined explained that their managers did not have time to talk, either because of a recent reorganization, a recent acquisition, or a takeover threat.

The firms that agreed to participate were diverse. They ranged in size from $40 million to nearly $10 billion in annual sales (median = $2.6 billion). They were in different businesses, so none of them competed with any of the others to any significant extent. They also showed wide variation in a number of other ways, including the following: service versus manufacturing industries, capital-intensive versus labor-intensive production processes, high-technology versus low-technology products, rapid growth versus stability, varying customer bases (government versus commercial, consumer versus industrial marketing), and degree of diversification.

In each firm that agreed to participate, interviews were conducted first with corporate-level managers. Always included were the chief financial officer and/or controller, and among those interviewed in some firms were top-level general managers (chairman, president, chief executive officer, chief operating officer), staff officers (vice president–administration, vice president–planning, treasurer), and other financial staff (assistant controller, director of internal audit). The corporate interviews were used to gather information on the firm's businesses, its organization, its current business situation, and its control systems, including planning, budgeting, measurement, and incentive compensation, as they were applied to profit centers within the firm.

During these interviews, a small sample of profit centers (three to six) was chosen for further study.[2] I asked that the profit center managers have authority over the primary business functions of marketing and operations. I imposed no constraints on location except that I wished to conduct the interviews within North America. I allowed the number of profit centers selected to vary from the target of four as long as a cross-section of the North America-based profit centers in the corporation was included.

Like the corporate sample, the sample of 54 profit centers was diverse. The profit centers were in many industries. Their annual revenues ranged from $360,000 to $1.1 billion; the median was $58 million, and the average was $152 million. And their managers' authority ranged from being nearly complete, because the managers had almost total control of the operations that affected the profit centers' results, to highly restricted, because they relied on the use of many shared resources.

In each profit center studied, interviews were conducted with the profit center manager and, where possible, his or her immediate superior, controllers at both organizational levels, and other functional managers from whom useful information could be gathered. Most of the interviews were one hour in length, but the interviews with profit center managers typically took two hours, and some corporate interviews ran three or more hours. Some people were interviewed more than once.

Table A-1 shows the number of people interviewed in each corporation, classified according to role, and the number of hours of interviews conducted. Two hundred and three individuals were interviewed, in 311 meeting hours.

Two interviewers were present at a majority of the interviews. With only rare exceptions, we met with each interviewee individually so that we could cross-check the responses for accuracy and detail. In both the corporate and profit center interviews, I gathered as many relevant internal documents as I could as a further accuracy check on the interview data. These documents included accounting manuals, planning manuals, operating statements, descriptions of compensation agreements, consultants' reports, internal studies, and interoffice memoranda.

Later, after I had learned of the extent of earnings-management behavior at profit center organization levels, I sent a questionnaire (shown in Figure A-2) to the most senior

TABLE A-1
Summary of Interviews Conducted

Corporation	Number of People Interviewed (Interview Hours in Parentheses)							
	Corporate Level			Level of Immediate Superior		Profit Center Level		
	General Manager	*Control Staff*	*Other Staff*	*General Manager*	*Control Staff*	*General Manager*	*Control Staff*	*Total*
A	1(3)	2(4)	1(1)	4(6)	2(2)	5(10)	5(7)	20(33)
B	1(1)	2(5)	5(5)	2(2)	3(5)	3(3)	3(3)	19(24)
C	1(2)	1(3)	3(5)	1(1)	2(2)	6(13)	3(4)	17(30)
D	1(1)	3(6)	—	2(3)	2(2)	4(8)	4(5)	16(25)
E	—	4(6)	3(5)	3(3)	4(4)	6(11)	4(6)	24(35)
F	—	2(3)	4(4)	7(8)	4(4)	6(11)	—	23(30)
G	2(3)	1(2)	—	N/A		4(11)	1(1)	8(17)
H	1(1)	1(3)	—	2(3)	—	5(10)	2(2)	11(19)
J	—	2(5)	3(3)	2(3)	3(4)	5(11)	4(4)	19(30)
K	—	3(6)	2(3)	2(2)	5(7)	3(6)	1(2)	16(26)
L	1(2)	3(5)	2(2)	3(2)	1(1)	5(10)	3(3)	18(25)
M	—	5(9)	1(1)	1(1)	1(1)	2(3)	2(2)	12(17)
Totals	8(13)	29(57)	24(29)	29(34)	27(32)	54(107)	32(39)	203(311)

FIGURE A-2
Questionnaire Sent to Corporate Financial Officers

QUESTIONNAIRE ON THE ACCEPTABILITY OF SHORT-TERM EARNINGS MANAGEMENT PRACTICES

Division general managers engage in many practices intended to improve short-term operating results. Some of these practices are clearly acceptable. Others are judged by some or most companies to be unacceptable, although judgments as to the degree of severity of the infraction can vary widely. This questionnaire asks you to indicate how easy certain earnings management practices are to detect and whether or not they are felt to be acceptable in your corporation. Your responses will be compared with those from managers in other corporations.

All responses will be held strictly confidential.

Corporation: ______________________

Respondent: ______________________

FIGURE A-2 (*Continued*)

I. The first part of the questionnaire deals with your ability to detect managers' use of various earnings management practices. Detection can be achieved through any of a number of means, such as analysis of accounting records, examination of auditors' reports or communication with division controllers.

For each practice described on the next two pages, please indicate whether or not you are concerned about the practice and, if you are concerned, how easy it would be to detect it. Use the following scale:

A. The practice concerns me:

1. Very easy to detect. I would know right away.

2 - Easy to detect. I would become aware of the practice as soon as its effect reached a non-trivial amount (say, 1% of the profit center's pre-tax earnings).

3 - Somewhat difficult to detect. I would become aware of it if the effect was significant (say, 5% of the profit center's pre-tax earnings).

4 - Very difficult to detect. It would have to entail a large effect (say, 10% or more of the profit center's pre-tax earnings) before I could detect it.

B. The practice does not concern me:

5 - This is not something I monitor because it is an area totally within the general managers' discretion.

9 - Not applicable. This procedure is not practiced in any of our divisions (e.g., because of the characteristics of our business).

(circle one number for each)

EARNINGS MANAGEMENT PRACTICE	A. AREA OF CONCERN — Difficulty of detecting				B. NO CONCERN	
	Very Easy	Easy	Somewhat Difficult	Very Difficult	Within-GM Discretion	Not Applicable
1. Record services to be received next period as an expense in the current period	1	2	3	4	5	9
2. Change reserve balances (e.g. for inventory obsolescence, doubtful accounts)						
a. so that division profit for the period is increased	1	2	3	4	5	9
b. so that division profit for the period is decreased.	1	2	3	4	5	9
3. Use current period excess earnings (i.e. earnings exceeding budget targets) to invest in "pet" product-development projects that probably would not be funded if requests were made through normal channels.	1	2	3	4	5	9
4. Defer discretionary expenditures for two months (and into the next accounting period), in order for the profit center to reach its:						
a. quarterly earnings target	1	2	3	4	5	9
b. annual earnings target	1	2	3	4	5	9

FIGURE A-2 (*Continued*)

(circle one number for each)

EARNINGS MANAGEMENT PRACTICE	A. AREAS OF CONCERN — Difficulty of detecting: Very Easy	Easy	Somewhat Difficult	Very Difficult	B. NO CONCERN: Within-GM Discretion	Not Applicable
5. Offer more favorable terms of sales (e.g. discounts, liberal payment terms) at the end of a quarter to pull sales from the next quarter into the current quarter . . .	1	2	3	4	5	9
6. Order manufacturing to work overtime so that everything possible can be shipped before the end of the quarter	1	2	3	4	5	9
7. Sell excess assets at a profit	1	2	3	4	5	9
8. Record an expense in the period subsequent to the one during which the goods or services are consumed:						
a. by failing to record an invoice	1	2	3	4	5	9
b. by arranging with a supplier to delay receipt of an invoice	1	2	3	4	5	9
9. Increase discretionary expenditures because results for the period are above budget	1	2	3	4	5	9

II. This part of the questionnaire includes short descriptions of several specific earnings management practices. Please indicate, using the following scale, how each of the practices would be regarded in your company:

1 - Acceptable practice.

2 - Questionable practice. We do not encourage it, but it is tolerated.

3 - Minor infraction. The manager would be warned not to engage in the practice again.

4 - Serious infraction. The manager would be severely reprimanded.

5 - Totally unacceptable. The manager would be fired.

The impact of some practices is given as a percentage of division Profit Before Tax (PBT). Assume that the division in question accounts for 10% of your corporation's earnings.

Answer each question separately. (Assume the incidents are independent.)

FIGURE A-2 (*Continued*)

EARNINGS MANAGEMENT PRACTICE	JUDGMENT OF ACCEPTABILITY (circle one number for each)				
	Acceptable Practice	Questionable Practice	Minor Infraction	Serious Infraction	Totally Unacceptable
1. The division's buildings were scheduled to be painted in 1988. Since the division's earnings were way ahead of budget in 1987, however, the division general manager (GM) decided to have the work done in 1987. Amount: 1% of annual division PBT	1	2	3	4	5
2. The GM ordered his employees to defer all discretionary expenditures (e.g., travel, advertising, hiring, maintenance) into the next accounting period so that his division could make its budgeted profit targets. Expected amount of deferral: 1% of division PBT					
a. The expenses were postponed from February and March until April in order to make the first quarter target	1	2	3	4	5
b. The expenses were postponed from November and December until January in order to make the annual target.	1	2	3	4	5
3. On December 15, a clerk in the division placed an order for $3,000 worth of office supplies and the supplies were delivered on December 29. This order was a mistake because the division GM had ordered that no discretionary expenses be incurred for the remainder of the fiscal year, and the supplies were not urgently needed. The company's accounting policy manual states that office supplies are to be recorded as an expense when delivered. The division GM learned what had happened, however, and to correct the mistake, he instructed the accounting department not to record the invoice until February	1	2	3	4	5

	Acceptable Practice	Questionable Practice	Minor Infraction	Serious Infraction	Totally Unacceptable
4. In September, the GM realized that the division would need strong performance in the last quarter of the year in order to reach its budget targets.					
a. He decided to implement a sales program offering liberal payment terms to pull some sales that would normally occur next year into the current year; customers accepting delivery in the 4th quarter would not have to pay the invoice for 120 days	1	2	3	4	5
b. He ordered manufacturing to work overtime in December so that everything possible could be shipped by the end of the year	1	2	3	4	5
c. He sold some excess assets and realized profit of 0.5% of annual division PBT	1	2	3	4	5
5. At the beginning of December, 1986, the GM realized that the division would exceed its budgeted profit targets for the year					
a. He ordered his controller to prepay some expenses (e.g., hotel rooms, exhibit expense) for a major trade show to be held in March 1987 and to book them as 1986 expense. Amount: 0.5% of annual division PBT.	1	2	3	4	5
b. He ordered his controller to develop the rationale for increasing the reserve for inventory obsolescence. By taking a pessimistic view of future market prospects, the controller was able to identify some finished goods (worth 5% of annual division PBT) that conservative accounting would say should be fully reserved (i.e., written off), even though the GM was fairly confident the inventory would still be sold at a later date at close to full price. . .	1	2	3	4	5

FIGURE A-2 (*Continued*)

	Acceptable Practice	Questionable Practice	Minor Infraction	Serious Infraction	Totally Unacceptable
6. The next year, the division described in question 5b sold 70% of the written-off inventory, and a customer had indicated some interest in buying the rest of that inventory the following year. The GM ordered his controller to prepare the rationale for reducing the reserve for obsolescence by 1.5% of annual division PBT (i.e., writing up the remaining 30% of the previously written off goods to full cost). The GM's motivation for recapturing the profit was:					
a. to be able to continue working on some important product development projects that might have had to be delayed due to budget constraints	1	2	3	4	5
b. to make budgeted profit targets	1	2	3	4	5
7. In November of 1986, the division was straining to meet budget. The GM called the engagement partner of a consulting firm that was doing some work for the division and asked that the firm delay sending an invoice for work done until next year. The partner agreed. Estimated work done but not invoiced in 1986:					
a. 0.2 % of annual division PBT	1	2	3	4	5
b. 5% of annual division PBT	1	2	3	4	5

III. This part of the questionnaire asks for some relevant perceptions and attitudes. Please indicate the extent to which you agree or disagree with each of the following statements. (Circle one number in each row.)

	Strongly Disagree	Disagree	Neither Agree nor Disagree	Agree	Strongly Agree
1. Most GMs in my corporation are under considerable profit pressure	1	2	3	4	5
2. The stock market favors companies with a steady pattern of growth as compared to those with an irregular pattern of growth even if the long-term growth rates are the same.	1	2	3	4	5
3. To be safe, most GMs in my corporation usually set two levels of standards; one between themselves and their boss, and another between themselves and their subordinates	1	2	3	4	5
4. Most GMs in my corporation have their ways of "smoothing" income	1	2	3	4	5
5. In my corporation, internal and external auditors provide effective protection against profit center personnel engaging in unacceptable earnings management activities.	1	2	3	4	5
6. Allowing slack in budgets is good because it allows GMs to do useful things that cannot be officially approved.	1	2	3	4	5
7. To protect themselves, most GMs submit budgets that can be safely attained.	1	2	3	4	5

FIGURE A-2 (*Continued*)

	Strongly Disagree	Disagree	Neither Agree nor Disagree	Agree	Strongly Agree
8. At present, my corporation's profit performance is below the level that top management considers acceptable	1	2	3	4	5
9. In good business times, top management is willing to accept a reasonable level of slack in the operating budgets.	1	2	3	4	5
10. It is preferable that any slack in the corporation be held only at corporate level.	1	2	3	4	5
11. Annual profit budgets are commitments from our GMs to the corporation. They are expected to make their targets	1	2	3	4	5

	Never	Rarely	Sometimes	Frequently
12. My corporation makes public forecasts of earnings (or EPS)	1	2	3	4

a. If forecasts are made, the amount is: (check one)

___ Less than the earnings in the corporation's consolidated plan.

___ Equal to the earnings in the corporation's consolidated plan.

___ Greater than the earnings in the corporation's consolidated plan.

___ Not applicable.

Comments:
(optional)

financial executive with whom I had contact (generally the CFO). The primary purpose of this questionnaire was to verify some of the interview data collected, particularly about the types of earnings-management activities corporate managers consider acceptable.

Synthesis of Findings

The purpose of the research was to develop theory, but the theory development did not come exclusively after the data had been collected. Many of my views evolved over time. Some of the data confirmed views I held before doing the research, whereas other data surprised me and caused me to modify my beliefs or enrich them.

Early in the research, I was able to identify some common practices, such as weighting budget targets heavily and setting highly achievable targets. When the data converged early, I used later interviews to test the limits of the finding and to explore the reasons behind it.

In other cases, however, particularly where there were major differences across firms, additional interviews seemingly added only more variety and complexity. In these cases, I was able to make sense of some of the data only after many interviews and repeated reviews of my interview notes in which I sorted the data in multiple ways. On several occasions, I was forced to go back to firms for more information because the alternate data sorts revealed that data that had now become relevant were missing.

Limitations and Suggestions for Further Research

Because so little evidence has been gathered at profit center levels in divisionalized corporations, this study must be described as exploratory. To keep the findings in perspective, it is important to keep in mind the nature of the study and its limitations. One is a sample limitation. The findings are based on observations in only 12 corporations, which obviously do not span all industries. It is likely that other practices and rationales exist in other settings.

Second, I studied only a small sample of the profit centers in each corporation. I intended that the profit centers chosen for study represent a cross-section of profit centers in the firm. In several of the companies (but not all), however, corporate managers appeared to steer me away from managers in profit centers that were not performing well, giving reasons such as "they're too busy," or "the manager is too new." In some instances, it was possible to gather second-hand information on the poorer-performing profit centers, but it remains likely that the sample of 54 profit centers contains at least a slight underrepresentation of profit centers in difficulty.

Third, I conducted most of the interviews during a relatively favorable economic period. Since short-term pressure tends to become tighter when economic conditions worsen, a similar study conducted during a recession would probably report a somewhat different, and perhaps more striking, data distribution.

Finally, some would criticize my use of interviews for data collection with the observation that managers' responses are likely to be biased. I acknowledge this possibility. However, I was able to follow up the responses in some depth if the logic was not internally consistent; I posed the questions to multiple respondents to cross-check the answers for reliability; and I examined source documents where possible as a further cross-check. The number of conflicts I discovered in facts or perceptions was minimal.

Although these limitations are significant, this study was not designed to be the final word on the topic. Our knowledge about the important issues related to the design of motivational contracts for profit center managers is far from complete or reliable. Much work remains.

Perhaps most important, the issues raised and explored in this study need more field–study exploration in other samples of firms. Longitudinal studies of the phenomena studied here could provide more powerful insights and more convincing evidence about the causal factors at work. And in-depth, one-firm studies can be used to discover more about how and why the motivating-contract practices vary across profit centers within a firm.

With the current base of knowledge, surveys can probably be used to measure the variables identified as relevant in this study. Data collected in this way would yield larger data bases that could be used to understand better how and how strongly the variables are related.

The primary contribution of this study is useful exploratory theory. The trade-off framework developed includes many variables that should be part of a theory describing the use of motivating contracts in divisionalized corporations. The findings should be useful for informing managers who are making contract design decisions about the state of the art of contract design. They should also help researchers who are developing principal–agent models of organizational behavior identify the parameters that should eventually be included in the models and the relationships among them.

NOTES

1. Glaser and Strauss (1967); Glaser (1978).

2. Only two profit center managers were interviewed in corporation M (consumer durables), but five were actually selected for study in the corporate interviews. One group vice president later asked that he and his profit center managers be excused from participation because of a heavy workload.

References

Accounting Principles Board. *Basic Concepts and Accounting Principles Underlying Financial Statements of Business Enterprises.* Statement #4, 1970.

Anthony, R.N. *The Management Control Function.* Boston: Harvard Business School Press, 1988.

———. *Management Accounting,* 3rd edition. Homewood, Ill.: Richard D. Irwin, 1964.

Antle, R., and J.S. Demski. "The Controllability Principle in Responsibility Accounting." *Accounting Review* LXII (October 1988), pp. 700–718.

Antle, R., and A. Smith. "An Empirical Investigation of the Relative Performance Evaluation of Corporate Executives." *Journal of Accounting Research* 24 (Spring 1986), pp. 1–39.

Argyris, C. *Strategy, Change and Defensive Routines.* Cambridge, Mass.: Ballinger, 1985.

Argyris, C., and D. Schon. "Reciprocal Integrity: Creating Conditions That Encourage Personal and Organizational Integrity." In *Executive Integrity,* edited by S. Srivastva and Associates. San Francisco, Cal.: Jossey-Bass, pp. 197–222.

Arrow, K.J. "Control in Large Organizations." In *Behavioral Aspects of Accounting,* edited by M. Schiff and A.Y. Lewin. Englewood Cliffs, N.J.: Prentice-Hall, 1974.

Atkinson, A.A., and R.S. Kaplan. *Advanced Management Accounting,* 2d edition. Englewood Cliffs, N.J.: Prentice-Hall, 1989.

Baber, W.R., and J.A. Haggard. "Management's Use of Discretionary Spending To Manipulate Financial Accounting Income: The Case of Research and Development." Unpublished working paper, Columbia University Graduate School of Business, December 1987.

Baiman, S., and J.S. Demski. "Economically Optimal Performance Evaluation and Control Systems." *Journal of Accounting Research* (Supplement 1980), pp. 184–220.

Baiman, S., and J. Noel. "Noncontrollable Costs and Responsibility Accounting." *Journal of Accounting Research* 23 (Autumn 1985), pp. 486–501.

Baker, G.P., M.C. Jensen, and K.J. Murphy. "Compensation and Incentives: Practice vs. Theory." *Journal of Finance* XLIII (July 1988), pp. 593–616.

Balkin, D.B., and L.R. Gomez-Mejia. "The Strategic Use of Short-Term and Long-

Term Pay Incentives in the High-Technology Industry." In *New Perspectives on Compensation,* edited by D.B. Balkin and L.R. Gomez-Mejia. Englewood Cliffs, N.J.: Prentice-Hall, 1987, pp. 237–246.

Barrett, E.M., and L.B. Fraser III. "Conflicting Roles in Budgeting for Operations." *Harvard Business Review* 55 (July–August 1977), pp. 137–146.

Bart, C.K. "Budgeting Gamesmanship." *The Academy of Management Executive* II (1988), pp. 285–294.

Beaver, W.H. *Financial Reporting: An Accounting Revolution.* Englewood Cliffs, N.J.: Prentice-Hall, 1981.

Bellah, R.N., R. Madsen, W.M. Sullivan, A. Swidler, and S.M. Tipton. *Habits of the Heart: Individualism and Commitment in American Life.* Berkeley: University of California Press, 1985.

"Bonus Program is Boosting Cash Flow." *Industry Week,* January 7, 1980, pp. 43–48.

Brickley, J.A., S. Bhagat, and R.C. Lease. "The Impact of Long-Range Managerial Compensation Plans on Shareholder Wealth." *Journal of Accounting and Economics* 7 (1985), pp. 115–129.

Brindisi, L.J., Jr. "Creating Shareholder Value: A New Mission for Executive Compensation." *Midland Corporate Finance Journal* 2 (Winter 1985), pp. 56–66.

Brown, P., G. Foster, and E. Noreen. *Security Analyst Multi-Year Earnings Forecasts and the Capital Market.* Sarasota, Fla.: American Accounting Association, 1985.

Bruns, W.J., Jr., and K.A. Merchant. "The Dangerous Morality of Managing Earnings." Unpublished working paper, Harvard Business School, November 1988.

Chakravarty, S.N. "Unreal Accounting." *Forbes,* November 16, 1987, pp. 74–75.

Chesley, G.R., "Elicitation of Subjective Probabilities." *Accounting Review* L (April 1975), pp. 325–337.

Cheung, S.N.S. "The Contractual Nature of the Firm." *Journal of Law and Economics* 26 (April 1983), pp. 1–21.

Chow, C.W. "The Effects of Job Standard Tightness and Compensation Scheme on Performance: An Exploration of Linkages." *Accounting Review* LVII (October 1983), pp. 667–685.

"Cooking the Books." *Dun's Business Month* 120 (January 1983), p. 40.

Costello, T.W., and S.S. Zalkind. *Psychology in Administration.* Englewood Cliffs, N.J.: Prentice-Hall, 1963.

Culbert, S.A., and J.J. McDonough. *The Invisible War: Pursuing Self-Interests at Work.* New York: John Wiley & Sons, 1980.

Curran, J.J. "Companies That Rob the Future." *Fortune,* July 4, 1988, pp. 84–89.

Curtis, D.A. "The Modern American Accounting System." *Financial Executive* 1 (January/February 1985), pp. 58–62.

Dalton, G.W. "Motivation and Control in Organizatons." In *Motivation and Control in Organizations,* edited by G.W. Dalton and P.R. Lawrence. Homewood, Ill.: Richard D. Irwin, and the Dorsey Press, 1971, pp. 1–35.

DeAngelo, L.E. "Managerial Competition, Information Costs, and Corporate Governance: The Use of Accounting Performance Measures in Proxy Contests." *Journal of Accounting and Economics* 10 (January 1988), pp. 3–36.

Dearden, J. "Measuring Profit Center Managers." *Harvard Business Review* 65 (September–October 1987), pp. 84–88.

———. "The Case Against ROI Control." *Harvard Business Review* 47 (May–June 1969), pp. 124–135.

Dobrzynski, J.H. "The Lessons of the RJR Free-For-All." *Business Week,* December 19, 1988, pp. 30–31.

Donaldson, G. *Managing Corporate Wealth: The Operations of a Comprehensive Financial Goals System.* New York: Praeger, 1984.

Dreyfus, P. "Go with the (Cash) Flow." *Institutional Investor,* August 1988, pp. 55–59.

Dunbar, R.L.M. "Budgeting for Control." *Administrative Science Quarterly* 16 (March 1971), pp. 88–96.

Eaton, J., and H.S. Rosen. "Agency, Delayed Compensation, and the Structure of Executive Remuneration." *Journal of Finance* XXXVIII (December 1983), pp. 1489–1505.

Eccles, R.G. *The Transfer Pricing Problem: A Theory for Practice.* Lexington, Mass.: Lexington Books, 1985.

Edwards, J.B. *The Use of Performance Measures.* Montvale, N.J.: National Association of Accountants, 1986.

Ehrenberg, R.G., and G.T. Milkovich. "Compensation and Firm Performance." In *Human Resources and the Performance of the Firm,* edited by M. Kleiner et al. Madison: Industrial Relations Research Association, University of Wisconsin, 1987, pp. 87–122.

Elliott, J., and W. Shaw. "Big Baths as Accounting Procedures to Manage Perceptions," *Journal of Accounting Research* (Supplement 1988), forthcoming.

Etzioni, A. *The Moral Dimension: Toward a New Economics.* New York: Free Press, 1988.

Fama, E.F. "Agency Problems and the Theory of the Firm." *Journal of Political Economy* 88 (1980), pp. 288–307.

Florkowski, G.W. "The Organizational Impact of Profit Sharing." *Academy of Management Review* 12 (1987), pp. 622–636.

Foulkes, F.K. "Why Bonus Plans Are Good For Business." *Personnel* 62 (August 1985), pp. 72–73.

Fried, D., M. Schiff, and A. Sondhi. "A Closer Look at 'Surprise Writeoffs.' " In *Proceedings of the 1986 Accounting Research Convocation,* edited by R.W. Ingram. Tuscaloosa, Ala.: University of Alabama, 1986, pp. 35–39.

Glaser, B.G. *Theoretical Sensitivity: Advances in the Methodology of Grounded Theory.* Mill Valley, Cal.: Sociology Press, 1978.

Glaser, B.G., and A.L. Strauss. *The Discovery of Grounded Theory.* Chicago: Aldine, 1967.

Greenberg, J. "Determinants of Perceived Fairness of Performance Evaluations." *Journal of Applied Psychology* 7 (1986), pp. 340–342.

Hamner, W.C. "How to Ruin Motivation with Pay." *Compensation Review* 7 (1975), pp. 17–27.

Hand, J.R.M. "A Test of the Extended Functional Hypothesis." Unpublished working paper, University of Chicago Graduate School of Business, September 1988.

Hart, O., and B. Holmstrom. "The Theory of Contracts." In *Advances in Economic Theory,* edited by T. Bewley. Cambridge, Eng.: Cambridge University Press, 1987.

Hay Group. *Contingent Compensation Survey.* Philadelphia, Penn.: Hay Group, 1988.

Hayes, R.H., and W.J. Abernathy. "Managing Our Way to Economic Decline." *Harvard Business Review* 58 (July–August 1980), pp. 67–77.

Hays, L. "Du Pont Will Start Pay-Incentive Plan for All Fibers Business Workers in '89." *The Wall Street Journal,* October 6, 1988, p. A4.

Healy, P. "The Effect of Bonus Schemes on Accounting Decisions." *Journal of Accounting and Economics* 7 (1985), pp. 85–107.

Hector, G. "Yes, You *Can* Manage Long Term." *Fortune* (November 21, 1988), pp. 64–76.

Henderson, R.I. *Compensation Management: Rewarding Performance.* Reston, Va.: Reston Publishing, 1985.

Henrici, S. "The Perversity, Peril and Pathos of ROI." *Financial Analysts Journal* (September–October 1983), pp. 79–80.

Hertenstein, J.H. "Management Control System Change: The Adoption of Inflation Accounting." In *Accounting and Management: Field Study Perspectives,* edited by W.J. Bruns, Jr., and R.S. Kaplan. Boston: Harvard Business School Press, 1987, pp. 17–48.

Hill, C.W.L., M.A. Hitt, and R.E. Hoskisson. "Declining U.S. Competitiveness: Reflections on a Crisis." *The Academy of Management Executive* II (1988), pp. 51–60.

Hirschman, A.O. *Exit, Voice and Loyalty: Responses to Decline in Firms, Organizations, and States.* Cambridge, Mass.: Harvard University Press, 1970.

Hirst, M.K. "Accounting Information and the Evaluation of Subordinate Performance: A Situational Approach." *Accounting Review* LVI (October 1981), pp. 771–784.

Hofstede, G.H. *The Game of Budget Control.* Assen, The Netherlands: Van Gorcum, 1967.

Holmstrom, B.R. "Incentive Compensation: Practical Design from a Theory Point of View." In *Incentives, Cooperation and Risk Sharing,* edited by H.R. Nalbantian. Totowa, N.J.: Rowman & Littlefield, 1987, pp. 176–185.

Holmstrom, B.R., and J. Tirole. "The Theory of the Firm." In *Handbook of Industrial Organization,* edited by R. Schmalensee and R. Willig. Amsterdam: North Holland, 1989.

Hopwood, A. *Accounting and Human Behaviour.* Englewood Cliffs, N.J.: Prentice-Hall, 1974.

Horngren, C.T. "Cost and Management Accounting: Yesterday and Today." In *Research and Current Issues in Management Accounting,* edited by A. Hopwood and M. Bromwich. London: Pitman, 1986, pp. 31–43.

Horngren, C.T., and G. Foster. *Cost Accounting: A Managerial Emphasis.* Englewood Cliffs, N.J.: Prentice-Hall, 1987.

Hrebiniak, L.G., and W.F. Joyce. "The Strategic Importance of Managing Myopia." *Sloan Management Review* (Fall 1986), pp. 5–14.

Hudson, R.L. "SEC Charges Fudging of Corporate Figures is a Growing Practice." *The Wall Street Journal,* June 2, 1983, p. 1.

Ivancevich, J.M., A.D. Szilagyi, Jr., and M.J. Wallace, Jr. *Organizational Behavior and Performance.* Santa Monica, Cal.: Goodyear Publishing, 1977.

Jensen, M.C. "Takeovers: Their Causes and Consequences." *Journal of Economic Perspectives* 2 (Winter 1988), pp. 21–48.

———. "Agency Costs of Free Cash Flow, Corporate Finance and Takeovers." *American Economic Review* 76 (May 1986), pp. 323–329.

Jensen, M.C., and W.H. Meckling. "Theory of the Firm: Managerial Behavior, Agency Costs and Ownership Structure." *Journal of Financial Economics* 3 (1976), pp. 305–360.

Jensen, M.C., and K.J. Murphy. "Performance Pay and Top Management Incentives." Working paper #88-059, Harvard Business School, May 1988.

Jereski, L. "Wishful Thinking by the Numbers." *Forbes,* October 19, 1987, p. 67.

Johnson, H.T., and D.A. Loewe. "How Weyerhaeuser Manages Corporate Overhead Costs." *Management Accounting* (August 1987), pp. 20–26.

Kanter, R.M. "From Status to Contribution: Some Organizational Implications of the Changing Basis for Pay." *Personnel* (January 1987), pp. 12–37.

———. *Men and Women of the Corporation.* New York: Basic Books, 1979.

Kaplan, E. "Wall Street Zeros In On Cash Flow." *Dun's Business Month* (July 1985), pp. 40–41.

Kendrick, J.W. "Group Financial Incentives: An Evaluation," In *Incentives, Cooperation and Risk Sharing,* edited by H.R. Nalbantian. Totowa, N.J.: Rowman & Littlefield, 1987, pp. 120–136.

Kerr, J. "Assigning Managers on the Basis of the Life Cycle." *Journal of Business Strategy* 2 (Spring 1982), pp. 58–65.

Kohn, A. "Incentives Can Be Bad for Business." *Inc.* (January 1988), pp. 93–94.

Kopelman, R.E., and L. Reinharth. "Research Results: The Effect of Merit-Pay Practices on White Collar Performance." *Compensation Review* (1982), pp. 30–40.

Kotter, J.P. *The General Managers.* New York: Free Press, 1982.

Lambert, R.A., and D.F. Larcker. "Executive Compensation, Corporate Decision-Making and Shareholder Wealth: A Review of the Evidence." *Midland Corporate Finance Journal* 2 (Winter 1985), pp. 6–22.

Larcker, D. "Short-Term Compensation Contracts and Executive Expenditure Decisions: The Case of Commercial Banks." *Journal of Financial and Quantitative Analysis* 22 (March 1987), pp. 33–50.

———. "The Association between Performance Plan Adoption and Corporate Capital Investment." *Journal of Accounting and Economics* 5 (1983), pp. 3–30.

Leibenstein, H. *Inside the Firm: The Inefficiencies of Hierarchy.* Cambridge, Mass.: Harvard University Press, 1987.

Leventhal, G.S., J. Karuza, and W.R. Fry. "Beyond Fairness: A Theory of Allocation

Preferences." In *Justice and Social Interaction,* edited by G. Mikula. New York: Springer-Verlag, pp. 167–218.

Levinthal, D. "A Survey of Agency Models of Organizations." *Journal of Economic Behavior and Organization* 9 (1988), pp. 153–186.

Locke, E.A. "Toward a Theory of Task Motivation and Incentives." *Organizational Behavior and Human Performance* 3 (1968), pp. 157–189.

Locke, E.A., G.P. Latham, and M. Erez. "The Determinants of Goal Commitment." *Academy of Management Review* 13 (1988), pp. 23–39.

Locke, E.A., K.N. Shaw, L.M. Saari, and G.P. Latham. "Goal Setting and Task Performance: 1969–1980." *Psychological Bulletin* 90 (1981), pp. 125–152.

Longenecker, C.O., and D.A. Gioia. "Neglected at the Top—Executives Talk About Executive Appraisal." *Sloan Management Review* 29 (Winter 1988), pp. 41–47.

Lowe, E.A., and R.W. Shaw. "An Analysis of Managerial Biasing: Evidence from a Company's Budgeting Process." *The Journal of Management Studies* 5 (October 1968), pp. 304–315.

Maccoby, M. *The Gamesman.* New York: Free Press, 1986.

Maciarello, J.A. *Management Control Systems.* Englewood Cliffs, N.J.: Prentice-Hall, 1984.

Magee, R.P. *Advanced Managerial Accounting.* New York: Harper & Row, 1986.

Maher, M.W. "The Use of Relative Performance Evaluation in Organizations." In *Accounting and Management: Field Study Perspectives,* edited by W.J. Bruns, Jr., and R.S. Kaplan. Boston: Harvard Business School Press, 1987, pp. 295–315.

Mahoney, T. "Compensation Preferences of Managers." *Industrial Relations* 3 (1964), pp. 135–144.

"Management Bonuses: Do You Need Them?" *Chief Executive* (November 1979), pp. 18–21.

Martin, T.L., Jr. *Malice in Blunderland.* New York: McGraw-Hill, 1973.

Mason, K. "Four Ways to Overpay Yourself Enough." *Harvard Business Review* 66 (July–August 1988), pp. 69–74.

Mauriel, J.J., and R.N. Anthony. "Misevaluation of Investment Center Performance." *Harvard Business Review* 44 (March–April 1966), pp. 98–105.

McKeown, J.C. "An Empirical Test of a Model Proposed by Chambers." *Accounting Review* XLV (January 1971), pp. 12–29.

Mendenhall, R.R., and W.D. Nichols. "Bad News and Differential Market Reactions To Announcements of Earlier-Quarters Versus Fourth Quarter Earnings." *Journal of Accounting Research* (Supplement 1988), forthcoming.

Merchant, K.A. "The Effect of Financial Controls on Data Manipulation and Management Myopia." Working Paper #9-786-022, Harvard Business School, January 1989.

———. *Fraudulent and Questionable Financial Reporting: A Corporate Perspective.* Morristown, N.J.: Financial Executives Research Foundation, 1987.

———. *Control in Business Organizations.* Cambridge, Mass.: Ballinger, 1985.

Merchant, K.A., and W.J. Bruns, Jr. "Measurements to Cure Management Myopia." *Business Horizons* (May/June 1986), pp. 56–64.

"Merit Increases Will Shrink Next Year As Emphasis Shifts to Incentive Pay." *The Wall Street Journal,* September 15, 1987, p. 1.

Mihalek, P.H., A.J. Rich, and C.S. Smith. "Ethics and Management Accountants." *Management Accounting* (December 1987), pp. 34–36.

"More Than Ever, It's Management for the Short-Term." *Business Week,* November 24, 1986, pp. 92–93.

Nalbantian, H.R. "Incentive Compensation in Perspective." In *Incentives, Cooperation and Risk Sharing,* edited by H.R. Nalbantian. Totowa, N.J.: Rowman & Littlefield, 1987, pp. 3–46.

National Association of Accountants. *Measuring Entity Performance.* Statement on Management Accounting Number 4D. Montvale, N.J., January 3, 1986.

National Commission on Fraudulent Financial Reporting. *Report of the National Commission on Fraudulent Financial Reporting.* Washington, D.C.: National Commission on Fraudulent Financial Reporting, October 1987.

Newman, W.H., E.K. Warren, and A.R. McGill. *The Process of Management,* 6th ed. Englewood Cliffs, N.J.: Prentice-Hall, 1987.

Opsahl, R.L., and M.D. Dunnette. "The Role of Financial Compensation in Industrial Motivation." In *Compensation and Reward Perspectives,* edited by T.A. Mahoney. Homewood, Ill.: Richard D. Irwin, 1979, pp. 79–88.

Otley, D.T. "Budgeting for Management Control." *Management Accounting* (U.K.) (May 1987), pp. 20–21.

Palepu, K. "Predicting Takeover Targets: A Methodological and Empirical Analysis." *Journal of Accounting and Economics* 8 (1986), pp. 3–35.

Pearce, J.L. "Why Merit Pay Doesn't Work: Implications from Organization Theory." In *New Perspectives on Compensation,* edited by D.B. Balkin and L.R. Gomez-Mejia. Englewood Cliffs, N.J.: Prentice-Hall, 1987, pp. 169–178.

Rappaport, A. *Creating Shareholder Value: The New Standard for Business Performance.* New York: Free Press, 1986.

Reece, J.S., and W.R. Cool. "Measuring Investment Center Performance." *Harvard Business Review* 56 (May–June, 1978), pp. 28–49.

Reibstein, L. "More Employers Link Incentives to Unit Results." *The Wall Street Journal,* April 10, 1987, p. 25.

Rich, J.T., and J.A. Larson. "Why Some Long-Term Incentives Fail." In *Incentives, Cooperation and Risk Sharing,* edited by H.R. Nalbantian. Totowa, N.J.: Rowman & Littlefield, 1987, pp. 151–162.

Ridgway, V.F. "Dysfunctional Consequences of Performance Measures." In *Information for Decision Making,* edited by A. Rappaport. Englewood Cliffs, N.J.: Prentice-Hall, 1982, pp. 378–383.

Rockness, H.O. "Expectancy Theory in a Budgetary Setting: An Experimental Examination." *Accounting Review* LII (October 1977), pp. 893–903.

"A Roundtable Discussion of Management Compensation." *Midland Corporate Finance Journal* 2 (Winter 1985), pp. 23–55.

Schroeder, M. "Watching the Bottom Line Instead of the Clock." *Business Week,* November 7, 1988, pp. 134, 136.

Sears, D. "Make Employee Pay a Strategic Issue." *Financial Executive* (October 1984), pp. 40–43.

Sharfman, M.P., G. Wolf, R.B. Chase, and D.A. Tanski. "Antecedents of Organization Slack." *Academy of Management Review* 13 (1988), pp. 601–614.

Sibson, R.E. *Compensation.* New York: AMACOM, 1981.

Sibson & Company, Inc. *Boards, Company Performance and Executive Pay.* Princeton, N.J.: Sibson & Co., 1987.

Simons, R. "Planning, Control, and Uncertainty: A Process View." In *Accounting and Management: Field Study Perspectives,* edited by W.J. Bruns, Jr., and R.S. Kaplan. Boston: Harvard Business School Press, 1987, pp. 339–362.

Solomons, D. *Divisional Performance: Measurement and Control.* Homewood, Ill.: Richard D. Irwin, 1965.

Speck, R.W., Jr. "Management Compensation Planning in Diversified Companies." *Compensation and Benefits Review* (March/April 1987), pp. 26–33.

Staubus, G.J. *Making Accounting Decisions.* Houston: Scholars, 1977.

Stedry, A.C. *Budget Control and Cost Behaviour.* Englewood Cliffs, N.J.: Prentice-Hall, 1960.

Stedry, A.C., and E. Kay. "The Effects of Goal Difficulty on Performance: A Field Experiment." *Behavioral Science* 11 (November 1966), pp. 459–470.

Stein, J.C. "Takeover Threats and Managerial Myopia." *Journal of Political Economy* 96 (February 1988), pp. 61–80.

Stewart, B. "Performance Measurement and Management Incentive Compensation. *Midland Corporate Finance Journal* 2 (Winter 1985), pp. 76–81.

Swinford, D. "'Unbundling' Divisional Management Incentives." *Compensation and Benefits Review* 19 (November/December 1987), pp. 57–61. (Reprinted from *Management Review* [July 1987].)

Treynor, J.L. "The Financial Objective in the Widely Held Corporation." *Financial Analysis Journal* 37 (March–April 1981), pp. 68–71.

Ubelhart, M.C. "Business Strategy, Performance Measurement and Compensation." *Midland Corporate Finance Journal* 2 (Winter 1985), pp. 67–75.

Uyterhoeven, H.E.R. "General Managers in the Middle." *Harvard Business Review* 50 (March–April 1972), pp. 75–85.

Vancil, R.F. *Decentralization: Managerial Ambiguity by Design.* Homewood, Ill.: Dow Jones-Irwin, 1979.

Walsh, F. J., Jr. *Measuring Business-Unit Performance.* Research Bulletin No. 206. New York: The Conference Board, Inc., 1987.

Wang, P. "Claiming Tomorrow's Profits Today." *Forbes,* October 17, 1988, p. 78.

Wattenberg, B.J. "Their Deepest Concerns." *Business Month* (January 1988), pp. 27–35.

Weiss, A. "Incentives and Worker Behavior: Some Evidence." In *Incentives, Cooperation and Risk Sharing,* edited by H.R. Nalbantian. Totowa, N.J.: Rowman & Littlefield, 1987, pp. 137–150.

Williamson, O.E. *Corporate Control and Business Behavior.* Englewood Cliffs, N.J.: Prentice-Hall, 1970.

Wilson, S.R. "Motivating Managers with Money." *Business Horizons* XVI (April 1973), pp. 37–43.

Winter, R.E. "Trying to Streamline, Some Firms May Hurt Long-Term Prospects." *The Wall Street Journal,* January 8, 1987, p. 1.

Zimmerman, J.L. "The Costs and Benefits of Cost Allocations." *Accounting Review* LIV (July 1979), pp. 504–521.

INDEX

A

Accountability, authority and, 92, 95, 96, 108*n*4
Accounting earnings measures. *See also* Short-term bias problem
  controllability and, 87, 88–98, 104–107
  correlation with stock price, 191
  design of, 88–98
  inflation-adjusted, 56
  as performance measure, 46, 51–52, 58–59, *60*
  shareholder value and, 46
  short-term bias problem and, 59, *60*, 63
  vs. leading performance indicators, 69
  weighting of, important, 221
Accuracy. *See* Measurement accuracy
Achievability. *See* Budget targets; Developmental milestones, achievement of; Performance standards
Acquisitions, adjustments for, 121–122
Acts of nature, adjustments for, 125–126
Adjustments for uncontrollables, 87–107
  acquisitions and, 121–122
  acts of nature and, 125–126
  after measurement period, 87–88, 109–140
  benefits and costs of, 130–131
  bonus awards and, 116, 117
  changes in industry volume and, 122–123, 126, 127
  decision makers in, 117–118
  deemphasis of budget targets and, 137–140
  direction of, 129
  divestment and, 121–122
  excessive compensation and, 204–206
  favorable events and, 204–206
  foreign currency fluctuations and, 122, 126
  insurance program and, 121
  method of, 126–129
  no-adjustment philosophy and, 109
  operations consolidation and, 111
  purposes of, 113, 116–117
  symmetry in, 204–206
  top management and, 119–122
  trade-offs for subjectivity in, 109, 130–137
  upper reward cutoffs and, 202
  variety of factors adjusted for, 109, 113, *114–115*, 119–126
Allocation basis
  for bonus pool, 118, 149
  for bonus pool, and corporate performance, 149
  for corporate G&A expenses, 100, 101–102, 108*n*8
Annual performance. *See* "Make-the-budget-or-else" contracts; Short-term incentive contracts
Anthony, R.N., 20*n*4, 21*n*5, 47*n*2
Antle, R., 108*n*5, 140*n*5
Argyris, C., 227*n*3
Arrow, K.J., 21*n*12
Asset accounts, in profitability measures, *93*, *114*
Attention-direction, and risk-sharing, 151–152
Audit ratings, *66*, *68*. *See also* Leading performance indicators
Authority
  accountability and, 92, 95, 96, 106–107, 108*n*4
  earnings management feasibility and, 172
Autonomy, as reward, 213, 218

B

Baber, W.R., 194*n*10
Baiman, S., 48*n*8
Bart, C.K., 194*n*12, 15
Bellah, R.N., 207*n*1, 227*n*1
Bonus awards
  adjustments for uncontrollables and, 110–113, 116, 117, 118, 149
  corporate performance and, 149–151
  in short-term incentive contracts, 38–39, 50*n*26
Bookings, *66*, *68*, *82*. *See also* Leading performance indicators
Bottom-line performance measure. *See also* Accounting earnings measures; Shareholder value
  asset and liability accounts in, 92, *93*
  choices of, 56–59
  importance of, 55–56
Brickley, J.A., 85*n*6
Brindisi, L.J., Jr., 62*n*7
Brown, P., 192
Budget games, 194*n*12, 201
Budget targets. *See also* Highly achievable budget targets; "Make-the-budget-or-else" contracts
  achievability of, and excessive compensation, 203–204
  actual achievement of, *33–34*, 35

References in italic refer to tables or figures.

Budget targets (*continued*)
  as commitments, 155–156
  dangers of optimistic budgets, 157
  deemphasis of, 77–78, 84, 137–140
  nonmotivational purposes and, 154–160
  short-term bias problem and, 77–78, 84
  subjective probability of achieving, *31–32,* 49*n*22
  uncontrollables and, 1, 124–125, 137–140
Business Month, 194*n*16

C
Capital charge rate, in profit measure, 97
Career advancement, 41–42, 218–219
Cash awards, 213, 216, 218, 222. *See also* Bonus awards
  size of, 223
Cash flow
  as performance measure, 56, 57–58, 61*n*3
  rewards for generation of, 223
Chesley, G.R., 49*n*22
"Cliff" plans, 160*n*1
Codes of conduct, 189–190
Collection of receivables, *66, 68. See also* Leading performance indicators
Communication
  contract design and, 14, 21*n*12
  between profit center and corporate staff, 100
Compensation committee, contract design and, 224
Compensation consistency, and upper reward cutoffs, 147
Compensation consultants, contract design and, 224
Competitive factors
  adjustments for, 123–125
  risk limitation for, 124–125
Constraints. *See under* Contract design
Contract costs
  of adjusting for effects of uncontrollables, 130–131
  for cost-benefit analysis, 121–122
  of line-item accountability, 107
  of long-term written contracts, 74–75
  of short-term performance pressure, 188–190
  unnecessary, and contract design, 15, 20
  of using leading performance indicators, 82
Contract design. *See also* Controllability; Design trade-offs; Nonmotivational purposes; Shareholder value
  categories of problems in, 13–15
  choices available in, 12, 13
  comparison of two corporations' contracts, 220–224
  conflicting advice about, 15–17
  constraints and trade-offs in, 44–47, *45*
  cutoff levels and, 145
  deviation of actual contracts from ideal, 42–44
  displaced motivation and, 14, 21*n*15
  effective processes for, 224–225
  effects of missing ideal qualities, *29*
  elements in, 12
  in highly flexible contracts, 217–220
  for high risk, high reward, 211–216
  ideal characteristics in, 23–28, *29*
  multiple contracts and, 28–42
  optimal contracts and, 143
  parties participating in, 224
  situational factors in, *210,* 214–216, 219–220, 223–224
  types of flows in, 7
  use of upper cutoffs in, 202
  variation in, 19, 143–144, *210*
  wise trade-offs in, 6, 47
  written vs. unwritten contracts and, 11–12
Contract effectiveness
  dysfunctional outcomes as evidence of flaws and, 190–193
  excessive compensation and, 203–206
  foregone motivation and, 197–203
  incidence of earnings management and, 162–186
  incidence of myopia and, 162–186
  monitoring of dysfunctional outcomes and, 225–226
  operating managers' criticisms and, 163–165
  trade-offs for short-term pressures and, 186–190
Controllability. *See also* Adjustments for uncontrollables; Influence
  in ideal contract, 24–26
  inability to isolate, as design constraint, *45,* 46
  as lacking in actual contracts, 42–43
  line-item accountability and, 92–98
  long-term contracts with little effect, 79–80
  performance measurement in terms of, 94–95, 97–98
  trade-offs and, 4–5
"Cooking-the-books" actions, 169
Cool, W.R., 20*n*4
Corporate controls
  contract design process and, 224
  cost of, and budget targets, 157–158
  earnings management feasibility and, 174–178, 180
Corporate general and administrative (G&A) expenses, 97, 100–102
Corporate performance. *See* Risk-sharing, corporate

Corporation A (diversified luxury goods)
achievement of budget targets at, *31, 33*
adjustments for uncontrollables at, 116, 118, 129, 205, 218–219, 220, 223
annual bonus contract at, 218
bases for assignment of awards at, *40*
contract design choices at, *36–37,* 211, 217–220
earnings management at, 171, *173,* 181
form of rewards at, *40*
long-term contract at, 72–73, 74, 75
managerial retention at, 153
non-use of flexible planning at, 127
performance measures at, *91, 93,* 98, 100, 101
reward cutoffs at, 220
sandbagging at, 78
short-term bias problem at, 219–220
short-term performance pressure at, 181, *182*
simplicity of contract plan and, 71
subjectivity at, 132
use of leading indicators at, *68,* 219–221
value of attention-directing at, 151
Corporation B (electronic equipment)
accountability for worldwide performance at, 104–106
achievement of budget targets at, *31, 33,* 156–157
adjustments for uncontrollables at, 116–117, 118, 119–121
bases for assignment of awards at, *40*
corporate risk-sharing at, 150
earnings management at, *173,* 176–177, 185–186
features of motivational contracts at, *36–37*
form of rewards at, *40*
investment myopia at, 168
measurement-differentiation issue at, 83
performance measures at, 61, *91, 93*
reward cutoffs at, 202
short-term performance pressure at, 53, *182*
use of leading indicators at, *68*
value of attention-directing at, 151
Corporation C (distribution)
achievement of budget targets at, *31, 33*
adjustments for uncontrollables at, 109–111, 121, 123–126
bases for assignment of awards at, *40*
earnings management at, 170, *173*
factors in design choices at, 223
features of contracts at, *36–37*
form of rewards at, *40*
performance measures at, *91, 93*
recognition awards at, 140*n*1
short-term bias at, 81
short-term performance pressure at, *182*
subjectivity at, 136
unwritten long-term contract at, 41
use of leading indicators at, *68*
Corporation D (diversified industrial products)
achievement of budget targets at, *31, 33,* 35, 156–157
adjustments for uncontrollables at, 118, 122–123, 126–127
bases for assignment of awards at, *40*
earnings management at, 170, *173,* 183
features of contracts at, *36–37*
form of rewards at, *40*
investment myopia at, 168
performance measures at, 61, *91, 93,* 101, 102, 103
reward cutoffs at, 147, 201
short-term performance pressure at, 54, *182,* 183, 184–185
subjectivity at, 133, 135
use of leading indicators at, *68*
Corporation E (diversified chemicals)
achievement of budget targets at, *32, 33*
adjustments for uncontrollables at, 118, 121, 124, 128
bases for assignment of awards at, *40*
earnings management at, 171, *173,* 189
expense control at, 69–70
features of contracts at, *36–37,* 38
form of rewards at, *40*
investment myopia at, 165, 166, 168
performance measures at, 58, 61, *91, 93,* 98, 101, 102, 103
short-term performance pressure at, *182,* 191
use of leading indicators at, *68*
Corporation F (hospitality)
achievement of budget targets at, *32, 34*
adjustments for uncontrollables at, 118, 137–140
bases for assignment of awards at, *40*
earnings management at, *173,* 174
features of contracts at, *36–37*
form of rewards at, *40*
performance measures at, *91, 93,* 94–95, 98
performance pressure at, 54, *182*
use of leading indicators at, *68*
Corporation G (electrical connectors)
achievement of budget targets at, *32, 33, 34,* 156
adjustments for uncontrollables at, 116, 117
bases for assignment of awards at, *40*
earnings management at, *173,* 174
features of contracts at, *36–37*
form of rewards at, *40*
managerial retention purposes of plan at, 153

Corporation G (*continued*)
performance measures at, *91, 93,* 102
performance pressure at, *182*
reward cutoffs at, 201
short-term bias at, 80–81
use of leading indicators at, *68*
Corporation H (high tech)
achievement of budget targets at, *32, 34,* 155, 158
adjustments for uncontrollables at, 109, 118, 213, 216
bases for assignment of awards at, *40*
contracts used at, 212–214
earnings management at, *173*
features of contracts at, *36–37,* 210, 211–216
form of rewards at, *40*
investment myopia at, 168
long-term contract used at, 73–74, 75
no-adjustment philosophy at, 111–113
penalties for missed budget target at, 30
performance measures at, *91, 93,* 95–98, 103, 213
performance pressure at, 54
reward cutoffs at, 145–146, 147, 201, 216
short-term bias at, 214–215
short-term performance pressure at, 52, 53, *182,* 184, 187, 188
use of leading indicators at, *68*
Corporation J (consumer products)
achievement of budget targets at, *32, 34,* 35, 155
adjustments for uncontrollables at, 117, 118, 121
bases for assignment of awards at, *40*
corporate risk-sharing at, 199
earnings management at, 169, *173,* 174, 181
features of contracts at, *36–37,* 38
form of rewards at, *40*
long-term contract at, 76, 79
performance measures at, *91, 93*
reward cutoffs at, 146
short-term bias in, 166–168
short-term performance pressure at, 181, *182,* 185, 187
use of leading indicators at, *68*
value of attention-directing at, 152
Corporation K (electronic systems)
achievement of budget targets at, *32, 34,* 158, 160*n*11
adjustments for uncontrollables at, 117–118
bases for assignment of awards at, *40*
corporate risk-sharing at, 151
earnings management at, *173,* 175, 189
excessive compensation at, 203–204
factors in design choices at, 223
features of contracts at, *36–37*
form of rewards at, *40*
long-term contract at, 80
performance measures at, *91, 93,* 102
performance pressure at, *182*
reward cutoffs at, 145, 146, 148, 200–201
simplicity of contract plan at, 71
subjectivity and, 133–135
use of leading indicators at, *68*
value of attention-directing at, 152
Corporation L (specialty chemicals)
achievement of budget targets at, *32, 34,* 155, 158, 160*n*11
adjustments for uncontrollables at, 118
bases for assignment of awards at, *40*
corporate risk-sharing at, 198
earnings management at, *173,* 186
excessive compensation at, 205–206
factors in design choices at, 223
features of contracts at, *36–37*
form of rewards at, *40*
long-term contract at, 76
measurement-differentiation issue at, 83
performance measures at, 59, *91, 93,* 103–104
reward cutoffs at, 145
short-term performance pressure at, 53, *182*
subjectivity at, 133, 135, 136–137
use of leading indicators at, *68*
Corporation M (consumer durables)
achievement of budget targets at, *32, 34*
bases for assignment of awards at, *40*
earnings management at, *173,* 175, 176
features of contracts at, *36–37*
form of rewards at, *40*
long-term contract at, 80
performance measures at, 57–58, *91, 93*
performance pressure at, 54, *182,* 187
simplicity of contract plan at, 71
use of leading indicators at, *68*
value of attention-directing at, 152
Cost-benefit analysis. *See also* Trade-offs
costs of, 121–122
Costello, T.W., 49*n*20
Cost-plus contracts, 138–140
Costs. *See also* Contract costs; Expense control
control, 157–158
for corporate G&A expenses, 97, 100–102
as uncontrollables, 48*n*8
Creativity, and performance pressure, 53–54, 159
Criticisms of contracts from operating managers, 163–165, *164,* 193*n*1, 198

Customer satisfaction, 67, *68*. *See also* Leading performance indicators

D
DeAngelo, L.E., 194*n*17
Dearden, J., 56, 108*n*5
Debt-equity swaps, 195*n*23
Delayed compensation, 160*n*4
Demski, J.S., 108*n*5
Design constraints. *See under* Design trade-offs
Design trade-offs
  for accounting earnings measures, 88
  in adjustments for uncontrollables, 109, 130–137
  in assigning corporate G&A expenses, 102–104
  constraints and, 2, 44–47, *45*
  controllability and, 4–5
  inability to measure shareholder value and, 3–4
  of leading performance indicators, 70–71
  with long-term unwritten contracts, 77
  with long-term written contracts, 74–75
  of reward cutoffs, 200–203
  of short-term performance pressures, 186–190
  situational factors and, 214–216, 219–220
Developmental milestones, achievement of, *66,* 67, *68*. *See also* Leading performance indicators
Discretionary expenditures, 171, 175
Divestment, adjustment for, 121–122
Divisional income statement form, *89*
Divisionalization, and role of profit center managers, 9–10
Dobrzynski, J.H., 48*n*4
Donaldson, G., 9, 48*n*3, 49*n*15, 160*n*9, 227*n*2
Dunbar, R.L.M., 49*n*17
Dysfunctional outcomes
  barriers to learning in monitoring of, 225–226
  as evidence of contract flaws, 190–193

E
Earnings management
  acceptability of practices, *178–180,* 194*n*14
  accounting methods of, 169–170, 194*n*8–9
  challenges to corporation managers from, 192–193
  corporate controls and, 175, 177–180
  costs of, 188–189
  evidence of, 168–186
  as evidence of dysfunction, 162–163
  feasibility of, 172, 174–180
  incidence of, 169, 172–186, *173,* 193*n*6
  operating methods of, 170–172
  questionnaire on acceptability of, *178–179*
  reward cutoffs and, 202
  severity of short-term pressure and, 180–186
Earnings pattern, and short-term performance pressure, 186–187, 194*n*16
Eaton, J., 160*n*4
Eccles, R.G., 108*n*4
Economic factors
  risk limitation for, 122, 124–125, 205
  short-term performance pressure and, 187–188, 194*n*16–17
Elliott, J., 194*n*11
End-of-period promotions, 176, *177*
Enforcement rules, 21*n*12
Etzioni, A., 49*n*21, 85*n*9
Excessive compensation, 203–206
  from asymmetric adjustments for uncontrollables, 204–206
  for incorrect calibration of target awards, 203–204
  uneasiness about, 205–206
"Excuse culture," subjective evaluations and, 135–137
Expense control, 67, *68,* 69–70. *See also* Leading performance indicators
External auditors, and earnings management, 175, 176
Externality problem, 21*n*15

F
Fairness, 140*n*6, 199
Favoritism, 133–135
Federal excise tax, 110
Federal income tax, 98–100
Financial reporting
  budget targets and, 155–156
  fraudulent, and moral tone, 195*n*18
Fixed and variable expenses, separation of, 127
Flexibility
  in budgeting, and adjustments for uncontrollables, 126–128
  in contract design, 217–220
  earnings management and, 169–170, 172, 174
Forbes magazine, "Numbers Game" section, 194*n*8
Foregone motivation, 197–203
  reward cutoffs and, 200–203
  risk-sharing and, 198–200
Foreign currency fluctuations, adjustment for, 122, 126
Free cash flow theory, and short-term pressure, 165

Fried, D., 194*n*11
Frustration, and corporate risk-sharing, 198–199, 207*n*1

G
Gamesmanship, 194*n*12, 201
Generally accepted accounting principles (GAAP), and earnings management, 169
Gioia, D.A., 140*n*6
Goal congruence
accounting measures and, 59, *60*
in ideal contract, 24
as lacking in actual contracts, 42
leading indicators and, 69, 70, 71
long-term unwritten contracts and, 76–77
as term, 47*n*2
Goals, disciplinary vs. predictive functions of, 160*n*9
"Gresham's Law of Planning," 11, 21*n*7

H
Haggard, J.A., 194*n*10
Hand, J.R.M., 195*n*23
Hay Group, 21*n*9
Healy, P., 194*n*9
Hector, G., 195*n*26
Highly achievable budget targets
control costs and, 157–158
corporate financial reporting and, 155–156
creativity and, 159
excessive compensation and, 203–204
managers' incentives for, 78, 154–155
nonmotivational purposes of, 154–160
resource planning and, 156–157
sense of achievement and, 159
total compensation package and, 158
Hirst, M.K., 84*n*1
Hofstede, G.H., 50*n*25
Holmstrom, B.R., 48*n*4
Hopwood, A., 62*n*8
Horngren, C.T., 47*n*2

I
Ideas, funding of, 165–166
Incentives. *See* Rewards
Income statement form, divisional, *89*
Incomplete performance measure, defined, 84*n*1. *See also* Short-term bias problem
Industry volume, adjustment for, 122–123, 126, 128
Inflation-adjusted accounting, 56
Influence. *See also* Adjustments for uncontrollables; Controllability
line-item accountability and, 92, 106, 108*n*5
worldwide product performance and, 105–106
Influence/authority match, and accountability, 106–107
Insurance program, adjustments for, 121
Interperiod adjustment, 129
Inventory control, 67, *68*. *See also* Leading performance indicators
Investment myopia
accounting earnings measures and, 64–65
challenges to corporation managers from, 192–193
evidence of, 165–168
as evidence of dysfunction, 162–163
in growing corporations, 80–81
long-term written contracts and, 71, 84
quarterly earnings disclosures and, 192
Ivancevich, J.M., 49*n*13

J
Johnson, H.T., 108*n*8
Johnson & Johnson, 141*n*9

K
Kanter, R.M., 160*n*2
Kay, E., 49*n*17
Kopelman, R.E., 49*n*14
Kotter, J.P., 85*n*8

L
Labor contract, adjustment for expiration of, 111
Larcker, D., 85*n*2, 6
Leading performance indicators, 66–67
in reduction of short-term bias, 81–82
selection of, 70, 71, 85*n*5
standardized sets of, 67, 82–83
tailoring of, 82–83, 214, 219–221
trade-offs of, 70–71
used in studied corporations, 67, *68*, 69–71, 85*n*4, 219–221
varied over profit centers, 67
Leibenstein, H., 61*n*2
Liability accounts, in profitability measures, *93*, *114*
Line-item accountability, 90–92. *See also* Corporate general and administrative expenses; Federal income tax; Worldwide product performance
choices of items for, *91*, *93*
controllability principle and, 92
for corporate managers, 88–90
at the influence margin, 98–106
items included in earnings measures, 90–92, *91*, 108*n*3
profit center managers' roles and, 88–90, 92, 106, 108*n*5
Locke, E.A., 49*n*19
Loewe, D.A., 108*n*8

Longnecker, C.O., 140*n*6
Long-term incentive contracts. *See also* Long-term unwritten contracts; Long-term written contracts
  costs of, 74–75
  problems for implementation of, 74–75
  purpose of rewards in, 222
Long-term unwritten contracts, 39, 41–42
  reinforcement of, 76
  short-term bias and, 75–77, 84
Long-term written contracts
  administration of, 74, 75
  bases for assigning rewards in, 39, *40*
  costs of, 83
  feasibility of, 214–215
  form of rewards in, 39, *40*
  managerial retention and, 152–153
  short-term bias and, 71–75, 83–84, 214–215
  trade-offs required with, 74
  used in studied corporations, 72–74
Lower reward cutoffs
  corporate survival and, 160*n*1
  earnings management and, 185–186
  motivational costs of, 200–201
  used in studied corporations, 144–145

M
Maher, M.W., 140*n*2
"Make-the-budget-or-else" contracts, 29–35
  actual achievement and, 33–35
  performance standards in, 30–31
  subjective probability and, *31–32*, 49*n*22
Management-by-exception philosophy, 157–158
Management-by-objectives (MBO) system, 67
Managerial retention
  adjustments for uncontrollables and, 116
  excessive compensation and, 206
  as nonmotivational purpose of contract, 152–153
Market share, *66, 68,* 82. *See also* Leading performance indicators
Mason, K., 48*n*4, 227*n*2
Mauriel, J.J., 20*n*4
Measurement accuracy. *See also* Objectivity; Subjectivity
  accounting measures and, 58, *60*
  as lacking in actual contracts, 43
  objectivity and, 26
  verifiability and, 26
Mendenhall, R.R., 195*n*24
Merchant, Kenneth A., 47*n*1, 50*n*27, 85*n*3, 140*n*3, 193*n*7, 195*n*18
Mihalek, P.H., 193*n*6
Moral tone, 189–190, 194*n*18
Motivation
  in control of profit center managers, 10–11
  use of contracts for, 11–15, 21*n*8
Multiple motivational contracts
  categories of, 28–42
  management of, 225–227
  variation among, 2
Myopia. *See* Investment myopia; Operating-decision myopia; Short-term bias problem

N
Nichols, W.D., 195*n*24
Noel, J., 48*n*8
Nonmotivational purposes, 143–160
  corporate G&A expenses and, 101–102
  design constraints and, *45,* 46–47
  for highly achievable budget targets, 154–160
  limitation in range of results/rewards link and, 144–148
  managerial retention and, 152–153
  risk-sharing and, 148–152
  trade-offs and, 5–6
  upper reward cutoffs and, 220

O
Objectivity. *See also* Measurement accuracy; Subjectivity
  adjustments for uncontrollables and, 126–128, 131
  leading performance indicators and, 71
  of results measures, 26
Operating-decision myopia
  accounting earnings measures and, 65
  distribution profit centers and, 80–81
  earnings management as, 172
Operations consolidation, adjustment for, 111
Organizational interdependence, and corporate risk-sharing, 152

P
Performance measures. *See also* Accounting earnings measures; Controllability; Earnings management; Profit measure
  accuracy and, 26
  cash flow measure in, 220
  controllability and, 24–26
  as element of contracts, 12
  financial, in short-term incentive contracts, 38
  goal congruence and, 24
  no-adjustment philosophy and, 112–113
  operating center management of, 193*n*4
  profitability ratio vs. residual income measures, 59, 61

Performance measures (*continued*)
in terms of controllable profit, 94–95, 97–98
Performance standards. *See also* Adjustments for uncontrollables; Budget targets; Subjectivity
achievability of, 221–222
budget games and, 194*n*12
as challenging, 26–27, 43
as element of contracts, 12
flexible plan-versus-actual comparison in, 122–123
in long-term unwritten contracts, 77
in long-term written contracts, 75
in "make-the-budget-or-else" contracts, 30–31
minimum, 144–145, 156, 213
optimum motivation and, 27, 49*n*17
preset, 26–27, 43
revision of, 124
in short-term incentive contracts, 38
uncertainty of, 133–135
upper cutoff in, 145–148
Personal performance, rating of, and uncontrollables, 129
Personnel staff, in contract design process, 224
Planning uncertainty, and contract choices, 215–216
Price, adjustments for, 123–125
Price-earnings ratio, 187
Product quality, 67, *68*. *See also* Leading performance indicators
Profitability measures vs. residual income measure, 59, 61
Profit center, defined, 21*n*5
Profit measures. *See also* Performance measures
accounts included in, *91*, 108*n*3
labels for, and line-items used in, *91*
profit before tax as, 95–98
Profit-sharing plans, 85*n*7, 198

R

Rappaport, A., 42, 62*n*7
Recognition awards, 140*n*1
Reece, J.S., 20*n*4
Reinharth, L., 49*n*14
Relative performance evaluation, and uncontrollables, 48*n*8
Research and development (R&D). *See also* Investment myopia
budget targets and, 168
earnings management and, 175, 194*n*10
Residual income-type measures vs. profitability ratio, 59, 61
Resource planning, 156–157. *See also* Investment myopia
Restricted stock awards, in long-term contracts, 72–73, 218
Restructuring costs
adjustment for, 119–122
subjectivity problem and, 136–137
Results measures. *See* Performance measures; Profit measures
Results/rewards link, limitation in range of, 144–148
Return on assets (ROA), 59, 61, 95–98
Return on net asset (RONA), 12
Return on operations (ROO), 168
Return on shareholders equity (ROE), 72–73. *See also* Shareholder value
Reward cutoffs. *See* Lower reward cutoffs; Upper reward cutoffs
Rewards
bases for assignment of, 39, *40*, 41, 76
cash awards and, 222
as element of contracts, 12
form of, 39, *40*, 41
incorrect calibration of, 203–204
linkage to actions, 79–80
in long-term unwritten contracts, 41, 76
in long-term written contracts, 39, *40*
meaningfulness of, 27–28, 43–44
minimum cost and, 27–28
in short-term incentive contracts, 38–39, 50*n*26
timeliness and, 27, 49*n*20
types of, and adjustments for uncontrollables, 140*n*1
uneasiness about undeserved, 205–206
Ridgway, V.F., 85*n*5
Risk limitation. *See* Adjustments for uncontrollables
Risk-sharing, corporate, 148–152, 160*n*2
motivational costs of, 198–200, 207*n*1–2
Risk-taking. *See also* Contract design, for high risk, high reward
employee accountability and, 25, 48*n*9
high cash reward potential and, 216
reward cutoffs and, 202
ROA measures. *See* Return on assets
ROE measures. *See* Return on shareholders equity
RONA measures. *See* Return on net assets
ROO. *See* Return on operations
Rosen, H.S., 160*n*4

S

Safety ratings, *66*, *68*. *See also* Leading performance indicators
Sales, earnings management and, 170–171, 176, *177*
Sales growth, *66*, 67, *68*. *See also* Leading performance indicators

Salespeople, performance indicators and, 147
Sandbagging, 78, 96–97
Shareholder value
accounting earnings measures and, 46
inability to measure, 3–4, 44, *45,* 46
as performance measure, 56–57, 62*n*7
return on shareholders equity (ROE) and, 72–73
risk-sharing and, 199–200
vs. corporate wealth, 48*n*3
Shaw, W., 194*n*11
Shortsightedness, and upper reward cutoffs, 145
Short-term bias problem, 59, *60,* 63–84, 84*n*1
deemphasis of budget targets and, 77–78, 84
design trade-offs and, 214–215, 219–220
effects of, 64–65
leading performance indicators and, 66–71, 81–83
long-term unwritten contracts and, 75–77, 84
long-term written contracts and, 71–75, 83–84
prevention of myopic actions and, 65–66
severity of, 80–81
solutions to, 65–78
uniform set of contracts and, 215
Short-term incentive contracts, 35–39
differences among, 38–39
limit in range of results/rewards link in, 144–148
major features of, *36–37*
return-on-assets (ROA) measure in, 61
similarities among, 35–38
Short-term/long-term balance. *See* Goal congruence; Short-term bias problem
Short-term performance pressure. *See also* "Make-the-budget-or-else" contracts; Short-term bias problem; Short-term incentive contracts
advantages of, 52–55
costs of, 188–190
creativity and, 53–54
culture of deception and, 183–184
dysfunctional outcomes and, 163–165
earnings management and, 180–186, *182*
funding of ideas and, 165–166
prevention of sloppiness and, 54–55
from short-term contracts, 184
trade-offs of, 186–190
Sibson, R.E., 50*n*26
Simons, R., 141*n*9
Simplicity
accounting measures and, 58, *60*
in ideal contract, 28
as lacking in actual contracts, 44
leading performance indicators and, 71, 85*n*5
Situational factors, and contract design, *210,* 214–216, 219–220, 223–224
"Skunkworks," 159
Slack. *See* Highly achievable budget targets
Sloppiness, and short-term performance pressure, 54–55, 78
Smith, A., 140*n*5
Social control, 79, 85*n*7
Solomons, D., 89
Special payments, 129
Stability, and upper reward cutoffs, 146
Standard corporate and industry practices, and upper reward cutoffs, 148
Stedry, A.C., 49*n*17
Stewart, B., 62*n*7
Stock market, short-term performance pressure and, 187–188, 190–192, 194*n*16–17, 195*n*23–26
Stock option plan
in long-term contracts, 73, 80, 213
managerial retention and, 153
in uncontrollable long-term contracts, 80
Subjective-probability estimates, 160*n*6
Subjectivity. *See also* Measurement accuracy; Objectivity
adjustments for uncontrollables and, 109, 126, 128–129, 130–137
advantages of, in performance evaluation, 131–133
annual bonus awards and, 218–219
leading performance indicators and, 70
long-term unwritten contracts and, 77
minimum performance standards and, 218–219
perceived fairness and, 140*n*6

T
Taylor, Frederick, 191
Teamwork, and risk-sharing, 199
Tirole, J., 48*n*4
Top management. *See also* Corporate controls
adjustments made for decisions by, 119–122
in contract design process, 224
knowledge about profit-centers' businesses and, 214, 220
line-item accountability for, 88–90
management of sets of contracts and, 225–227
motivational contracts for, 16
shareholder value vs. corporate wealth and, 48*n*3
Trade-offs. *See* Design trade-offs

U
Ubelhart, M.C., 62*n*7
Uncontrollable factors. *See* Adjustments for uncontrollables
Uniformity of contracts across profit centers, 215, 223
Unrealized gains (or losses), 171, 194*n*11
Unreported profits, 183, 184, 194*n*15
Upper reward cutoffs
  earnings management and, 185
  motivational costs of, 200, 201
  in performance standards, 145–148
  purposes of, 222
  tempering of growth and, 216

V
Vancil, R.F., 20*n*4, 50*n*26, 103, 108*n*4
Variable and fixed expenses, separation of, 127
Verifiability, 26, 71
Vertical compensation equity, and upper cutoffs, 146–147
Vertical integration, and contract design choices, 22*n*25

W
Weiss, A., 207*n*1
Windfall gain, 145
Worldwide product performance, accountability for, 104–106
Write-offs, 194*n*11

Z
Zalkind, S.S., 49*n*20
Zimmerman, J.L., 48*n*8